STRATFORD-UPON-AVON STUDIES 10

General Editors

JOHN RUSSELL BROWN
& BERNARD HARRIS

Already published in this series:

AMERICAN THEATRE

New York

St Martin's Press

1967

© EDWARD ARNOLD (PUBLISHERS) LTD 1967

First published 1967

First published in
the United States of America in 1967

First published in Great Britain by
Edward Arnold (Publishers) Ltd

Library of Congress Catalog Card Number 67–25727

Printed in Great Britain by
Butler & Tanner Ltd, Frome and London

Contents

Preface

THIS volume follows *American Poetry* in the *Stratford-upon-Avon Studies* series. Like the earlier book it presents American achievement to readers on both sides of the Atlantic.

Ten critics and scholars have collaborated for this study of *American Theatre*. Each of the book's ten chapters has been especially commissioned by the General Editors to form part of a comprehensive, up-to-date and varied account of the large theme; the aim is to provide not one view but several, to use different approaches, to concentrate attention on individual writers, on influences, on ideological and social conditions, on theatrical idioms and on theatrical history. Half the book's authors are American, the other half English; some of them point to considerable achievements of American dramatists, others attempt to show the way ahead.

John Gassner's first chapter is a wide and authoritative survey of Realism that seeks to correct some notions of what is often seen as the hallmark of American theatre. A study of O'Neill follows, by Arnold Goldman, that tries to define the theatrical style of this first undoubted master, considering his development as a dramatist, his methods of characterization and that pervasively important element of style—rhythm. James Rosenberg takes up a subsidiary theme from this chapter in a more general account of European influences, including the way Broadway transforms transplanted dramatic texts. Later in the volume, European influences are again considered by Brian Way in a chapter on 'Absurd' elements in Edward Albee's earlier plays. Besides Albee and O'Neill, Arthur Miller and Tennessee Williams are also considered in separate chapters, Miller by Eric Mottram who gives a detailed account of his ambitions and achievements as a political dramatist, and Tennessee Williams by George Brandt who traces cinematic influences in his stage-plays.

Several chapters are on general themes, as Gassner's on Realism and Rosenberg's on European influences. So, too, Katharine Worth considers the theatrical writings of four poets, MacLeish, Lowell, cummings and William Carlos Williams, and Morris Freedman the economic and social pressures on dramatists. Near the beginning of the

6

book is Gerald Weales' account of the Group Theatre and its plays and at the end Richard Duprey's assessment of 'Today's Dramatists'; here individual writers are seen comparatively, within a collaborative effort of the 1930's and among the individual and emergent careers of the 1960's.

As in earlier volumes of the series, a prefatory note to each chapter gives bibliographical and, sometimes, biographical information, and suggestions for further reading. Works listed here are referred to by their author's name in the following chapters. In these notes and also in the text, '1920/1' means 'performed 1920, first published 1921'.

The General Editors gratefully acknowledge the generous help given during the planning of this volume by Robert Corrigan of New York University.

JOHN RUSSELL BROWN
BERNARD HARRIS

Acknowledgements

THE editors and publishers wish to express their thanks to the following for permission to reprint extracts from copyright works:

the Executors of the Eugene O'Neill Estate, Jonathan Cape Ltd. and Random House Inc. for extracts from *The Plays of Eugene O'Neill*; Carlotta Monterey O'Neill, Jonathan Cape Ltd. and Yale University Press for extracts from *Long Day's Journey into Night* and *Hughie* by Eugene O'Neill; Miss Audrey Wood of Ashley Famous Agency, Curtis Brown Ltd. and New Directions Publishing Corporation for extracts from *Sweet Bird of Youth*, *The Glass Menagerie*, *Summer and Smoke*, *Cat on a Hot Tin Roof*, *The Night of the Iguana*, *A Streetcar Named Desire* and *Camino Real* by Tennessee Williams; Ashley Famous Agency and Viking Press Inc. for extracts from *The Collected Plays of Arthur Miller*; Ashley Famous Agency for extracts from *The Misfits*, *After the Fall*, *Incident at Vichy*, *The Shadows of the Gods*, *The Family in Modern Drama* and *The Man Who Had All the Luck* by Arthur Miller; Ashley Famous Agency, *Esquire*, *The New York Times*, *The Observer* and *The Guardian* for quotations from these publications by Arthur Miller; Methuen and Co. Ltd. and Grove Press Inc. for the extract from *The Birthday Party* by Harold Pinter; Brandt & Brandt, New York, for the quotation from *Awake and Sing!* by Clifford Odets; Indiana University Press for quotations from *him* by e. e. cummings in *From the Modern Repertoire: Series Two* edited by E. Bentley; the author and *Partisan Review* for quotations from *My Kinsman, Major Molineux* by Robert Lowell; New Directions Publishing Corporation for extracts from *Tituba's Children* and *Many Loves* by William Carlos Williams; Editions Gallimard, Hamish Hamilton Ltd. and New Directions Publishing Corporation for extracts from *La Nausée* by Jean-Paul Sartre; Jonathan Cape Ltd. and William Morris Agency Inc. for extracts from *The American Dream* and *Zoo Story* by Edward Albee; Calder & Boyars Ltd. and Grove Press Inc. for extracts from *Rhinoceros* and *Amédée* by Ionesco; Faber & Faber Ltd. for the quotation from *Waiting for Godot* by Samuel Beckett; the author, William Heinemann Ltd. and Farrar, Straus & Giroux Inc. for the extract from *On the Contrary* by Mary McCarthy; Jonathan Cape Ltd. and Harper & Row Inc. for extracts from *O'Neill* by Arthur and Barbara Gelb; Peter Owen Ltd. and New York University Press for extracts from *O'Neill and His Plays* edited by O. Cargill, N. B. Fagin and W. J. Fisher; Dover Publications Inc. for the extract from *Eugene O'Neill: The Man and His Plays* by Barrett H. Clark; the American Educational Theatre Association Inc. for the extract from 'Eugene O'Neill: An Exercise in Unmasking' by

Eugene M. Waith; MacGibbon & Kee Ltd. and Alfred A. Knopf Inc. for quotations from *The Fervent Years* by Harold Clurman; the author and his agent, James Brown Associates Inc. and the Bobbs-Merrill Company Inc. for quotations from *The Story of the Misfits* by James Goode; the author, *The Reporter*, January 2, 1964, for the extract from 'What's the Matter with Edward Albee?' by Professor Tom F. Driver; the University of Minnesota Press for the quotation from *Recent American Drama*, University of Minnesota Pamphlets 7, by Alan Downer; the editors, Peter Owen Ltd. and the Bobbs-Merrill Company Inc. for extracts from *Directors on Directing* edited by Toby Cole and Helen Krich Chinoy; Methuen and Co. Ltd. and Hill & Wang Inc. for the quotation from *Brecht on Theatre* by Bertolt Brecht, translated by John Willett; Eyre & Spottiswoode Ltd. for the extract from *Theatre of the Absurd* by Martin Esslin; Alfred A. Knopf Inc. for the quotation from *The Seesaw Log* by William Gibson.

Note

The most comprehensive collection of American plays is *Best American Plays*, ed. J. Gassner, 7 vols. (1939–64). A smaller collection is *Critics' Choice: New York Drama Critics' Prize Plays, 1935–1955*, ed. J. Gaver (1955).

A selection of books on American Theatre, in general, is listed below; for works on present-day dramatists see the prefatory notes to Chapters IV, VI and X.

B. Atkinson, *Broadway Scrapbook* (1947);

J. Mason Brown, *Dramatis Personae: a Retrospective Show* (1963);

A. S. Downer, *Fifty Years of American Drama, 1900–1950* (1951);

H. Clurman, *Lies Like Truth* (1958);

Eleanor Flexner, *American Playwrights, 1918–1938: the Theatre Retreats from Reality* (1938);

E. M. Gagey, *Revolution in the American Drama* (1947);

J. Gassner, *The Theatre in Our Times* (1954) and *Theatre at the Crossroads* (1960);

L. Langner, *The Magic Curtain* (1951), a history of the Theatre Guild;

W. Kerr, *Pieces at Eight* (1952), collected dramatic criticism;

J. W. Krutch, *The American Drama Since 1918* (1939; revised ed. 1957);

Mary McCarthy, *Mary McCarthy's Theatre Chronicles, 1937–1962* (1963);

F. H. O'Hara, *Today in American Drama* (1939).

Two anthologies are particularly useful: *American Drama and Its Critics*, ed. A. S. Downer (1965) and *American Playwrights on Drama*, ed. F. Frenz (1965).

Realism in the Modern American Theatre

JOHN GASSNER

*

REALISM has been often equated, rather carelessly, with the modernity of the American theatre, and as a result much error has crept into American dramatic history and criticism. The main cause of confusion is careless use of the term itself, a failure to examine the meaning of realism in the light of its multivalent and relativistic character. And a related source of the glib generalizations that have afflicted our evaluation is, in the first place, insufficiency of direct experience with the theatre, and, secondly, sheer ignorance of historical fact. The latter, moreover, is nothing less than the compounding of errors when generalizations that are valid for only one period are copied by later historians, misunderstood, and passed on as simple fact to still another generation of unoriginal historians and critics.

Prevailing confusions start with the assumption that American realism is a twentieth-century, more specifically post-1918, phenomenon, for which the American drama has been alternately praised and scorned. Actually, realism came into vogue in the last quarter of the nineteenth century in a large number of plays and with considerable variety. In some of the plays (in James Herne's *Shore Acres*, for example) the authors and producers emphasized local colour, local character types and local speech. Character drama began to make its appearance with realistic portrayals in James Herne's *Margaret Fleming* (1890), in which a woman reconciled herself to her husband's infidelity and accepted responsibility for his illegitimate child when its mother died. Here character drama involved a departure from strict Victorian convention that suggests the growing influence of Ibsenism. Frailty of character was observed with noteworthy objectivity in Eugene Walter's *The Easiest Way* (1909), in which a young woman with a questionable past proved unequal to the task of mending her ways. Character traits were treated with some degree of psychological observation when Clyde Fitch made jealousy his theme in *The Girl with the Green Eyes* and habitual prevarication the subject of *The Truth*; and the American drama deviated into psychological drama in *The Witching Hour* (1908) by Augustus Thomas, a courtroom melo-drama in which mental telepathy determined the turn of the action, and in William Vaughan Moody's *The Faith Healer*, in which the key to a character's power to effect cures by suggestion was convincingly related to self-confidence rather than to magic or to plain charlatanism.

Psychological interest began to be assimilated into social reality after Herne's *Margaret Fleming*, as is the case in Moody's *The Great Divide* in which a New England young woman, once forced into yielding to a man of the 'Wild West', reluctantly overcomes her Puritan condition-ing and realizes that she is in love with him. (Regrettably, the public saw only a bowdlerized version.) And a number of plays unmistakably qualified as 'social drama' from one point of view or another as American drama began to describe social tensions arising from conflict between capital and labour, represented by Steele MacKaye's *Paul Kauvar* (1887), monopolistic malpractice to which Charles Klein called attention in *The Lion and The Mouse* (1905), and political corruption, plainly indicated, if sentimentally resolved, in Clyde Fitch's *The City*. Even the problems of racial discrimination associated especially with the south-eastern region of the United States won recognition in the American theatre with Edward Sheldon's *The Nigger* (1909), in which a Southern political figure learns to his dismay that he is not a pure-blooded 'Anglo-Saxon'.

If these and other pieces have been almost completely neglected in the American theatre since World War I and scorned by its dramatists, they nevertheless sustain my contention that realism was not of post-1918 vintage. If these plays have been considered unmodern, it is not because they were unrealistic in matter but pseudo-realistic in manner. This is partly a question of idiom and style, and partly of outlook. Nothing dates so rapidly as colloquialism when it is associated with local and temporal modes of jocularity, sentiment, pseudo-refinement, circumlocution and cliché; and the worst offences against dramatic dialogue arise from the sentimentalities of a place and a period. Victorian drama suffered acutely from them until the arrival of Wilde and Shaw in the English theatre. American realistic drama suffered from them until the advent of O'Neill with his short plays of the sea presented by the avant-garde Provincetown Players after 1914.

A related defect early in American realism was the forced optimism, characteristic of American society, which encouraged 'happy endings', problems lightly resolved, and malefactors quickly converted to virtue, usually through the love of a pure (preferably married) woman. Fundamentally, then, early American realism proved intellectually confining, dramatically inconsistent, and critically lax. And, with changes in idiom and manners, ordinary American dramatic realism still suffers from these defects—despite noteworthy sporadic engagements to the psychological and sociological realities of the twentieth century.

One of the most successful modes of encompassing it appeared in comedy and farce after 1920. Anticipated at best only two or three times on the American stage, most notably by Langdon Mitchell's *The New York Idea* (1906), genuine comedy-of manners was virtually an innovation of the American theatre of the 1920's. Its foremost proponents, Philip Barry and S. N. Behrman, were characteristically divided in their aims, the urbane Barry wavering between his comic élan and a striving for spiritual drama consonant with his early Catholic background, Behrman between sophistication and social conscience. Barry's best comedies of the 'twenties, *Holiday* and *Paris Bound*, followed in the 1930's by *The Animal Kingdom* and *The Philadelphia Story*, expressed a civilized writer's protest against conventional adulation of wealth and social position, as well as against righteousness in matters of morals and mores regardless of whether maintained by 'right wing' or 'left-wing' moralists. Invariably in Barry's comedies characters arrived at a position of reasonableness and tolerance after cutting through thickets of circumspection and pride, as when the heroine of *Paris Bound* comes to realize that even she, the marmoreal American upper-class matron, is susceptible to seduction. At the same time the 'reality principle' was well served by the author's supplementary theme that even an adulterous episode (on the part of her normally faithful husband) was insufficient reason for jettisoning a happy marriage.

Behrman's concern with divided or conflicting dispositions served realism with comic penetration in *The Second Man* (1927), in which the leading character, a middle-aged writer who allowed himself to be kept by a wealthy woman, rejected the flattering love of a young woman because he realized that he could not live up to her idealistic view of his character; he preferred the comfortable love of a middle-aged woman who expected little of him. Next, responding to the social conflicts of the 1930's, Behrman studied fundamental contrasts of character and attitude with realistic detachment. In *Biography* (1932), an overly tolerant woman and an overstrenuous reformer separate on coming to understand their fundamental incompatibility. A fitting conclusion to Behrman's involvement with political themes, which thrust Behrman over the borderline between comedy and *drama* in his anti-fascist play *Rain from Heaven*, was *No Time for Comedy* (1938). In this somewhat self-critical work, a popular playwright who endeavours to write a drama about the Spanish Civil War in order to please his conscience comes to acknowledge the truth of his wife's realistic view that his talent is exclusively comic. Insight into the realities of character was apt to be sustained by wit or, at least, urbane dialogue in the best work of Barry and Behrman. A characteristic example appears in Barry's *The Philadelphia Story*; when a young radical exclaims that he is 'not a Communist', his mistress drily adds that he is 'Just a pin-feather on the left wing.' If the talents of a Bernard Shaw eluded them, they at least manifested the flair for meaningful modern high comedy that Somerset Maugham had in *The Circle* and *The Constant Wife*. Rarely did American playwrights equal Barry's and Behrman's comic deftness; only two instances occur to the present writer—Robert Sherwood's essentially European comedy of a psycho-analyst's discomfiture by an Austrian archduke, *Reunion in Vienna*, and Howard Lindsay and Russel Crouse's *Life with Father*, the domestic comedy of a crotchety turn-of-the-century patriarch.

Less distinctively expert in the art of high comedy, other post-1918 American playwrights exhibited the particular zest for blunt-edged realism that has been considered both characteristically American and post-Victorian. This appeared with considerable verve in Maxwell Anderson's vigorous *What Price Glory?* (1924), a collaboration with Laurence Stallings, a journalist and former World War I marine officer. In the twenties and in later decades, the subject of politics, as practised on the rough American scene invigorated American comedy quite often. Among the best examples one would include Maxwell Anderson's attack on Congressional 'log-rolling' *Both Your Houses* (1933); Garson Kanin's hilarious picaresque comedy, *Born Yesterday* (1946), in which a crude business 'operator' who keeps corrupt legislators in his pay is defeated by his naïve mistress and a liberal *New Republic* reporter; *State of the Union* (1945), an exposé of the compromises involved in choosing candidates for the presidency of the United States, by Howard Lindsay and Russel Crouse; and another treatment of the same theme, *The Best Man* (1960), by Gore Vidal. Attractive regional comedy was the special achievement of Sidney Howard, a realistic craftsman with an exceptionally fine ear for colloquial dialogue and dialect. Howard's *They Knew What They Wanted* (1924), a naturalistic variation on the Paolo and Francesca theme, was a particularly adept folk-comedy set among the wine-making Italian population of California. Local colour, however, was secondary to the theme of the marriage of a prosperous elderly Italian and a young waitress both of whom settle realistically for what they want most—the former desiring a child even if it was fathered by his young handyman, the latter seeking economic security after much privation and weariness.

The most distinctively American type of comic writing appeared in a brash and mainly farcical genre by means of which popular play-wrights—notably Charles MacArthur and Ben Hecht (especially in *The Front Page*, which dealt with 'yellow journalism') and George S. Kaufman and his collaborators, especially Moss Hart—amused their audiences with the foibles and extravagances of American life. Thus, *Merton of the Movies* and *Once in a Lifetime* reduced the Hollywood motion picture industry to absurdity, and *June Moon* made the industry of 'tin-pan alley' music publishing and promotion a source of scornful low-comedy. Even serious subjects such as the economic depression of the 'thirties was apt to be reduced to blithe extravaganza, as in the case of Kaufman and Hart's immensely successful *You Can't Take It With You* (1936). It must be observed, moreover, that the comic essence of the writing of these and similar pieces was almost invariably devoid of wit but replete with the gross repartee of the 'wisecrack'. The heroine of *Born Yesterday* gave classic expression to this primitive élan when in rebelling against her arrogant racketeer lover, she told him to 'Drop dead!'.

That realism should play an important role in psychological and social drama was undoubtedly inevitable. But it is hardly surprising that psychological problems or insights would also call for expression-istic forms of treatment once these became familiar to American play-wrights from the practice of Strindberg and later European playwrights. Direct realistic or naturalistic treatments of character problems rarely rose above the level of George Kelly's *Craig's Wife* (1925), a study of an unloving wife obsessed with a desire for material possessions, or

Sidney Howard's *The Silver Cord* (1926), an exposé of matriarchal possessiveness. Honest and forthright dramas of this calibre were free from both Victorian sentimentalism and prudery, and could be considered creditable examples of low-grade critical realism.

Beyond this minor achievement the theatre could rise only on the momentum of personal passion or an impassioned naturalism not altogether alien to poetic feeling and imagination in the case of O'Neill (notably in *Desire Under the Elms*, *The Iceman Cometh* and *Long Day's Journey Into Night*), Tennessee Williams (indubitably in *A Streetcar Named Desire* and less certainly in *Summer and Smoke*, *Cat on a Hot Tin Roof* and *The Night of the Iguana*), Arthur Miller (in *Death of a Salesman* and *A View from the Bridge*), and Edward Albee, in *Who's Afraid of Virginia Woolf?* It is noteworthy, moreover, that in the case of each author, the poetic or imaginative element, whatever its source in the temperament and experience of the playwright, found inspiration or example from significant European departures from realism.

The development of modern American drama and theatre was anything but exclusively realistic in aim and orientation. We merely formed that impression because playwriting after 1918 inevitably reflected the bourgeois character of the audiences and the social challenges to which American writers responded—first, in reaction to the materialism of the prosperous 1920's, and subsequently to the economic distress, class conflict and reformatory or revolutionary zeal of the depressed 1930's. Actually, the formative modernism of the American avant-garde was strongly drawn to the aesthetic ideals and methods of the so-called art theatres of Europe that constituted a reaction against the rigors of naturalism. After 1890 the torch of progress in dramatic art passed into the hands of neo-romanticists, symbolists, expressionists and surrealists. The avant-garde 'little theatre' movement in the United States after 1914 was drawn to the visionary art of Gordon Craig and the pictorial poetry of Max Reinhardt, the symbolism of Maeterlinck and Andreyev, and the expressionism of Strindberg and his German followers. In general, the progressive movement represented in New York by the Provincetown Players, the Neighborhood Playhouse, Washington Square Players and the early Theatre Guild (founded in 1918), as well as by perhaps a dozen little theatres in other cities, amalgamated *two* modern trends. It moved in two opposite directions, the *realistic* and the *anti-realistic* or poetic.

Both tendencies appeared alternately and in some sort of fusion in the work of O'Neill, and it is evident that the realistic playwriting to which he returned repeatedly after romantic and symbolist divagations differed greatly from the humdrum realistic endeavours of his playwright colleagues. The poetic atmosphere in his one-act sea-pieces and *Anna Christie*, the sense of ironic fate in *Beyond the Horizon*, and the tragic intensity of *Desire Under the Elms*, *Mourning Becomes Electra*, *The Iceman Cometh*, *A Moon for the Misbegotten*, *Long Day's Journey Into Night*, and *A Touch of the Poet* made O'Neill the most genuinely imaginative American *realist*. Conversely, the impressiveness of his expressionistic experiments, their superiority to most American playwrights' expressionistic dramas, must be attributed chiefly to the naturalistic concreteness of background and millieu in *The Emperor Jones*, *The Hairy Ape*, *All God's Chillun Got Wings*, *The Great God Brown* and *Strange Interlude*. Their very expressionism is often merely an extension or intensification of specific fact—'Emperor Jones's' chain-gang memories and atavistic fears, the confused 'Hairy Ape's' (Yank's) increasingly desperate alienation, the underlying racial tensions of the Negro husband and his neurotic white wife in *All God's Chillun*, the artist's schizoid condition in the bourgeois world of *The Great God Brown*, the frustrations of the characters in *Strange Interlude*.

In neither the preponderantly naturalistic nor expressionistic plays is the realism devoid of poetry or the poetry devoid of realism. And O'Neill's particular defect is the same in both styles of theatre—namely, a want of language that made him a prose John Webster or at best a tongue-tied Shakespeare. O'Neill was his own severest critic when he made his *persona*, the youngest son Eugene in one of his last plays *Long Day's Journey Into Night*, exclaim that he found himself incapable of distilling his poetic experience adequately:

> I couldn't touch what I tried to tell you [he tells his father], I just stammered. That's the best I'll ever do . . . Well, it will be faithful realism, at least. Stammering is the native eloquence of us fog people.

But a substantial cause of this deficiency was also O'Neill's sometimes too zealously pursued intention to give his characters dialogue suitable to their time, place and social background. This was an essentially naturalistic objective, and it is present in both his realistic and expressionistic writing. It is hardly surprising, of course, in the case of a writer who went as far afield as any major modern playwright in search of imaginative forms of drama only to return to realistic theatre

B

in his last works, including the two nowadays considered his major masterpieces, *The Iceman Cometh* and *Long Day's Journey Into Night*.

O'Neill was, as a matter of fact, least effective when he was deliberately literary, whereas he often achieved an emotionally potent low-grade poetry in his colloquial dialogue. Thinking of leaving the stony New England soil and joining the gold-rush in California, one of the Cabot sons in *Desire Under the Elms* ruminates in the sunset:

> Gold in the sky—in the West—fields o' gold in Golden Gate— Californi-a!—Golden West!—. . . Here—it's stones atop o' the ground—stones atop o' stones—makin' stone walls—year atop o' year. . . . If we plowed in Californi-a, they'd be lumps o' gold in the furrow.

Later, as he leaves the farm for freedom, the other son exults, 'The halter's broke—the harness is busted—the fence bars is down—the stone walls air crumblin' and tumblin!'. Given these characters and their milieu, the rhythms and images could hardly have been improved.

Drawn to classic themes, O'Neill felt compelled to 'modernize' them, giving the Hippolytus-Phaedra myth[1] a New England peasant-drama incarnation, and setting the Oresteian legend[2] in a New England brahmin environment immediately after the Civil War as well as reducing the events to Freudian 'Oedipus Complex' attachments and hostilities, so that O'Neill's Orestes (Orin) is mother-fixated and his Electra (Lavinia) father-fixated. Moreover, O'Neill dipped repeatedly into the sources of contemporary alienation in social and family tensions. Despite repeated disavowals of realism in the 1920's, O'Neill was the supreme realist of the American theatre. He proved himself its most effective poet precisely when he refrained from poeticizing the drama and losing himself in a maze of pseudo-philosophical rhetoric and abstract banalities about Life, Death, Truth and the loss and recovery of Faith—to be found in *Lazarus Laughed*, *Dynamo* and *Days without End*, in which he was at best only a poet *manqué*. Like other American playwrights, he needed solid ground for whatever genuine drama and poetry he was capable of producing. Even Thornton Wilder, who had less regard for dramatic naturalism than O'Neill, was most successful as a playwright when he combined fantasy and a theatricalist structure borrowed from the Orient with simple naturalistic scenes in *Our Town*; and the most poetic scene, in which the dead in the village

[1] In *Desire under the Elms*.   [2] In *Mourning Becomes Electra*.

burial grounds receive the newly interred heroine of the play, owes its poignancy to homely speech and detail.

That O'Neill's case was not unique was evident in the career of the more or less regional playwrights. The ablest of these were Lynn Riggs, best known as the author of *Green Grow the Lilacs*, which became the source of *Oklahoma!*, and Paul Green, whose weakest products were fantasies such as *Tread the Green Grass* while his strongest work, with or without a vein of symbolism, was rooted in the social realities of the South; they sustain *The House of Connelly*, *Potter's Field*, his dramatization of the Richard Wright novel *Native Ground*, and numerous one-act pictures of Negro and 'poor white' life. Paul Green's most genuinely poetic writing will be found in the speeches he gave to the sadistic chain-gang captain of *Hymn to the Rising Sun*, a powerful naturalistic drama of protest against the penal system of the South. In the theatre of 'social significance' and protest during the 1930's the same fusions of realism and imagination in poetry were apparent. Clifford Odets combined naturalism with expressionist technique and a bristling rhetoric in *Waiting for Lefty* (1935), his short masterpiece of revolutionary protest. Irwin Shaw fused social protest with expressionist fantasy in his stirring anti-war drama *Bury the Dead*, during the same brief period of social militancy between 1933–9. And its chief poet in the theatre, Clifford Odets, was also its foremost realist. It is characteristically American that as a social realist in *Awake and Sing!*, *Paradise Lost*, *Golden Boy* and *Rocket to the Moon* he should have distilled his 'poetry' out of common city life and speech. Urban naturalism of this order did not appear in England until more than a quarter of a century later, in the work of Arnold Wesker and his contemporaries.

In the case of O'Neill, it was largely private vision and a sense of personal bedevilment that sublimated realism in his work—a realism that would otherwise have been merely prosaic and banal. In the case of Odets, it was mainly public vision and agitation, shared with a number of other playwrights of the 'thirties, including Elmer Rice, Lillian Hellman, Sidney Kingsley and even the inveterately bohemian William Saroyan in *My Heart's in the Highlands* and *The Time of Your Life*, both produced in 1939. The playwrights who won the greatest reputation after 1940 derived the same augmented or sublimated realism from private or public sources, although these were not mutually exclusive. (They were not mutually exclusive in the case of O'Neill and Odets either, since O'Neill expressed a keen sense of milieu in dramas of the sea and New England along with his family trauma and private disenchantments, and Odets's social passion had components of highly personal longing and frustration.) In the work of Arthur Miller the dominant influence has been moral passion and a strong sense of social responsibility. In the dramatic élan of Tennessee Williams, William Inge and Edward Albee, the concern with milieu has been decidedly secondary to the expression of private tensions and sensibility. In the careers of these four writers, generally regarded as the most gifted and productive of post-1945 American dramatists, these pressures have resulted in the naturalism or realism of their successful plays. And, as in the case of O'Neill, it is their deviations into bald fantasy and extreme symbolism in Williams's *Camino Real* and Albee's *Tiny Alice* that have had unsatisfactory results.

When we consider the career of Miller we find him hankering for status as a dramatic poet and a tragedian, but bent upon achieving that status only in terms of the common man's condition. The story of Willy Loman, the marginal hero of Miller's *Death of a Salesman*, is that of a common man trapped by the commonplace values and pressures of his society. Willy is uncommon only in the intensity with which he endeavours to overcome his littleness with unrealistic claims and dreams for himself and his favourite son. Miller believed that Willy's passion for self-respect qualified him for tragic stature and hoped that the play was an authentic tragedy. At best, it was 'bourgeois tragedy', the essence of which is realism and pathos. The same thing may be said of the same author's first successful play *All My Sons*, which revolved around a petty producer of aeroplane parts, of the Salem Witchcraft trial drama *The Crucible*, and of the Brooklyn dockyards drama *A View from the Bridge*, in which Miller followed blueprints for tragedy along Aristotelian lines but with ordinary characters rather than classic heroes.

Except in *All My Sons*, a 'well-made' play, revolving around the discovery of the war-profiteer's guilt by his own idealistic son, Miller added a more or less imaginative formal dimension to his playwriting or found some other means of augmenting and enriching it. This was most conspicuously the case in *Death of a Salesman*, in which realistic scenes involving Willy Loman and his family in the present alternated with scenes involving them in the past. Being memory scenes, they were fragmentary and impressionistic; and when Willy imagined events in a feverishly disturbed state of mind, since he had been on the verge of committing suicide even before the start of the play, the memories became expressionistically distorted. In *Death of a Salesman*, produced in 1949, Miller combined verisimilitude with poetic structure in order to provide insight into his commonplace character's state of mind and materialistic values, which reflect a narrow American middle-class world of success worship and constitute a commentary on it. Even the prose of Miller's convincingly colloquial dialogue acquired moments of poetic illumination or dramatic punctuation as a result of the imaginative structure.

Miller employed similar means of judicial review, fragmentation and expressionistic dramatization of past events in *After the Fall*, pro-duced in 1964 after a nine years' interim during which he had no new plays on the stage. Here the dramatic structure was once more realistic-ally motivated by a character's emotional crisis, which required a crucial decision on his part. The character was the author himself and a review of his life opened up the entire question of guilt, individual responsibility for the evil in the world, and the impulse towards des-truction residing in the human heart. The structure was somewhat muddled and the narrating character's assertions banally worded, but the dramatist thrust aerial roots from the ground of commonplace reality, so that the work, no matter how flawed, possessed an impres-siveness rarely present even factitiously in American playwriting.

A moderate but unusual structural element appeared in Miller's naturalistic drama, *A View from the Bridge*, in the form of a prologue and a narrative matrix consisting of a lawyer's reminiscences of life as he once knew it on the Brooklyn waterfront, when passions ran strong and violence flared up among the inhabitants. The central action con-cerned a dockworker whose unconscious desire for his wife's young niece ends in betrayal of his Sicilian relatives and in a fatal hand-to-hand encounter with one of them. These events acquired an added dimension from the narrator's ruminative memory. No such modification of realistic structure appeared in Miller's *The Crucible*, but its seventeenth-century New England background and formal speech provided a distancing effect that increased the stature of its simple farmer-hero and strengthened the tragic significance of his struggle against the Salem witch-hunt. At the risk of some stiffness and archaism in the writing of this work, Miller once more succeeded in maintaining realism of content and point of view without succumbing to trans-parent commonplaceness of effect. He was less successful in *Incident at*

Vichy (1965), but attained some dramatic dignity by choosing an event of great moment—the deportation of suspected Jews from Nazi-dominated Vichy. Individual reactions of prisoners culminate in the guilt-inspired sacrifice of an Austrian nobleman which enables a Jewish psychiatrist to escape.

One could wish only that Miller's earnestness and engagement to moral issues had been less heavy-handed. A commendable lightness of touch appeared in a number of sensitive stage pieces produced in New York after the end of World War II. Those the present writer recalls with the greatest regard were George Kelly's *The Deep Mrs. Sykes*, Robert Anderson's *Tea and Sympathy*, Carson McCullers's *Member of the Wedding*, William Inge's *Come Back, Little Sheba* and Tennessee Williams's beautiful memory play *The Glass Menagerie* and only slightly overdone *Summer and Smoke*, a novelistic account of the deterioration of an idealistic small-town Southern spinster. For the most part, however, the American drama continued to exhibit the same laboriousness that characterized Odets's social and Miller's moral seriousness. This tendency vitiated even efforts at producing fantasy such as Paddy Chayefsky's folk-play *The Tenth Man* and biblical drama *Gideon*. William Inge narrowly escaped it in his mid-western dramas *Picnic*, *Bus Stop* and *The Dark at the Top of the Stairs*, but succumbed to it in later dramas of frustration or personal trauma. Edward Albee's powerful naturalistic drama *Who's Afraid of Virginia Woolf?* could have been improved by the exercise of more restraint and finesse, and the lack of these qualities became conspicuous in the most productive and poetic of post-1945 American playwrights, Tennessee Williams.

It has been generally observed that Tennessee Williams showed exceptional skill in the writing of American dialogue that is at once poetic and colloquial. He proved himself especially adept in conveying the sensibility of female characters in as many as half a dozen full-length plays and in several powerful one-act dramas such as *Portrait of a Madonna* and *The Lady of Larkspur Lotion*. Williams has published poetry and is fond of quoting the symbolist poets, and he has evinced a particular attachment to D. H. Lawrence, not merely because of the latter's obsessive concentration on sexuality but his fine feeling for magical and musical prose. He has been without doubt the most consistently poetic writer of prose drama in the American theatre, and this is evident not only in his early impressionistic masterpiece *The Glass Menagerie* (1944–1945), but in the patently naturalistic plays that succeeded it, from *A*

Streetcar Named Desire to *The Night of the Iguana*, including his folk-comedy of sex and love, *The Rose Tattoo*.

Next to his dialogue as a factor in the sublimation of naturalism, which became increasingly lurid as a result of his fixation on sexuality, has been Williams's penchant for utilizing the theatrical nature of a play as a formal feature of the work. This tendency is most conspicuous when he uses the device of direct address to the audience. *The Glass Menagerie* frames the dramatic action with a narration and commentary by one of the principal characters, the youth who left home and now, while in the Merchant Marine, recalls the pathetic inability of his mother and painfully shy sister to cope with reality. In *Sweet Bird of Youth*, the 'hero', a young man who has made a sorry mess of his life and is about to be castrated for infecting the daughter of a Southern senator with venereal disease, says to the audience, as he moves to the forestage, 'I don't ask for your pity, but just for your understanding—not even that! No, just for your recognition of me in you, and the enemy, time, in us all.'

In all his plays, moreover, Williams's theatrical imagination effect-uated itself by means of 'symbols'. These are visual rather than merely verbal, as in the case of poetry solely intended for reading or recitation. The symbol that illuminates or underscores reality in Williams's plays is apt to be something *seen*, as in the case of the photograph of the father who left the feckless family of *The Glass Menagerie* in the lurch when he 'fell in love with long distance' and absconded. Williams wants the picture to light up whenever there is occasion to remember him as one who escaped the stalemate of his life and his wife's social pre-tensions and nagging. At times the symbol becomes action. Thus, in *The Night of the Iguana*, a lizard is caught and tied under the porch of a Mexican inn for fattening before it is eaten by the natives; it is liberated by the sodden ex-clergyman of the play who regards it as a symbol of all helpless nature, both human and animal, victimized by the insensitive and case-hardened characters who persecute him, too. In *Summer and Smoke* the most prominent scenic feature is a fountain 'in the form of a stone angel' standing in the centre of the Southern town of 'Glorious Hill'. It symbolizes 'Eternity' and it represents, so to speak, the virginal idealism of the heroine Alma ('Soul' in Spanish). As a child she plays in front of the statue with the wild boy whom she attempts to convert to spiritual aspiration and good behaviour. As a frustrated spinster at the end of the play, when she has lost him, she meets a lonely young travelling salesman and accompanies him to a casino for a belated fling at life: 'She faces the stone angel and raises her gloved hand in a sort of valedictory salute,' writes Williams.

In *Orpheus Descending*, it is plain that Williams counts heavily on analogies between ancient Greek myth and the tragic events of his modern story set in the South. His heroine, a lively, life-loving young woman of Italian extraction, is its abducted Eurydice, who has been compelled to marry a rich old man (the Hades or Pluto of the play) who is dying but won't give her up to life and kills her when she tries to leave him. And Williams's Orpheus is a young guitar-player who does not succeed in his effort to release her from her bondage, but loses her to 'Death' just as they are about to escape. Subsequently, having been falsely accused of murdering the woman, he is tracked down by bloodhounds and torn to pieces by them, in a conclusion that parallels the dismemberment of Orpheus by enraged Maenads. In Williams's own recurring 'mythology', Orpheus, the artist-man, is invariably destroyed by Woman or because of her; and Eurydice or Beauty, whether masculine or feminine (or epicene), is usually the victim of callous people and a benighted, grasping society. Williams, in brief, strives to transfigure the naturalism that pervades his work in lurid details of action or report, in pungent dialogue, and in candid portraiture. Noteworthy flashes of poetic dialogue, portraits of sensitive, usually frail heroes and heroines, vivid theatrical presentation now and then vitiated by archness, and a veritable pattern of symbolic references and equivalences—it is this combination of poetic strategies that enabled him to serve the poetic theatre and the realistic drama simultaneously. The modern American theatre has rarely failed to reveal this tendency at least once in a season, as it recently did, in the poet and Harvard scholar William Alfred's *Hogan's Goat* (late in 1965), even when an American author aspires to create poetic drama. The poetic passages in *Hogan's Goat* appear in a matrix of lusty Irish characterizations and a strenuous knockdown struggle for power between a young and an elderly politician in late nineteenth-century Brooklyn. *Hogan's Goat* stands at the opposite pole of poetic drama as the contemporary English theatre has known it in the fastidious dramatic literature of Eliot, Fry and others.

In the American theatre, we must conclude, realism or naturalism has remained a vital force by proving to be something other than it was assumed to be. It was, at its best, not an apotheosis of the humdrum but sometimes a leap into the ether of speculative or visionary drama, sometimes an underground convulsion in the case of psychological drama, sometimes an explosion above ground in the case of social drama. This was apparent even in the case of some documentary or slice-of-life plays like Elmer Rice's *Street Scene* (1929), in which the surface realism was stirred by a gust of pity for characters caught in the underbrush of banal and boring poverty, or Sidney Kingsley's *Dead End* (1935), in which compassion and zeal for reform swept through an oppressive picture of the crime-breeding slums of New York. And it has been even more apparent in plays by O'Neill, Odets, Hellman, Miller, Williams, Inge, Albee and others for which one could claim dramatic or even some literary stature.

On the one hand, this mode of realism could be passionately critical, anti-heroic and 'debunking'—that is, deflating, or derogatory; it could live up to Mary McCarthy's terse definition in her 'American Realist Playwrights' essay that 'Realism is the depreciation of the real.' It was drama and comedy of exposé and protest in a direct line of descent from Ibsen (Miller has been especially linked to Ibsen), from Strindberg (O'Neill proudly acknowledged indebtedness to Strindberg in both his realistic and expressionist phases), or from Chekhov, who was Odets's unacknowledged and domesticated forerunner. As Miss McCarthy has put it, 'The strength and passion of realism is its resolve to tell the whole truth.' In comparatively significant American realism this has been the case whether the dramatist exposed a representative individual (as Miller did in *All My Sons* and *Death of a Salesman*), a group or a family (as Odets did in *Awake and Sing*, O'Neill in *Long Day's Journey Into Night* and Albee in *Who's Afraid of Virginia Woolf?*), or a milieu (as Lillian Hellman did in *The Little Foxes*).

On the other hand, as I have attempted to show, significant American dramatic realism has manifested various admixtures of realism and poetry or poetic coloration, some histrionic imaginativeness, or some transcendence of descriptiveness and photographic reduplication of commonplace reality. This has appeared even in representations of sordid conditions and gross situations, as in *The Iceman Cometh, A Streetcar Named Desire* and *The Night of the Iguana*. The 'higher realism' cannot be attempted, as both Miller and Williams have shown, without running the risk of some questionable posturing as an 'artist', some artificial inflation of the subject or the emotion attending it, and a resort to poetic language as a sort of varnish on a cadaver. And ironically in such cases the author has been apt to be saved as an effective dramatist (that is, as an 'artist'), by authenticity in some passage, scene or (supremely in the case of *The Iceman Cometh* and *Long Day's Journey Into Night*) some particular play. In such instances the 'prose' that a playwright like O'Neill or Williams could honestly write could prove more poetic through its sheer power as drama than the 'poetry', towards which he could only gesture in a resolve to achieve artistic eminence by an act of will, or hubristic attempt to hoist himself up into the empyrean by his bootstraps.

Against the dubious results of this forced 'artistry' there has been a critical reaction that has tended to emphasize the superior value of realistic writing in the American theatre. This tendency has occurred, interestingly enough, at the very time that, in journalistic commentary or play reviewing as well as in academic quarters, it has been fashionable to deplore realism and exalt the virtue of anti-realistic stylization as an aesthetic panacea for the theatre's ailments. The reaction, comparable to the reaction in England against the vogue of poetic drama under the leadership of Eliot and Fry, was particularly signalized by the recovery and actual growth of Eugene O'Neill's reputation in the 1950's. Exceptional regard for him was entertained as a dramatic realist, rather than an expressionist, on the strength of his last plays, most notably *Long Day's Journey Into Night*, which such unsentimental judges as the *New Republic* critic Robert Brustein and Mary McCarthy acclaimed as his greatest work and one of the great plays of the twentieth century. Miss McCarthy's tribute to him was also a moderate compliment to American realists in general, which even extended to minor writers such as Paddy Chayefsky and William Inge, on the strength of such plays as *Middle of the Night* and *Come Back, Little Sheba*, unstrained exercises in authentic emotional and environmental verisimilitude free of stagey symbolism. Concerning *Long Day's Journey Into Night* Miss McCarthy's comment was apt:

A *Long Day's Journey Into Night*, sheer dogged prose from beginning to end, achieves in fact a peculiar poetry, and the relentless amassing of particulars takes on, eventually, some of the crushing force of inexorable logic that we find in Racine or in a Greek play. The weight of circumstance itself becomes a fate of nemesis. This is the closest, probably, that realism can get to tragedy.

We may well regret that American playwrights, such as Miller and Williams, who have manifested to a lesser degree the same kind of talent for rendering reality on the stage, have felt the need to conceal or apologize for their strong points, and exhibit various degrees of inadequacy as stylists or 'stylizers'. Nevertheless, in view of the need to surmount the banality of surfaces, their discontent with mere verisimilitude and their endeavours to extend their range of expression beyond descriptiveness and 'fourth-wall' naturalism are laudable. Variety of presentation and expression is a necessity of the theatre if it is to arouse or retain interest, and this is particularly true of contemporary realistic theatre in America, which offers audiences neither the glamour nor the diversions of romantic drama, spectacle or musical and balletic entertainment. There have been instances in American drama, moreover, when its documentary character or its closeness to raw experience and the commonplaces would have proved tiresomely obvious and restrictively painful without some theatrical distancing of the material by formal and stylistic means. This has been an effective strategy of American realism not merely in *The Glass Menagerie* and *Death of a Salesman*, but in many less well known American plays ever since the 1920's. Thus, Sophie Treadwell resorted to it in *Machinal*, with her treatment of a sordid murder case, by making moderate use of expressionistic technique to convey the desperation of the murderess who married her unpleasant employer under dire economic pressure; John Howard Lawson in *Roger Bloomer*, to project the theme of sexual repression in the case of a commonplace American youth; Sidney Howard in *Yellow Jack* (written in 1928, but first produced in 1934), to recount in semi-documentary form the story of the struggle against yellow fever in Cuba; the authors of Federal Theatre's 'living newspaper' documentary dramas on such subjects as public *versus* private ownership of electric power and city slums, in *Power* and *One-third-of-a-nation* . . . during the New Deal period of the 'thirties; and more recently Jack Gelber in *The Connection*, an uncompromisingly naturalistic treatment of drug addiction encapsulated in a theatrical, Pirandellian framework involving the making of a documentary motion picture about that very subject. Provided the reality of the central situation is not diminished or seriously obscured, realism is served well by being served imaginatively. In endeavouring to prevail with both verisimilitude and some transcendence of verisimilitude, talented American playwrights pursued an essentially sound objective and expressed a characteristic compulsion to deal with reality in contemporary terms on the stage.

Note

Biography. *Eugene O'Neill* was born on 16 October, 1888, in New York City, and died in Boston, Mass., on 27 November, 1953. The son of James O'Neill, Shakespearian actor and romantic idol, Eugene grew up in New London, Connecticut, in preparatory school and on the road with his father's companies. An early first marriage ended in divorce after a separation during which O'Neill led an adventurous life at sea as a deck hand and later 'able seaman'. A period of dissipation in New York's Lower East Side ended with his entry into a tuberculosis sanatorium for treatment. This enforced rest appears to have set the seal on his determination to write. O'Neill attended Professor Baker's graduate Drama Workshop at Harvard University in 1914–15, though his only previous higher education had been an incomplete undergraduate year at Princeton. In summer of 1916, O'Neill was 'discovered' by a group of earnest amateurs who were to become, with his help, the Provincetown Players. A series of one-Act plays, of which 'Bound East for Cardiff' (1916) is the most memorable, was followed by *Beyond the Horizon* (1920), *The Emperor Jones* (1920/1), *The Hairy Ape* (1922), *Desire Under the Elms* (1924), *Marco Millions* (1928/7), *The Great God Brown* (1926), *Strange Interlude* (1928), the trilogy *Mourning Becomes Electra* (1931) and others. A period of withdrawal from the stage preceded World War II and no new production of an O'Neill play was given from 1935 until 1946, when *The Iceman Cometh* was performed. O'Neill died of pneumonia in 1953, a merciful release after years of progressive immobilization from a disease similar in appearance to Parkinson's. A number of plays, in various stages of composition, were discovered among his papers, including what is today perhaps his best known play, *Long Day's Journey Into Night* (1956, written 1939–41). Four of these have been published and performed since his death, and he is known to have destroyed others, relating to a projected eleven-play 'cycle'.

Editions. Quotations in this chapter are from *The Plays of Eugene O'Neill* (New York, Random House, 1951), 3 vols.; *Long Day's Journey Into Night* (New Haven, 1956); and *Hughie* (New Haven, 1959). Other texts are: *Thirst and Other One-Act Plays* (1914); *Lost Plays of Eugene O'Neill* (1950 and 1958); *A Moon for the Misbegotten* (1952); and *A Touch of the Poet* (1957).
In England, O'Neill's plays are published by Jonathan Cape (sixteen vols.; 1922–1962).

Criticism. O. Cargill, N. B. Fagin and W. J. Fisher have collected essays on *O'Neill and His Plays* (1961); this volume contains a bibliography. J. Gassner has also edited *O'Neill: A Collection of Critical Essays* (1964). Book-length studies of O'Neill include B. H. Clark, *Eugene O'Neill, The Man and His Plays* (revised version, 1947); E. Engel, *The Haunted Heroes of Eugene O'Neill* (1953); Doris Falk, *Eugene O'Neill and the Tragic Tension* (1958); A. and Barbara Gelb, *O'Neill* (1962); Doris Alexander, *The Tempering of Eugene O'Neill* (1962); and J. H. Raleigh, *The Plays of Eugene O'Neill* (1965). Two short studies are Mary M. Colum, 'The Drama of the Disintegrated', *The Forum* (1935) and E. Mottram, 'Men and Gods: a Study of Eugene O'Neill', *Encore*, (1963).

28

The Vanity of Personality: the Development of Eugene O'Neill

ARNOLD GOLDMAN

★

bitter: 1 a: having or being a peculiarly acrid, astringent, or disagreeable taste suggestive of an infusion of hops that is one of the four basic taste sensations 1 b: distasteful or distressing to the mind: *galling* 2: marked by intensity or severity a: accompanied by severe pain or suffering b: vehement, relentless also: exhibiting intense animosity c: (1) harshly reproachful: sharp and resentful (2) marked by cynicism and rancor d: intensely unpleasant esp. in coldness or rawness 3: expressive of severe pain, grief, or regret.

Webster's Dictionary

I

THE underlying movement of an O'Neill drama—perceptible first in the speech of characters, but extending equally to their relationships, to episodes and to total structures—is a fluctuation and oscillation, a flow and ebb forever turning back upon itself. It is the movement which L. C. Knights, describing the language of *Macbeth*, has characterized as a 'sickening see-saw rhythm'.[1]

This rhythm is found in individual characters either as a relationship between portions of their speech or thought, or between speech and thought. The easiest recognizable form is simple contradiction. Nina Leeds broods to herself in *Strange Interlude* (1928):

Sam must give me a divorce . . . I've sacrificed enough of my life . . . what has he given me? . . . not even a home . . . I had to sell my father's home to get money so we could move near his job . . . and

[1] L. C. Knights, *Some Shakespearean Themes* (1959), p. 121.

29

then he lost his job! . . . now he's depending on Ned to get him another! . . . my love! . . . how shameless! . . .

(*Then contritely*)

Oh, I'm unjust . . . poor Sam doesn't know about Ned . . . and it was I who wanted to sell the place . . . I was lonely there . . . I wanted to be near Ned . . .   (1, 93)

Self-delusion perceived; admission accompanied by remorse. Surface and underlying reality approach efficient description of this and similar pendular motions in O'Neill only when the characteristic emotions are attached: if the flow of self-justification originates in a feeling of being hurt and can end in a hurting of others, the ebb has as the object of its animus only the self.

All major O'Neill characters are divided against themselves, something which was already apparent to Mary Colum in 1935:

[O'Neill] has put with intensity on the stage one aspect of American life that no other writer has managed to express at all . . . that common character in American life, the disintegrated person . . .

[Strindberg's] disintegrated people were all madmen. But O'Neill contrives to present his people as disintegrated and yet holding on to sanity.   (p. 358)

Not all of 'his people'; the oscillation in Ella Downey, in *All God's Chillun Got Wings* (1924), resonates out of control and becomes schizoidal. She is torn to bits between a real love for her Negro husband Jim (if and only if he remains subservient) and an equally real '*mean, vicious [and] jealous hatred*' of him (II, 337). She wants and does not want him to pass his bar exams. As *both* poles of the rhythm acquire radical reality—one of Nina's was a lie, even if the expression of a truly felt grievance—the rhythm acquires dramatic complexity: Ella can love Jim if he fails in the 'white' world, partly because in so doing he remains for her the asexual security to which she fled from that world, partly because it will preserve him from her residual racial prejudice (Negroes should know their place) at the same time as it confirms it (Negroes are not capable of rising), and partly because he will then be the kind of failure she feels herself to be and to deserve. Ironically, like Jay Gatsby trying to make himself over into the social type he imagines Daisy Buchanan will desire, Jim is trying to 'become white' to satisfy Ella, to overcome his feelings of inferiority. The 'resolution' the play allows

Ella is a regression into childhood—'I'll be just your little girl, Jim' (II, 342)—but her fragile, pitiful 'happiness' leaves him baffled, blocked, in an intolerable position.

In Ella's regression, the ending of *All God's Chillun* is like those in many O'Neill plays. Similar are the regression to insanity in 'Where the Cross Is Made' (1918/19), to savagery in *The Emperor Jones* (1920/1) and to 'hopeless hope' in *The Straw* (1921). In each case, as in *Days Without End* (1934), the regression appears as 'the straw' at which the mind clutches to escape a situation of intolerable bafflement. The closest analogy to Ella Downey, however, is of course Mary Tyrone in *Long Day's Journey Into Night* (1956, written 1939–41), whose mind leaps, under the influence of morphine, further and further into her past, reverting first (Act III) to her wedding day and then (Act IV), 'Back before she even knew me,' as her husband James sadly admits (p. 137), to her student days in the convent.[2]

Mary Tyrone remains, however, sane, where Ella Downey does not, and the greater complexity of her speech-patterning is the measure, for us, of her sanity. Even at the outer limit of her 'dope dream' the emotional variegation is still present—within the escape there is no escape—and her long monologue which ends the play, while it removes her entirely into her past, robs her at the last of fantasy-gratification. What she remembers is precisely the advice of Mother Elizabeth that precipitated her exposure to the world: that she leave the convent 'for a year or two' to put 'to the test' her wish to become a nun (p. 175). Mary's barely submerged resentment preserves the troubled motion of her speech (and mind) to the very end.

Mary's language—and the structure of the play in so far as she helps comprise it—is a complex rhythm of admission and denial of her narcotic addiction, counterstressed with blame and exoneration of her husband James (for calling in the 'quack' doctor who first gave her morphine to ease the pains of childbirth), her older son Jamie (for, as she imagines, having deliberately and fatally infected his brother Eugene with measles), and her younger son Edmund (whose birth, she claims, broke her health). Admission is excused by 'the things life has done to us' (p. 61) and is even justified as a proof of the burdens of her

[2] Both the 'Ella' and 'Jim' of *All God's Chillun* and the 'Mary' and 'James' of *Long Day's Journey* have the forenames of O'Neill's parents. His mother was born Mary Ellen (Quinlan), but always used the name Ella, and was so called by family and friends.

life. But she meets with '*stubborn defiance*' (p. 69), and denial, the attacks on her which the others make, provoked as much by her own excuses and accusations as by their chagrin at once again having allowed themselves to believe her cured.

*   *   *

In two consecutively written plays, *Strange Interlude* and *Dynamo* (1929), O'Neill supplied his characters with 'thoughts' as well as speech. Here the added dimension can be seen working to the same purpose for more normative personalities than Ella and Mary Tyrone, troubling and upsetting the linear narrative flow.[3] Kenneth Macgowan, writing in 1929, noted that 'To the dramatic contrasts and conflicts of ordinary spoken dialogue O'Neill added the contrasts and conflicts of thoughts' (Cargill, p. 452).

These 'asides' spoken in *Strange Interlude* while all the characters 'freeze' (the director, Philip Moeller's idea) have taken a beating from critics from the first performance on, and will do wherever the 'contrasts and conflicts', the ruffling of verbal texture, is not recognized as their primary purpose. But the notion that the primary function of the asides in *Strange Interlude* is to reveal the true feelings which the characters otherwise hypocritically suppress is a stick to beat the play: where it is observed, the play can be called simplistic and, where it is not, O'Neill's failure to realize his intention. The fact is that the play is extremely outspoken in ordinary dialogue, and that, while Nina's father, the family friend Charlie and her husband Sam Evans are shockable, Nina—and Ned Darrel only to a lesser degree—is perfectly willing to shock. Nina and Ned's more acerbic 'thoughts' are not different in kind from much of what they do say to others in the play.

The asides add, as Joseph Wood Krutch noted in his review, 'depth' and 'solidity' (Cargill, p. 185), but they do it by obstructing what we would conventionally imagine to be the smooth flow of narrative— viz. what really gets said. (Some of the Theatre Guild, who first produced the play, wanted all the asides cut.) The play has a broken, dimensional movement; and the language, because of the ubiquity of

[3] Part way between the 'spoken thoughts' under stress and the fully-fledged unspoken thoughts of 1928–9, is the scene in *Welded* (1924) where Michael and Eleanor Cape sit side by side, a spotlight on each the only stage lighting, and '*speak, ostensibly to the other, but showing by their tone it is a thinking about oneself*' (II, 452).

the asides, can flow back and forth, poisoning itself and suggesting the dividedness of personality—not only split, but warring—'yet holding on to sanity'. It is telling that the threat of insanity is held only over the healthiest (and dullest) mind in the drama, and the supposed hereditary taint never does visit him. Some of the characters, much of the time, are in highly emotional states, but the rhythms of those who are not are equally variegated by the technique. The play moves vertically as well as horizontally, and the verticals include half-heard and half-understood dialogue as well as the conscience, desire and further observation and reflection which constitute the asides. The structure follows a similar pattern, being the flux and reflux of Nina's spiritual fortunes: (down), up, further down, further up, etc.

Despite some clearly expressed and felt *truths*—as that (in the lines quoted at the beginning of this chapter) Nina Leeds really moved 'to be near Ned'—it is significant that by about midpoint in the play, before the oscillations become so strong as to possess whole scenes radically, one almost loses any sense of what the 'true selves' of the persons in *Strange Interlude* are. What do they really want and what are they really after? Does Nina love Ned, as she says? For a while it seems really doubtful, so capable are they of self-contradiction. This is a kind of dramatic modernity which the increasing hyperboles of fluctuation then drive out of the play; internal flux is externalized. For five Acts Nina takes on a ruling passion for domination—for total control of 'my three men' (I, 133), for 'one complete male desire . . . husband! . . . lover! . . . father!' (I, 135). But in attempting to add 'son' to this group, Nina overextends herself and in the last Act all but the fantasy-father desert her.

★   ★   ★

The self-frustration of desire, the abandonment of one aim for another, larger one, and the discovery that what has been desired is, when attained, only a version of what was fled from, are similarly functions of the key O'Neill trope. There is a prime case of the third of these in *Dynamo*, where Reuben Light, in reaction against the stern religion of his minister-father, flees into the arms of the dynamo, only to discover that it is the same demanding God. It seems apparent that O'Neill's brother Jamie represented this type in life, and of the plays which levy most heavily on Jamie, *A Moon for the Misbegotten* (1947/52, written 1941-2)—written to give Jamie 'his final due', said Carlotta

c

O'Neill (Gelbs, p. 848)—presents the most extensive dramatic treatment of the subject.

Exhausted and near-derelict, Jamie Tyrone idealizes the giant farmer's daughter Josie Hogan as different from the class of women he knows best—whores. But his idealization leaves him unsatisfied, which—coupled with his knowledge of worldly attitudes—renders him cynical. Cynicism awakens desire for her, which can be countered by immediate revulsion, coupled with re-idealization or, if met by her acquiescence, assault on her as just another whore. The assault is then recognized as beyond reasonable measure, repented of, and the cycle begins again. It is really a parallel attitude to Nina Leeds's desire for a 'complete male desire': Jamie wants a mother *and* a whore.

In the mechanism behind Jamie, which produces the see-saw of emotion, the battle of attractions and repulsions, the operative terms are self-mockery, self-derision, self-defeat, self-laceration, self-torture— all terms used by O'Neill and the last of the masks of the ages of man worn in *Lazarus Laughed* (1927). Arthur and Barbara Gelb have recorded a revealing reminiscence of Carlotta O'Neill's which demonstrates that this complex was the particular involvement O'Neill himself experienced when writing *A Moon for the Misbegotten*:

> One night during the time O'Neill was working on the script [of *A Moon for the Misbegotten*], Carlotta was in her room listening to a Hitler speech on the radio. . . .
> 'Gene came in and asked if he could lie down beside me and listen. . . . [He] was terribly distressed by it.'
> When the speech was over, Carlotta tried to soothe her husband. Suddenly he sprang from the bed.
> 'Goddam whore!' he shouted, and ran from the room.
> A few seconds later Carlotta heard him weeping in his own room. Controlling her mortification, she went to comfort him, and found him lying, face down on the floor.
> 'He implored me to forgive him,' Carlotta said. 'He told me he hadn't known what he was saying, and explained that he had been reliving his days with Jamie—the days they had spent in whorehouses together. . . .'   (p. 849)

The self-torment, which psychoanalysts—including G. V. Hamilton, O'Neill's own—have related to unresolved Oedipal conflict and to 'death-wish' (Gelbs, p. 597), comprises a linguistic nexus for O'Neill's aesthetic and philosophical beliefs as well as his characterizations and his own personality. In an interview of 1922 with Oliver M. Sayler, O'Neill said,

> The theatre to me *is* life—the substance and interpretation of life.
> . . . [And] life is struggle, often, if not usually, unsuccessful struggle;
> for most of us have something within us which prevents us from
> accomplishing what we dream and desire. And then, as we progress,
> we are always seeing further than we can reach.   (Cargill, p. 107)

And two years later he wrote in his playbill essay for the Provincetown Players' production of Strindberg' *The Spook Sonata,*

> it is only by means of some form of 'super-naturalism' that we may
> express in the theatre what we comprehend intuitively of that self-
> defeating, self-obsession which is the discount we moderns have to
> pay for the loan of life.   (Cargill, p. 108)

Casting and rehearsal for *Welded,* O'Neill's first production in two years—he had averaged three productions a year for the seven years from 1916 to 1922—were then in progress. *Welded* has an upbeat ending, underscored by its 'stage directions': '*It is as if now by a sudden flash from within they recognized themselves, shorn of all the ideas, attitudes, cheating gestures which constitute the vanity of personality*' (II, 487). But it is the 'self-obsession' of modern, married life which is the play's subject. The two main characters are each surrounded by '*a circle of light*' which,

> *like auras of egoism, emphasize and intensify* ELEANOR *and* MICHAEL
> *throughout the play. There is no other lighting. The two other people and
> the rooms are distinguishable only by the light of* ELEANOR *and* MICHAEL.
> (II, 443)

The lighting is a direct theatrical use of 'super-naturalism' to express 'self-obsession'. The problem, as it presents itself to the playwright-husband, is the apparent collapse of his 'dream' of ideal, integrated marriage into what O'Neill was shortly to be calling, in his preliminary notes on the characterization of Electra in Greek drama, 'undramatic married banality'. Michael Cape cries in Act I of *Welded,* 'It seems at times as if some jealous demon of the common-place were mocking us' (II, 452). After an Act of tearing down, husband and wife exeunt to find consolation and satisfaction elsewhere, she with an old admirer (II. i)—an anticipation of Nina Leeds and Charlie Marsden—he with a prostitute (II. ii)—an anticipation of Dion Anthony and Cybele in *The*

Great God Brown (1926). From the prostitute Michael appears to receive
a revelation:

> WOMAN. I was thinkin' of the whole game. It's funny, ain't it?
> CAPE. (*slowly*) You mean—life?
> WOMAN. Sure. You got to laugh, ain't you? You got to loin to
> like it.
> CAPE. (*this makes an intense impression on him. He nods his head several
> times*) Yes! That's it! That's exactly it! That goes deeper than
> wisdom. To learn to love life—to accept it and be exalted—that's
> the one faith left to us!   (II, 478)

It looks like a 'solution' has been found, but the counter-demands of his
marriage flood back in Act III: the vanity of personality which desires
domination, which fears loss of self, *versus* the need for union and for
loss of mere self. Each conflicts with and cannot eradicate the other;
alternatives are then entertained and rejected: they cannot part for good.
A 'modern', casual relationship is as dream-denying as any other sub-
lunar solution—'If there's nothing left but—resignation!—what use is
there? How can we endure having our dreams perish in this?' (II, 486).

Despite the nominal happy ending (O'Neill often claimed that such
endings were meant only as temporary respites), the total impression of
the play is the non-ethical one of its title. Michael and Eleanor are
'welded', not in permanent happiness, but in the cyclic rhythm of
idealism, dissatisfaction, dissociation and return which is the play's
completed structure. Haunting, the return of the curse of the old life,
wars against exorcism, the play's main positive thrust. (*Exorcism*,
produced in 1920 but never published, is the title of O'Neill's play
about his suicide attempt.) O'Neill's later, and last drama of modern
married life, *Days Without End*, ends with the actual casting-out of the
cynical, life-denying *alter ego* 'Loving' at the foot of the Cross.

★   ★   ★

That the self-defeat of an O'Neill hero is defeat of a 'dream' is
mirrored in a personal conflict between his sense of the mystery and
wonder of life and his cynical revulsion from it, between romance
and 'reality'. This conflict is directly posed in various plays and sophisticated, more disillusioning statements of it appear during the latter
'twenties—a stronger sense of the illusoriness of the romance. In
Marco Millions (1928/7), after the Princess Kukachin has finally been

disabused of her illusions about the materialistic Polo, the Emperor
Kublai is moved to comment,

> My hideous suspicion is that God is only an infinite, insane energy
> which creates and destroys without other purpose than to pass
> eternity in avoiding thought. Then the stupid man becomes the
> Perfect Incarnation of Omnipotence and the Polos are the true
> children of God! (*He laughs bitterly*) Ha! (II, 426)

God abandons the side of romance and wonder and begins to appear on
the other side, hitherto a god-less materialism. When in O'Neill's very
next play, *The Great God Brown*, the self-torturing Dion Anthony,
agreeing to prostitute his creative talent by working for the businessman Brown, follows him out of the room saying, 'Lead on, Almighty
Brown, thou Kindly Light!' (III, 283), we witness an extrapolation of
Kublai Kaan's 'hideous suspicion'. O'Neill's altering emphasis appears in
Brown's stealing from Anthony the mask of his 'creative life'. It also
appears, directly coupled with the 'electricity' God, in the plot of
Dynamo. In *Strange Interlude*, an incipient Manichaeanism enters with
Nina Leeds's division of God into 'God the Mother', the beneficent
deity, and 'God the Father', the maleficent. In a metaphor echoing
Kublai's purposeless materialism, Nina calls life 'the electrical display of
God the Father' (I, 199).

The discovery of 'truth' gradually ceases to hold romantic promise in
O'Neill. The antiphonal conflict of *Days Without End*—'to get at the
real truth' versus 'nothing to hope for' when you find it (III, 495)—
contains the last suggestion that action will follow from intellectual
discovery. In the next play, *The Iceman Cometh* (1946), the question is
what to do with the horrible truth. The salesman Hickey believes that
the inhabitants of Harry Hope's 'hotel' should be made to see that their
'pipe dreams' of re-entering ordinary life are illusions. But to Larry
Slade, the derelict 'Old Foolosopher' who believes they should be left
alone in their dreams, Hickey is selling Death. In neither case are the
dreamers going to 'do' anything—it is only a question of whether
the life of 'tomorrows' is happier than one which knows there is no
tomorrow.

The Iceman's action appears to bear Larry out: the truth once discovered is quickly forgotten, a process facilitated by the revelation of
Hickey's 'personal' reason for his views (he has murdered his too-
understanding wife). But Larry is forced to abandon his own philosophy

of near-apathetic non-interference by his undesired moral revulsion at Don Parritt's confession that he betrayed his mother to the police:

> LARRY. (*snaps and turns on him, his face convulsed with detestation. His quivering voice has a condemning command in it*) Go! Get the hell out of life, God damn you, before I choke it out of you! Go up——!
>
> (III, 720)

The imperative is thrust up from the depths: go upstairs and kill yourself—which Parritt does.

The double ending of *The Iceman Cometh* is ironically normative. Life mocks both extremes. There are limits to human nature in all directions: the truth-seller has an ineradicable ego conditioning his philanthropy (and besides, humanity cannot bear his kind of reality), and the quietist can arrive at a pass where options close and even he must admit involvement and play God.

II

The see-saw rhythm of dialogue is thus carried over into both the thematic content of plays and into their structures. In terms of character it creates radical ambivalences which become O'Neill's *forte* in the creation of characters (the more single-minded are nearer pasteboard figures).[4] O'Neill came to found the very being of his people on ambivalences and polarities and he seems to have felt he could do without ordinarily conceived 'true self' in characters—or even without the discovery of true self (by character or audience) as dramas unwind. If Jamie Tyrone's revelation of himself to his brother Edmund in the final act of *Long Day's Journey* appears to contradict this, it is in fact a revelation precisely of radical disintegration. What Jamie discovers is that he has *no* real self:

> Want to warn you—against me. Mama and Papa are right. I've been rotten bad influence. And worst of it is, I did it on purpose . . . to make a bum of you. Or part of me did. A big part. The part that's been dead so long. That hates life. . . . Wanted you to fail. Mama's baby, Papa's pet!
>   . . . I love you more than I hate you. . . . I'd like to see you become the greatest success in the world. But you'd better be on your guard. Because I'll do my damndest to make you fail.

[4] Polo and Brown, affected by a near-cosmic and yet socially satirical thrust, would play well as Brechtain conceptions.

... And when you come back [from the sanatorium], look out for me. I'll be waiting to welcome you with that 'my old pal' stuff, and give you the glad hand, and at the first good chance I get stab you in the back. (pp. 165-6)

It is a triumph of his 'live' self that Jamie can, with the aid of drink, bring himself to discover this to Edmund, for it cannot do his announced motive any good. This triumph is yet another self-defeat and is, as Jamie himself knows, only momentary. Despite a classic 'recognition scene', which we might expect to integrate Jamie, we continue to believe in the radical, self-destructive disunity of his soul.

From a very early point in his development, O'Neill appears not to have needed to work with heroes, or characters who would win through to positions of audience-shared satisfaction. In a letter of 1919, he wrote disparagingly to Barrett Clark of Smitty, the protagonist of *The Moon of the Caribbees* (1918), implying that his criticism is what constitutes the play's significance, while the more 'heroic' treatment of the same character in *In the Zone* (1917/19) is a deficiency:

Smitty in the stuffy, greasepaint atmosphere of *In the Zone* is magnified into a hero who attracts our sentimental sympathy. In *The Moon*, poised against a background of that beauty, sad because it is eternal, which is one of the revealing moods of the sea's truth, his silhouetted gestures of self pity are reduced to their proper significance, his thin whine of weakness is lost in the silence which it was mean enough to disturb, we get the perspective to judge him—and the others—and we find his sentimental posing much more out of harmony with truth, much less in tune with beauty, than the honest vulgarity of his mates. To me, *The Moon* works with truth, and *Beyond the Horizon* also, while *In the Zone* substitutes theatrical sentimentalism.

(Clark, p. 58-9)

What provided O'Neill with the 'perspective to judge' in *Beyond the Horizon* (1920) was the decision to make Robert, the younger Mayo brother, stay on the farm and marry Ruth Atkins, though he desires the romance of the sea. O'Neill revealingly compared Robert Mayo with his antitype, the sentimental land-desiring sailor he had recently portrayed in *The Long Voyage Home* (1917):

At exactly the right moment, when I was floundering about in the maze of [*Beyond the Horizon*, Olson, who served as his model in *The Long Voyage Home*] ... turned up in my memory ... I thought,

'What if he had stayed on the farm, with his instincts. What would have happened?' But I realized at once that he never would have stayed, not even if he had saddled himself with the wife and kids. It amused him to pretend he craved the farm. He was too harmonious a creation of the God of Things as They are. . . .

And from that point I started to think of a more intellectual, civilized type—a weaker type from the standpoint of the above-mentioned God—a man who would have [an] inborn craving for the sea's unrest, only in him it would be conscious, too conscious, intellectually diluted into a vague, intangible, romantic wanderlust. His powers of resistance, both moral and physical, would also probably be correspondingly watered. He would throw away his instinctive dream and accept the thralldom of the farm for, why almost any nice little poetical craving—the romance of sex, say.

(Gelbs, p. 335–6)

It is thus hard to doubt that the driving energy behind *Beyond the Horizon* was critical, just as the portrayal of the Olson-type in the play, Robert's elder brother Andrew, who does go to sea but for whom it means nothing, is basically critical. We watch a twin process of degeneration and deterioration, and Robert's recognition that only death can take him 'beyond the horizon' is the play's only enlightenment. This scene, the last, was cut in the initial production, but restored by O'Neill to the published text, and he stressed, in occasional comments, that Robert's vision was to be taken seriously. Whatever that vision may imply (on a scale from delusion to mystical experience), it does not proceed developmentally from the bondage of the plot: it is release.

★   ★   ★

In 'Eugene O'Neill: An Exercise in Unmasking', Eugene Waith has put the case for 'development' in the plays:

the characteristic movement . . . [is] toward discovery or revelation or both—a kind of unmasking.

Toward the end of an O'Neill play there almost always comes a moment when the principal characters are for the first time fully revealed to the audience, and often it is only then that they fully understand themselves or their relationships to each other and to the world they live in. These recognition scenes are O'Neill's high points. . . . O'Neill seems to have thought of his characters' coming to terms with life as movement forward or back. (Gassner, p. 33)

This view allows Waith to comment that *Desire Under the Elms* (1924) depicts Eben Cabot and Abbie Putnam 'mov[ing] through a sequence of false attitudes toward each other to true understanding and love' (p. 36). Yet it is possible that the web of life created by and for them leaves them no such release and that any positive state of mind in which the play may leave them cannot communicate itself to us so unambiguously.

Abbie murders her and Eben's child to 'prove' her love for him, to prove she did not want a child to steal the farm Eben has so stolidly (and greedily) maintained was his by right. (Barrett Clark thought (p. 99) she would have murdered her husband, old Ephraim Cabot, instead.) Eben then turns her in to the police:

EBEN. I woke him up. I told him. He says, 'Wait 'til I git dressed.'
I was waiting. I got to thinkin' o' yew. I got to thinkin' how I'd
loved ye. It hurt like somethin' was bustin' in my chest an' head.
I got t' cryin'. I knowed sudden I loved ye yet, an' allus would
love ye! (1, 266)

Eben can now 'love' Abbie precisely *because* he has just informed on her (compare Don Parritt's betrayal of his mother in *The Iceman*) and because he intends, as we discover momentarily, to share her punishment: 'I got t' pay fur my part o' the sin' (1, 267). Regression and relaxation, masochism and revenge may be absent from Eben and Abbie's minds, but not from ours. The 'love' here offers itself as another 'poetical craving', not exempt from the mire of '*ideas, attitudes [and] cheating gestures which constitute the vanity of personality*'.

The ending of *Desire* shares its ambiguity between subjective elation in the protagonists and wider, darker ramifications of their personalities which the play has beforehand canvassed—and by which ramifications the drama has obtained its tensile strength—with *Beyond the Horizon, The Straw, Anna Christie* (1921/2), *Welded* and a number of later plays.[5] If *Desire* contains no technical facility (masks, unspoken thoughts —both to make their appearance in the years immediately following) for showing alternatives to what Abbie and Eben say they feel, it does surround them with irony, Ephraim Cabot's—'Ye make a slick pair o' murderin' turtle-doves' (1, 267)—and the Sheriff's—the play's curtain-

---

[5] It is perhaps the apparent unconsciousness of its own previous canvass which makes the discovery-of-faith ending of *Days Without End* finally unsatisfactory. The hero is not 'integrated' at the end, as Mary Colum thought (Colum, p. 359), his devil is merely cast out.

line, 'It's a jim-dandy farm, no denyin'. Wish I owned it!' (1, 269). This ironical environment so isolates the presumptive lovers that it almost deflects the tragedy into 'tragical satire'. It is easy to imagine the mind which created Robert Mayo being witheringly sardonic towards his turtle-doves; that the cynicism is self-reflexive on 'the world', which takes such views, does not impair its force. O'Neill, as might be expected, took one and then another side in public, nor are the dramas neutral—they do not project a synthesis of sympathy and criticism, a view which makes both possible to an integrated mind. If *Desire Under the Elms* wins through, it is to a position of ambiguity, a poise *between* false and true 'attitudes' at the end. The former cannot be discounted, nor the latter denied Eben and Abbie. This ultimate ambivalence rids the play of injected 'acceptance' and frees O'Neill, on the other hand, from having to work with totally unredeemed material.

The ambivalence is equally relevant to Lavinia Mannon in the trilogy *Mourning Becomes Electra* (1931). The plays proceed by an ever-narrowing series of options, whose necessary shrinkage is a measure of 'Vinnie's' fate. Each 'event' in the plot is an attempt to bring about an *ending*, and each time (until the last) unforeseen factors intervene to prevent any ending. Each time, as well, it comes to seem possible to choose between less and less. There were many possible reactions to the discovery of a mother's adultery—Vinnie's helps goad hers into the murder of her father. There is a more restricted range of reactions to a mother who has murdered your father—Vinnie drives hers to death, but has to account for the chagrin of her brother. With the brother Orin going mad and threatening her, Vinnie has a few alternatives left—to do as he wishes and live only with him, or to run off with Peter, or to find a way to marry Peter and stay where she is. She attempts the last; Orin dies; and so she is closer to freedom than she has ever been, but closer to 'fate' as well. Peter deserts her, unable in his Puritanism to meet her at the passionate level she desires and needs. Love before everything, she is now crying, only to discover she has come full circle and is implicitly justifying the mother she had hounded to death. Her choice is now simple: she may walk out on her entire life in search of love (and in so doing admit she was wrong in persecuting her mother), or she may board herself up in the Mannon mansion, turning her back on the only thing in life she has come to desire, in fulfilment of her duty. Electra becomes Mourning.

When Lavinia does go inside, we may feel, with Eric Mottram, that her action sets the seal on the trilogy as 'a modern masochistic play of self-punishment' (p. 34); but we should also feel, at the cost of dividing ourselves, that her action was essentially right, necessary. 'By the title,' O'Neill insisted, 'I sought to convey that mourning befits Electra; it becomes Electra to mourn; it is her fate; black is becoming to her and it is the color that becomes her destiny' (Gelbs, p. 433).

Mourning Becomes Electra, more than any play O'Neill wrote to 1935, does—if only by compounding them—avoid categories. That such evasion was uppermost in O'Neill's mind from the very start is demonstrable. To George Jean Nathan he wrote,

> It has been one hell of a job . . . to conjure a Greek fate out of the Mannons themselves (without calling in the aid of even a Puritan Old Testament God) that would convince a modern audience without religion or moral ethics; to prevent the surface melodrama of the plot from overwhelming the real drama . . . and finally to keep myself out of it. . . . [It is] a valid dramatic experience with intense tortured passions. . . .   (Cargill, pp. 55-6)

In a letter to the *New York Tribune* in 1921, O'Neill denied any necessity for Freudian or Jungian bases for the 'psychology' of *Diff'rent* (1920/1), his first study of New England 'repression' and violence.[6] He was after, he claimed, 'life that swallows all formulas'.[7] In its major thrust, the fate of Electra-Lavinia, *Mourning Becomes Electra* does bypass even Freudian categories.

★   ★   ★

There are moments, even scenes in O'Neill when formulization and even apparent polarities are felt to be abandoned for an undifferentiated totality of predicament. These moments are generally sprung out of extreme tension and blocked action, and occur in an interstice of time. The confrontation of Lavinia Mannon and her mother Christine is one such 'moment': their relation may smack of a categorical Electra-complex,[8] but the texture of their dialogue is sufficiently variegated to blot out simplicities.

[6] *The Rope* (1918/19) does anticipate *Desire Under the Elms* in being a study of father–son hatred and possessiveness in a New England setting; the sexual element is not, however, explicit.

[7] *New York Tribune* (13 February, 1921); Cargill, p. 105.

[8] 'I do not see any advance or gain in the introduction of the term "Electra complex", and do not advocate its use' (S. Freud (1920): *Works*, tr. and ed. J. Strachey, xviii (1955), p. 155).

Each seeks to dominate the other. It is a very uncomic version of the dialogue in *The Way of the World*, a 'war game': advantages taken, pursued, attack overextended, retrenched, abandoned, defences maintained, counterattack. There is no merely theatrical exposition, as no item from the past (or the off-stage present) enters only to flesh out the 'story'. Each entry is part of the present battle.

Hughie (1958/9; written 1941) shows O'Neill's eventual total mastery of speech which is *making* a relationship rather than just stating its existence. 'Erie' Smith, 'a teller of tales', runs a wider, if less intense gamut than the Mannons, to win over *and* dominate the new night clerk of his sleazy West Side hotel. It is the conflict between winning over and domination which turns Erie's speech into a force-field: he is torn between despising the man's lack of Broadway 'dope' and the need to enlist his companionship and sympathy. He berates, cajoles, flatters, in a complete cycle[9] of attitudes whose spring, like the husband in *Welded*, is his need and his cynical reaction. In the end a fascinating cyclic symbiosis is attained and 'life'—suspended for Erie since the death of the previous night clerk—can once more go on. The characters, like Lavinia and Christine Mannon and Erie Smith, who are involved in the agonies of suspended time need not understand 'all' and are most certainly not above or outside their situations. It is interesting to reflect that *Bound East For Cardiff* (1916), the play which brought the unknown O'Neill to the notice of the then unfounded Provincetown Players, not only contains such a 'moment', but is controlled by it, wholly polarized by the sheer fact of the dying sailor lying in his bunk. In a way, *Bound East* is Driscoll's, the onlooker's, play—as *Lazarus Laughed* is really Caligula's—and he and the dying Yank exist in a similar symbiosis as Erie and his two 'Hughies'.

The dialogue of Driscoll and of the other men, for whom he comes to stand proxy by virtue of his participation in the death agony, avoids, refuses to countenance the idea of death. (It assails them by threatening the 'illusion' of sea-life by which they are sustained.) No one protests harder than Driscoll, and Driscoll does not break through to any clearer conception, much less to resignation and acceptance. It falls to the dying man himself to bring about a momentary *éclaircissement*, by admitting he is going to die. It is this admission—and not, as Kenneth Macgowan thought, 'the fever of death' (Cargill, p. 450)—which releases the flood of reminiscence and worry which brings the play to

[9] See the review by Henry Hewes reprinted in Cargill, pp. 224-6.

its ultimate articulacy. But the flood ironically takes Yank away from death to illusion—the dream of owning a farm—and again ironically, the illusion is nourishing, sustaining. The whole pattern of *The Iceman* and *Hughie* is already there, in 1916.

III

If the agony for an O'Neill protagonist was the struggle to break out of the 'web', the nexus of fluctuation and ambivalence, to find a 'faith' which was not regression and 'pipe dream', it was in a manner O'Neill's problem, too. Success would mean the abandonment of the dramatic as it exists in the plays. Thus there is a sympathy for 'failure' in O'Neill which grows apace with wilder dreaming and more incisive analysis of dream and ideal.

Lazarus is O'Neill's attempt at characterization of a man who had come through; and because he 'had', nothing in the play tests him. Thus, the careful, Act-by-Act progression of deaths—his parents and relations (Act I), his followers (Act II), his wife (Act III), himself (Act IV)—while obviously 'structural', fails of dramatic tension. There is no pressure, let alone an increase of pressure, in any of these confrontations. Only the effect on Caligula, a recognizable self-torturing O'Neill type, incapable of sustained 'belief', rescues *Lazarus Laughed* for drama.

For the caught character, in the long play, the effort is a search, and the 'ending' takes on particular importance as a potential counterweight to the 'web'. *Mourning Becomes Electra*, with its endings which turn out not to be endings, might have been titled *Days Without End*, which O'Neill wrote next: it attempts parabolically the very question of 'end' (termination, purpose).

O'Neill titled three of this play's four Acts 'Plot for a Novel'. The hero, a novelist, is desperately searching for an 'ending' to the plot of *his* novel. That plot is a thinly disguised version of his own life, so he is also searching for a personal 'end'. That end, if it comes, will also be the end of O'Neill's play. *Days Without End*, by means of this aesthetic analogy, is by way of being a transcript of O'Neill's process of creation, which is presented almost directly in the first scene, when John and 'Loving', his visible *alter ego*, discuss possible 'endings'. John's predicament is similar to Michael Cape's in *Welded*, with the additional complication that a gratuitously committed adultery may alienate his wife if it is discovered.

The ending for which O'Neill settled, after many alterations, was religious conversion (to Catholicism). This is not illogical (as has been claimed), for it exists as an option—which Loving prevents—from early in the play. John has staked all on 'married love' and it has not, he knows not how, prevented his adultery. (He cannot admit that 'he' also hates his wife.) Some absolute outside marriage must stand as its guarantor—and this is the function of religion in the play, the force capable (as it turns out) of excluding the cynical self-hating portion of personality from life.

The ending is indeed melodramatic and naïve (in the context of the whole play), but possibly odder is the ambiguity caused by the 'split-personality' device. (The business of masks in *The Great God Brown* may similarly end in confusion). Other characters besides 'John' are allowed to hear 'Loving', the denyer, though only John can see him. That John, the 'romantic' side of personality, would be unable to prevent Loving from 'thinking' is a reasonable *donnée*, but that he (as visible deputy for the absent 'whole' self) cannot prevent Loving from speaking out his cynicisms makes him seem altogether more schizoid than it appears he is to be taken. The others tut-tut John for 'Loving's' interjections, but do not accept him for the tortured and radically disorganized person we do. If the point of making Loving audible was to display the other characters' insensibility to the protagonist's agony, it was done at the risk of making the protagonist a weaker man; but the weaker he is, the less final will we see his ultimate decision.

Days Without End was not quite O'Neill's last attempt at the Way Up as a solution, but from 1935 the Way Down, the search for absolute bottom—not wholly absent from earlier plays—so energizes his work that it nearly transfigures itself into something like the 'positive' value whose rejection begins it on its downward path.

The Gelbs have identified O'Neill's personal time of doing 'his best to hit bottom' as 'from early December of 1910 to May of 1911' (p. 155). This is the time in Argentina which the dying Yank in *Bound East* remembers with such fondness. But it is the other Yank, 'the 'airy ape' (1922), who explains to the real gorilla,

I ain't on oith and I ain't in heaven, get me? I'm in de middle tryin' to separate 'em, takin' all de woist punches from bot' of 'em. Maybe dat's what dey call hell, huh? But you, yuh're at de bottom. You belong. (III, 253)

It is of course Yank's shaken belief in his own 'belonging' which provides the play's motive force, and the scenes which display his search up and down 'society' looking for a new place to belong (and muddling this with revenge on his awakener) end only when 'de bottom' is reached, and he is crushed by a true ape.

'The bottom' reappears in 1928 as a 'dive for the gutter', when Ned Darrell interprets Nina Leeds's behaviour in the years just after the war-time death of her *fiancé*:

> She's piled on too many destructive experiences. A few more and she'll dive for the gutter just to get the security that comes from knowing she's touched bottom and there's no farther to go! (I, 35)

Orin Mannon and Mary Tyrone state similar intentions, which flower as Larry Slade's description of Harry Hope's:

> What is it? It's the No Chance Saloon. It's Bedrock Bar, The End of the Line Cafe, The Bottom of the Sea Rathskeller! Don't you notice the beautiful calm in the atmosphere? That's because it's the last harbor. No one here has to worry about where they're going next, because there is no farther they can go. It's a great comfort to them. Although even here they keep up the appearances of life with a few harmless pipe dreams. (III, 587)

Ironically, Larry's picture is more wish than reality, in that the 'harmless pipe dreams' do cause 'worry'. Though Larry is for the others having their dreams, he prides himself on having none and wishing for none: that will be the ultimate 'beautiful calm'.

Larry mocks all hopes, ideals and faiths as 'pipe' or 'dope dreams', in the metaphor O'Neill had used as early as *The Straw* (III, 350) and *The Hairy Ape* (III, 215 and 253), when his mother's narcotics addiction was still a closely-kept secret. (Only the release of *Long Day's Journey* revealed it.) The dope or (opium) pipe-dream is a metaphoric intersection of hope, ideal, fantasy and unconsciousness. These dreams are mocked and yet it is suggested that all life lives by them and that without them there is no life. There are, however, a cursed few, the self-tormentors, for whom the usual run of pipe-dreams is unsatisfactory, and for them only some final state of insentience, or 'Nirvana', can minister. And there remains one final turn of the screw: the desire for insentience can turn out to be the biggest pipe-dream of all, and the one which gives, as a 'dream', least satisfaction to the holder.

*   *   *

The state of total rest 'begins' in a kind of mystical experience:

EDMUND. I lay on the bowsprit, facing astern, with the water foaming into spume under me, the masts with every sail white in the moonlight, towering high above me. I became drunk with the beauty and singing rhythm of it, and for a moment I lost myself— actually lost my life. I was set free! I dissolved in the sea, became white sails and flying spray, became beauty and rhythm, became moonlight and the ship and the high dim-starred sky! I belonged, without past or future, within peace and unity and a wild joy, within something greater than my own life, or the life of Man, to Life itself; To God, if you want to put it that way. Then another time, on the American Line, when I was look-out on the crow's nest in the dawn watch . . . the moment of ecstatic freedom came. The peace, the end of the quest, the last harbor, the joy of belonging to a fulfillment beyond men's lousy, pitiful, greedy fears and hopes and dreams! . . . Like a saint's vision of beatitude. . . .

He grins wryly.

It was a great mistake, my being born a man, I would have been much more successful as a sea gull or a fish.   (p. 153)

Edmund Tyrone's language gathers up O'Neill's previous touchings on the subject; Yank's ('belonging') and Larry Slade's ('the last harbor'). Eric Mottram has characterized this passage as 'a sea ecstasy which [O'Neill] tried to make over into a religious experience . . . a central positive experience' (p. 31). Yet, as Mottram goes on to point out, Edmund's picture (in the context of his real present entrapment) is a 'narcotic escape'. Edmund's own phrase for it is that he is one of 'the fog people' whose 'native eloquence' is 'stammering' (p. 154). The 'fog person', like the pipe-dreamer, is an ambivalent conception—on the one hand the wanderer, lost between romance and reality, in the hell of this world; on the other, the person whose real element is an even peaceful, mistiness, beyond care and vexation.

The desire for total rest enters as early as *Strange Interlude*, when Nina Leeds, in the shambles of her failed dominations, succumbs to a regressiveness so powerful in its expression as to suggest something ultimate:

Charlie will come in every day to visit . . . he'll comfort and amuse me . . . we can talk together of the old days . . . when I was a girl . . . when I was happy . . . before I fell in love with Gordon Shaw and all this tangled mess of love and hate and pain and birth began!
(1, 191)

You're so restful, Charlie. I feel as if I were a girl again and you were my father and the Charlie of those days made into one. I wonder is our old garden the same? We'll pick flowers together in the ageing afternoons of spring and summer, won't we? It will be a comfort to get home—to be old and to be home again at last—to be in love with peace together—to love each other's peace—to sleep with peace together——! (*She kisses him—then shuts her eyes with a deep sigh of requited weariness*)—to die in peace! I'm so contentedly weary with life!
(1, 199–200)

Nina seems here not only to desire peace, but to have gained it, if in frustrated reaction and if at the cost of her vitality. The 'strange interlude' is over.

From the peace of rest in *Strange Interlude* to a positive extinction of 'ecstatic freedom' in *Long Day's Journey* and a negative desire for extinction in *The Iceman*—the spectrum adumbrates the climate of the Buddhist 'Nirvana'. That Nirvana represents an ultimate release from the antinomies of existence is undisputed, though whether it is a nihilistic and 'negative' conception or a 'positive' one is a matter of continuing debate.[10]

When O'Neill used the word, he was concerned to associate it with 'hope':

The Clerk's mind remains in the street to greet the noise of a far-off El train. Its approach is pleasantly like a memory of hope; then it roars and rocks and rattles past the nearby corner, and the noise pleasantly deafens memory; then it recedes and dies, and there is something melancholy about that. But there is hope. Only so many El trains pass in one night, and each one passing leaves one less to pass, so the night recedes, too, until at last it must die and join all the other long nights in Nirvana, the Big Night of Nights. And that's life.
(*Hughie*, p. 19)

(O'Neill has finally merged his archaic Broadway slang and his romantic style into poetry.)

In *Beyond the Pleasure Principle*, Freud broached a dichotomy central to his later thought. The 'pleasure principle', which he had earlier thought to be a uniform force of pain-avoidance, 'the tendency to keep intracerebral excitation constant' (Breuer's phrasing; Freud, *op. cit.*, p. 9), he now suggested could tolerate a rhythm of willed frustration and release. There was, however, a new principle, one in which the organism,

[10] See R. L. Slater, *Paradox and Nirvana* (Chicago, 1951).

in the grip of an autonomous force (ego-instinct) different from the sexual (object-instinct), willed a state of 'Nirvana'. Freud borrowed the phrase 'Nirvana principle' from Barbara Low's *Psychoanalysis* (1920; p. 73), and from it quickly grew his notion of the nature of destructive forces in personality and the controversial 'death-instinct' in sentient matter.[11] The 'Nirvana principle', unlike the 'pleasure principle', seeks only rest, vacuity, release from the cycle of existence into non-activity.

In *Mourning Becomes Electra*, Vinnie and Orin had projected (and even visited) a 'South Sea Island' as their escape from the Mannon 'fate'. O'Neill wrote his next two plays of 'religious finality [and] tender family sentiment',[12] *Days Without End* and *Ah, Wilderness!* (1933) concurrently at Sea Island, Georgia. The last plays were all written at the 'pseudo-Chinese' San Ramon, California home, 'Tao House'.[13] The relations between Tao and Buddhism are complex and hardly un-ravelled, but it is often asserted that the spread of Buddhism into China was facilitated by Taoist concepts which resembled the 'new' notions: 'Thus for the Buddhist terms they coined Chinese equivalents. The Primal Nothingness (*pên-wu*) of Taoism prepared the way for the understanding of the Buddhist negativism of the Nonego, the Void and *nirvâna*'.[14]

In interviews and letters to editors, O'Neill made 'positive' claims for the bleakest of his early tragedies. According to him, the 'poetical vision' of *Desire Under the Elms* 'illuminat[ed] even the most sordid and mean blind alleys of life' (Cargill, p. 55). The emphasis falls on the 'illumination'. Perhaps O'Neill was bending over backwards to reassure the optimists: *Desire* was threatened with closure by the happy few for whom 'pessimism' constitutes a clear and present danger to the

---

[11] See esp. pp. 55–6, 60–1. Freud was developing the notion of distinct 'Nirvana' and 'pleasure' principles as he wrote, and in parts of the manuscript they are indistinguishable. By 1921, however, the distinction was clearly categorical and had led already towards the later speculations concerning life- and death-instincts which informs *Civilisation and Its Discontents* (1930). Herbert Marcuse and Norman O. Brown are among those who have extended this aspect of Freud's thinking.

[12] See the analysis by John Howard Lawson in Chapter V of *Theory and Technique of Playwriting* (1936), pp. 129–41 (reprinted in Gassner, pp. 42–51).

[13] O'Neill slept on a 'huge ebony opium couch, converted into a bed' (Gelbs, pp. 824–5). O'Neill often wrote in bed, and a number of his plots came to him in dreams.

[14] H. Dumoulin, *A History of Zen Buddhism*, tr. P. Peachey (1963), p. 54.

THE VANITY OF PERSONALITY

American way of life. No such O'Neillian optimism is recorded apropos of the late plays. One may finally imagine, as Leslie Fiedler so unsparingly does of almost all major American writers, that O'Neill had 'a secret message', an ultimate drift of hardly bearable toughness and dread—that the only supportable end of life is life's end, living or actual death, and that for the self-tortured there is only the Void. Worse still, the life instinct which was so baffled in its own search for faith, takes its revenge at the last by preventing the death-instinct's attainment of Nothingness: 'Be God, there's no hope!' says Larry Slade, thinking of the now dead Don Parritt *with a bitter self-derision,* 'I'll never be a success in the grandstand—or anywhere else!' (III, 726). In the end, the drama and the bitterness are co-terminal. That the long disease of O'Neill's final, unproductive decade should have been a pro- gressive degeneration of motor processes only, leaving his mind to function 'normally', is, in relation to a lifetime of spiritual agony, almost too horrible even to contemplate.

Note

For general accounts of American Theatre and important collections of criticisms of performances, see the prefatory note to Chapter I.

The following books are a selection of those concerned with present-day American theatre:

R. Brustein, *Seasons of Discontent: Dramatic Opinions, 1959–1965* (1965);

A. S. Downer, *Recent American Drama* (1961);

R. A. Duprey, *Just Off the Aisle* (1962);

R. F. Gardner, *The Splintered Stage: The Decline of the American Theatre* (1965);

A. Lewis, *American Plays and Playwrights of the Contemporary Theatre* (1965);

G. Weales, *American Drama Since World War II* (1962).

L. Broussard's *American Drama: Contemporary Allegory from Eugene O'Neill to Tennessee Williams* (1962) is especially applicable to a theme of this chapter.

European Influences

JAMES ROSENBERG

★

It is difficult at best to discuss European influences on the American drama, since, for all practical intents and purposes, American drama is, started out as and remains essentially European. The same holds true for most of the general shape, pressure and texture of American society. It is no coincidence that President Abraham Lincoln, on the evening of his assassination in the leading legitimate theatre in Washington, D.C., was watching a British play—Tom Taylor's *Our American Cousin*—or that the leading 'American' playwright of the period was an Anglo-Irishman, Dion Boucicault, whose reputation had been made on the London stage, or that the most widely read novelist in the American South was (and may still be), Sir Walter Scott, or that the most admired native-born novelists and poets were those—like William Gilmore Simms and Sidney Lanier—who most closely imitated British models from the early nineteenth and late eighteenth centuries.

One of the reasons, after all, why the American drama was virtually stillborn in the nineteenth century was that it sprang full-blown from the brow of British drama at a time when the British drama was at its lowest ebb in history. The playwright-actor-managers who began to troupe the new continent in the latter half of the century were as often as not British in birth or origin and—despite a strenuous attempt to find an 'American' theme in plays dealing with such native heroes as Rip Van Winkle and Daniel Boone—their plays, whether original works, adaptations of novels or short stories, or 'versions' of Shakespeare, were firmly imitative of British models.

It is traditional, of course, to mark Eugene O'Neill as the fountainhead of American drama and the playwright who is still, in the minds of most critics, not only the greatest but the most representative

American playwright. Yet the fact remains that O'Neill, too, is largely a European playwright *manqué* and his work is a pastiche (except for, significantly, the highly autobiographical realistic family plays) of borrowed and mostly ill-digested bits of Strindberg and Georg Kaiser and Sophocles and Freud. Nor was O'Neill, as has been indicated, really the first American playwright; when we call him that, what we mean, I suppose, is that he seems to be the first one to regard his work as more of an art than a craft, the first one we would care to set alongside his English, French or German contemporaries without a lively sense of national embarrassment.

It is further significant that O'Neill is rarely, if ever, discussed by American critics without their first conceding rather uneasily that he is really a very bad and awkward writer. (In fact, the whole American mystique of the 'great' writer who is also a very 'bad' writer—Whitman, Dreiser, O'Neill—is surely worthy of full-scale investigation some day by a critic interested in the interrelationships between style and society.)

O'Neill's position as the most 'central' American playwright may, indeed, depend not so much upon any innate quality in his writing (certainly Thornton Wilder is a 'better' playwright in many important respects) as in the fact that he represents a sort of archetypal pattern of the American experience, both literary and historical—the rebellion of the son against the father. In O'Neill's case, it was an uneasy rebellion acted out not only in his work but in his life as well, with an Irish-born actor-father who spent a good part of his theatrical career starring in an adaptation of *The Count of Monte Cristo*. The ghost of James O'Neill and the theatrical romanticism he stood for is exorcised and destroyed over and over again in his son's plays, and yet perhaps the cruellest blight on the work of Eugene O'Neill is the fact that he is never really able, either in sensibility or style, to rid himself of that *Count of Monte Cristo* world which he so loathed and rebelled against.

Strindberg may be in his mind, but Edmond Dantes is in his heart; and the history of American drama may be contained in that formula.

In looking, then, at the pattern of European influences on the American drama, two main points emerge. One is that these influences have almost invariably been limited to the realm of technique, that American playwrights, in going to school to Ibsen, Chekhov, Strindberg, Shaw, etc., have picked up bits and pieces of technique and have rarely if ever absorbed any of the passionate response to life's textures which characterizes the work of the European masters. This may not be surprising in a nation so single-mindedly devoted to the mastery of skills and mechanical techniques which add up to a formula for success, yet this kind of technological concern is and always has been inimical to the nature of art. The other point is that American playwrights have long and consistently denied, or simply failed to see, the nature of a truly American theme and subject-matter which might give to their work, whatever its surface manifestations of avant garde techniques, the depth of quality which characterizes, again, the best work of the best European playwrights from Shakespeare to Samuel Beckett.

To take the second point first, it is revelatory to glance through the works of a handful of the most important American playwrights and note where their best work lies. Does it not become increasingly clear, for example, that the peak of O'Neill's achievement is to be found, not in the rather pretentious imitations of Continental expressionist and symbolist techniques, but in the very personal, and generally quite realistic, hunks of more or less raw autobiography—the early sea plays, *The Iceman Cometh, A Touch of the Poet, Long Day's Journey Into Night*? Is not the real heart and soul of Arthur Miller's achievement to be found in his early plays—*All My Sons* and *Death of a Salesman*—rather than in his later, strained attempts to become the poet laureate of the Lincoln Center? Similarly, has Tennessee Williams ever, except intermittently, recaptured the highly personal, lyrical note of his first real success, *The Glass Menagerie*? As for Thornton Wilder, is it not true that, while critics may prefer *The Skin of Our Teeth* or *The Matchmaker* (alias *Hello, Dolly!*), scarcely a day in the year goes by when *Our Town* is not being performed somewhere in the world. Similarly, the reputation of William Inge, such as it is, rests on the early *Come Back, Little Sheba* and *Picnic*, and it is quite clear that no play in Edward Albee's still-slender canon has quite equalled the impact of *Who's Afraid of Virginia Woolf?*

What does all this imply? Two things, I believe. One—striking, but not particularly germane to the present discussion—is that American playwrights (and American artists generally) tend to show a steady downhill pattern in their careers. In nine cases out of ten, their early (often quite autobiographical) work is their best, so that instead of showing a steady deepening and maturing of purpose and skill their careers frequently become a rather sad and often frantic attempt to recapture the magic and lost innocence of first things. More important,

I think, is the fact that one basic theme unites nearly all of the plays I mentioned in the preceding paragraph. Is it not noteworthy that almost all take as their world and their unifying metaphor the micro-cosm of the family unit, and that their basic dramatic tensions spring from the lacerating interpenetration of feeling between parents and children, husbands and wives, brothers and sisters? Now it may well be argued that the family as a focus for drama is scarcely a uniquely American concept; some critics have gone so far as to identify the *Agamemnon* of Aeschylus as the first domestic tragedy and have gone on from there to place such plays as *Othello* and *Ghosts* in the same line of development. Actually, to call such plays as the *Agamemnon* and *Othello* 'domestic tragedies' is to play with critical terms rather capriciously, for, while both may spring from the fundamental tensions of hatred and jealousy and love and revenge involving husbands, wives and children, they clearly are meant to take place in a much larger world than that enclosed within the walls of one house. And, while some American domestic dramas may exhibit cosmic longings (*Our Town* most notably), they generally have their greatest impact when frankly focused on the private, the personal, the purely interfamilial. The names of the husband and wife in Albee's *Who's Afraid of Virginia Woolf?* may be intended to suggest the Father and Mother of Our Country, but I suspect that few members of the audience ever responded to this play as some sort of myth of the American nation.

This is not, of course, to argue that modern Europeans do not also have families and that the family as a centre of dramatic interest is unknown to European playwrights. It is to argue, however, that the family is the basic unit of bourgeois life, that the United States is the one nation in the world which has never known anything other than a bourgeois structure (even Soviet Russia still has overtones of a bygone aristocracy), and that middle-class family life is therefore not only a natural, but indeed an inevitable, subject for American writers. The nearest thing to an aristocrat we have ever produced is perhaps a Thomas Jefferson or a John F. Kennedy, and it is significant that, in our own eyes as well as in those of the rest of the world, the representative American type is a Benjamin Franklin, an Abraham Lincoln, a Walt Whitman, a Mark Twain.

What has happened, however, is that American playwrights, themselves middle-class in their origins (we have few, if any, American aristocrats in the true sense, and not many products of our ghettoes and slums have made a real impact on our literature), have consistently struggled to get free from the only world which they are competent to deal with. The plays I mentioned earlier represent a return (often an unconscious one) to the womb of the family experience; they also represent, I believe, the best of American drama, by and large. There are obviously other plays, whose titles I did not list, which represent attempts, often pretentious and almost always disastrous, to move outside the small, constricting limits of the family unit on to a larger, more cosmic stage of action. Nevertheless, they are in the minority. Notice, for example, the extraordinary paucity of political plays in the field of American drama, plays in the tradition, say, of *Coriolanus* or *Fuenteovejuna* or *Danton's Death* or *An Enemy of the People*. (One of the most interesting, and revelatory, texts in modern American drama is Arthur Miller's adaptation of the latter play—now almost impossible to find, since its author has allowed it to go out of print and has not seen fit to include it among his collected works.) I suppose our American attempts in this line are represented by such plays as *Winterset* and *State of the Union* and *The Best Man*—at best, Mr. Miller's *The Crucible*—and their scope, as compared, say, with a *Danton's Death*, speaks for itself. And while it is probably asking too much of any modern playwright to equal the mythic and cosmological scope of an Aeschylus or Sophocles, certainly a play like Friedrich Duerrenmatt's *The Visit* comes much closer to taking on the proportions of a 'modern myth' than do such self-conscious and imposing American attempts as *Mourning Becomes Electra* or *J.B.* (What Aeschylus might do, if he were alive today, with such themes as atomic fission or international power politics is enough to make the imagination boggle.)

The great problem, obviously, is that American playwrights, by and large, have been ashamed of their bourgeois origins (just as all American artists have) and have generally felt that the family as a dramatic theme is both trivial and contemptible. Part of this stems from the sense that bourgeois culture, *per se*, is anti-art and, in the widest sense, anti-life; part of it stems from the more immediate awareness of the sentimental-izing and over-simplification of family life in such areas of our popular sub-culture as radio and television soap-operas, women's magazines, and many best-selling novels. The result is that most serious American writers have felt and still do feel that 'domestic drama' implies senti-mentality, over-simplification, triviality. They want to write *Lazarus Laughed* and *Dynamo* instead of *Long Day's Journey Into Night*, but, in rejecting the sentimentality and vulgarity of their fathers' middle-class world, they have all too often cut themselves off forever from the only vital source material upon which they can feed and grow.

The result has been that American playwrights, as well as directors and actors, unable to find the natural wellsprings of creativity, have turned more and more towards the mastery of sheer technique as the answer. A prime example of this is the now-famous Americanization of Stanislavski, in which what appeared to be a 'method', a sure-fire formula for success, was seized upon, institutionalized, virtually deified (which is to say, radically misunderstood), to the point where it is now a truism to say that American actors simply cannot play Shakespeare or Greek tragedy or Restoration Comedy or, indeed, any kind of drama which calls for something other than an emotion-centred, purely naturalistic style of performance. This is the triumph of methodology with a vengeance, and there is nothing quite parallel in the work of American playwrights, although O'Neill's attempts to impose masks and choruses and stylized sets and costumes upon essentially ordinary material, in such plays as *The Great God Brown* and *The Hairy Ape* and *The Emperor Jones*, represent the same kind of desire to master techniques and turn them into a method, without seeing that techniques 'work' only when they are the agencies of vision, not when they are merely admired as surface effects in their own right.

It is interesting, in this respect, to compare O'Neill's use of dialect in a play like *The Hairy Ape*—the artificial, comic strip type of 'dese' and 'dose' Brooklynese spoken by 'Yank'—with the dialect employed by the characters in, say, Harold Pinter's *The Caretaker*. In the speeches of Pinter's tramp, Davies, you hear the actual movements, the rhythmic and repetitive banalities of the inarticulate and semi-literate mind struggling to express itself. In the speeches of 'Yank' you hear a mechanical pattern of ungrammatical mispronunciations such as never existed on land or sea. O'Neill is not transcribing from life, he is writing a 'dialect part' for a stage 'type', and 'Yank's' dialect (like the Swedish dialect of old Chris Christofferson in *Anna Christie*) comes, not from the world of felt experience, but from a world populated by the stage Jew, the stage Irishman, the stage 'rube'. It is a language as artificial, 'stagey', and contrived as any of the purple passages in a melodrama like *The Count of Monte Cristo*, and it is noteworthy that just as O'Neill's dialect passages always smack of the footlights and the backdrop and the smell of greasepaint in the dressing-room, so too his serious 'big speeches' in his major plays always tend to slop over into the kind of 'poetical' rhetoric that his father spouted for years across the footlights of America.

Consider, in this regard, the following passages, one by O'Neill, one by Pinter. The first is a part of 'Yank's' final speech from *The Hairy Ape*; the second is a brief passage from *The Birthday Party*, in which Stanley describes his past career (?) as a concert pianist:

YANK. Say, yuh're some hard-lookin' guy, ain't yuh? I seen lots of tough nuts dat de gang called gorillas, but yuh're de foist real one I ever seen. Some chest yuh got, and shoulders, and dem arms and mits! I bet yuh got a punch in eider fist dat'd knock 'em all silly! (*This with genuine admiration. The gorilla, as if he understood, stands upright, swelling out his chest and pounding on it with his fist.* YANK *grins sympathetically.*) Sure, I get yuh. Yuh challenge de whole woild, huh? Yuh got what I was sayin' even if you muffed de woids. (*Then bitterness creeping in.*) And why wouldn't yuh get me? Ain't we both members of de same club—de Hairy Apes? . . . I s'pose yuh wanter know what I'm doin' here, huh? I been warmin' a bench down to de Battery—even since last night. Sure. I seen de sun come up. Dat was pretty, too—all red and pink and green. I was lookin' at de skyscrapers—steel—and all de ships comin' in, sailin' out, all over de oith—and dey was steel, too. De sun was warm, dere wasn't no clouds, and dere was a breeze blowin'. Sure, it was great stuff. I got it aw right—what Paddy said about dat bein' de right dope—on'y I couldn't get *in* it, see? I couldn't belong in dat. It was over my head. And I kept tinkin'—and den I beat it up here to see what youse was like. (III. 252)

STANLEY. Played the piano? I've played the piano all over the world. All over the country. (*Pause.*) I once gave a concert. . . . Yes. It was a good one, too. They were all there that night. Every single one of them. It was a great success. Yes. A concert. At Lower Edmonton. . . . I had a unique touch. Absolutely unique. They came up to me. They came up to me and said they were grateful. Champagne we had that night, the lot. . . . My father nearly came down to hear me. Well, I dropped him a card anyway. But I don't think he could make it. . . . No, I—I lost the address, that was it. . . . Yes. Lower Edmonton. Then after that, you know what they did? They carved me up. Carved me up. It was all arranged, it was all worked out. My next concert. Somewhere else it was. In winter. I went down there to play. Then, when I got there, the hall was closed, the place was shuttered up, not even a caretaker.

They'd locked it up. . . . A fast one. They pulled a fast one. I'd like to know who was responsible for that. . . . All right, Jack, I can take a tip. They want me to crawl down on my bended knees. Well, I can take a tip . . . any day of the week. (Act I; pp. 23–4)

Granted that the Pinter play was written some thirty-five years later than the O'Neill play and thus could be expected to exhibit a con-comitantly greater sophistication in playwriting technique (a dubious argument, in its own right), the fact remains that 'Yank's' talk is a dialect that never existed on this earth—or anywhere except behind the footlights—while Stanley's speech is a chillingly evocative portrayal of the rhythmic twistings and turnings and hesitations of sheer paranoia. One is a form of dramaturgical carpentry which barely transcends hack-work; the other is—albeit on a modest scale—verbal and dramatic art.

It is generally true, not only of O'Neill, but of American playwrights by and large, that their tendency has been to regard dialogue as a playwriting technique rather than as a mode of perception, to think of plot in terms of a 'yarn' rather than in terms, say, of Aristotle's *praxis*. The result has been that, while American playwrights have always been eager—often all too eager—to go to school to their European masters, the lesson they have come away with has usually been a lesson in technical vocational training, not a lesson in what may rather grandi-osely but not inaccurately be called the mysteries of vision.

For a specific instance, consider Strindberg's forays into neo-expres-sionism, in such plays as *The Dream Play* and *The Ghost Sonata*, and the use that subsequent American dramatists—O'Neill in particular—have made of these experiments. The strange horticultural transmogrifica-tions and hysterical instance on dietetic treason below stairs are all merely eccentric, if not downright ludicrous, unless they are informed by the sort of searing and passionate insight which transforms them from nonsense into metaphor. (This may, indeed, be defined as a formula for making poetry.) In O'Neill's case, it is clear, I think, that the most searing and passionate of his plays—the autobiographical family plays—are almost wholly devoid of the Strindbergian expres-sionistic devices which would change their prose statements into poetic imagery.

To take an even more striking instance, consider Albee's *Virginia Woolf*, where the playwright's evident desire to make use of Strind-bergian and Pirandellian insights is never quite achieved. The whole play is bathed in a sort of lunatic half-light of Pirandellian 'theatricalism' (note the recurrent rituals and the emblematic titles of the Acts), yet the commitment to a truly poetic vision is never fully made, and the play remains—for nearly all audiences and readers—a long, brilliant, nerve-wracking prose harangue, undeniably powerful, yet firmly rooted in an almost David Belasco type of naturalism.

*   *   *

Perhaps most significant of all is the history of some of the modern masters of the European drama in the American professional theatre. People—particularly people in a mercantile society—are identified by the products they buy (i.e. vastly more Americans buy *The Reader's Digest* than the *Tulane Drama Review*). To what extent has America 'bought' Ibsen, Strindberg, Chekhov, Shaw, Pirandello, Lorca, Brecht, etc.? A quick glance at the annals of Broadway—still, and probably forever, the only real home of American professional theatre— is enough to tell the story. It would be only a very slight exaggeration at best to say that none of the foregoing playwrights has ever had a success on Broadway. Some, like Lorca, have never even been attempted there. And certainly any Broadway producer who, given a choice between a new play by Neil Simon and an old play by Henrik Ibsen, chose the Ibsen would be regarded as legally certifiable; for the records of the New York stage will clearly demonstrate that it is not plays like *The Wild Duck* and *Rosmersholm* which reap the big rewards but rather plays like *Abie's Irish Rose* and *Life With Father* and *Lightnin'* and, of course, the big blockbuster musicals in the Rodgers and Hammerstein tradition. All, it might be added, sufficiently free of European taint to satisfy even the most earnest congressman on the House Un-American Activities Committee.

Nor is it merely the classic Europeans who are discussed with respect but left discreetly unproduced (to paraphrase Mark Twain on the weather, everybody talks about them but nobody does them). Most contemporary European playwrights who enjoy major reputations in their own countries have either failed notably on Broadway (Max Frisch, Ugo Betti) or remain totally unknown to the American public (Georges Schehadé). And those few who have enjoyed some moderate commercial success have generally done so through watered-down, Times Square-oriented 'adaptations' of their work.

Indeed, the whole story of those few European playwrights who *have* enjoyed some sort of commercial success in New York—Giraudoux, Anouilh, Duerrenmatt, chiefly—is one of the most fascinating and revelatory chapters in the history of the American theatre. Few play-goers on either side of the Atlantic realize, to this day, that the American public generally knows the foregoing playwrights through watered-down, sometimes quite distorted 'adaptations', rather than accurate and honest translations, of their works. *Tiger at the Gates*, interesting and valid though it may be, is rather a different play from *La guerre de Troie n'aura pas lieu* (about as different as the titles would suggest!). Even a modest little piece like *The Apollo of Bellac* has undergone something of a sea-change, and a character who is a mistress in the original becomes, in the 'translation', a wife! ('Bottom, thou art translated!')

Most extraordinary of all, however, is the story of the Maurice Valency-Lunt and Fontanne-Peter Brook 'adaptation' of Duerrenmatt's *The Visit*, as chronicled in some detail (and far more revealingly than intended) in Randolph Goodman's book, *Drama On Stage* (1959). Of particular interest is the interview with Valency, in which the major 'adaptations' from the German original are described, with the frequent reiteration of such phrases as 'it was felt that American audiences would not understand this sort of thing', 'it was thought that this was not in line with American tastes', etc. The 'adaptations' (or 'emasculations', as you prefer) range from relatively minor touches of glamorization—the title is changed from *The Old Lady's Visit* (the literal translation of the German) to *The Visit*; some twenty years are deducted from Claire's age; emphasis is subtly shifted from the *grotesquerie* of her prosthetic limbs to the *haute couture* splendours of her Castillo wardrobe—to somewhat larger concessions to 'American audiences'' supposed distaste for harsh humour and bitter satire—the dehumanizing 'comic strip' names of Claire's retinue are banalized into American-ese (Max, Mike, Bobby); specific mention of the castration of the two blind men is delicately omitted; Claire is deprived of a couple of husbands ('to save salaries', according to Valency!)—on up to major re-alignments of the entire action of the play—the second Act has been completely re-structured (at a considerable cost in dramatic and thematic values); the choral sequences in which the townspeople enact trees in the forest have been abandoned; and the final Euripidean ode by the assembled townspeople has likewise disappeared. (It is only fair to add, on the side of those involved in the English-language production of *The Visit*, that all the emendations and 'adaptations' were approved of by the author for the production.)

Perhaps the most important footnote of all is the fact that the Lunt and Fontanne *Visit* was, indeed, a very great box-office success and that the collaborators in this venture would seem, after the fact, to have been proved quite correct in their shrewd and cynical estimate of what 'the American public' wants in the way of a Broadway show. *Quod erat demonstratum*. And yet at the same time is it Quixotic to observe that today, only a decade or so after the New York success of *The Visit*, a number of plays (Peter Weiss' *Marat/Sade*, most notably) which are at least as 'far out' as the Duerrenmatt *Der Besuch der Alten Dame* have enjoyed and are enjoying real box-office success? It is unlikely that America will ever come to know Duerrenmatt's original play—surely one of the masterpieces of the modern theatre—and yet it is ironic to reflect that, if *echt* Duerrenmatt were to be attempted in New York today, it would very likely meet with few of the objections which troubled the Lunt and Fontanne company in the late 'fifties. And perhaps there is a Moral for America here.

Of all the major contemporary playwrights of Europe, none, perhaps, offers a more interesting or instructive case history than Bertolt Brecht. For one thing, Brecht has 'arrived' in America just about twenty years late, or just about the time most of his 'Epic' concepts and principles are beginning to be regarded as slightly old hat in most European theatrical capitals. Nor would he have 'arrived' in the United States even yet had it not been for the almost single-handed propaganda campaign waged on his behalf by Eric Bentley, a campaign which won the college campuses, then the tributary theatres, and finally, a year of two ago, swept up on to the beachheads of Shubert Alley and culminated in two disastrous productions of *Mother Courage* and *Arturo Ui*—productions so disastrous that all Broadway producers are now confirmed in their suspicions that Brecht is and always will be box-office poison. The doom of the *Mother Courage* production was spelled out with the signing of the attractive and youthful Broadway and Hollywood actress, Anne Bancroft, to enact the title role and the appointment of the brilliant choreographer, Jerome Robbins, as the director. This is not to denigrate the undeniable talents of either Miss Bancroft or Mr. Robbins, but simply to point out what the Broadway type of mind can never seem to grasp: that the acting talents which functioned beautifully in *Two for the Seesaw* and *The Miracle Worker* and the directorial skills which illuminated *West Side Story* and *Oh, Dad, Poor Dad* are not so much inadequate as just plain irrelevant to the Epic Theatre of Bertolt Brecht. Yet just this past summer the Stratford, Ontario, company presented a brilliantly successful *Mahagonny* (the first time, incidentally, this great work has ever been seen on the North American continent!) and in so doing also confirmed what many of us have suspected all along—that Epic Theatre, stripped of all its mumbo-jumbo about placards and lights and alienation effects, is made up of the basic ingredients that all great art always has been: skill and passion and, above all, a clear and burning intelligence.

*　　*　　*

The story of European influences upon the American drama is, then, a paradoxical one, a story of the envy and emulation of European ways, on the one hand, and yet, on the other, a story of the ultimate rejection of the European experience. It would be tempting to construct an elaborate psychological analogy, based on the relationship of the rebellious son to the father-figure, which I suggested in my earlier remarks on Eugene O'Neill and his father, but this is probably too simple an answer. Actually, the American theatre generally has been more in the position of one of Henry James's American heroes, simultaneously attracted to and repulsed by the corruption and richness and power of the European world. The real problem for American playwrights and directors and actors has been, not that they have refused to learn the lesson of the master, in a technical sense, but that they have been unwilling to pay the price of the lesson in tears and suffering and humiliation. The history of the American nation has been one of the avoidance of experience—particularly of any painful or upsetting experience. But this, needless to say, is a dangerously immature attitude, and out of it no very profound or useful insights can be expected to develop. For over two hundred years the American experience has operated in the mode of comedy—at times, almost of farce—but no person and no nation can stay young—which is to say, comic—forever. Time and destiny moves us all, men and nations, towards that tragic view of life which is one of the marks of maturity. And the time may be fast approaching—indeed, it may already be here—when American playwrights will be capable of speaking to the world out of the same depths of experience which nourished the work of Sophocles, of Shakespeare, of Racine, of Chekhov. And when you win through to this vision you see that form and content are ultimately one, and that all the so-called technical tricks of the game simply do not matter.

It may be, then, in looking back fifty or a hundred years from now, we shall see the most important European influences on the American drama, not in the plays of Ibsen or Strindberg, the theories of Brecht or Artaud, the 'method' of Stanislavski, but in the experiences of World War I and World War II and the international aftermath of those holocausts, which has moved America, much against its will, to the centre of the world stage where, surrounded by corpses and poetry, it must take up the position at the centre of life and death which has always been occupied by the great tragic heroes, from the days of Aeschylus to the Years of the Atom.

Note

The Group Theatre was in operation from 1931 to 1941, at first under the direction of Harold Clurman, Cheryl Crawford and Lee Strasberg; from 1937 under Clurman alone. The chronological list that follows contains information about all the original productions: opening date, author, play, director, number of performances. The parenthetical date following the title is the date of publication; where special publishing information is necessary, it comes at the end.

28 September, 1931. Paul Green. *The House of Connelly*. Strasberg & Crawford. 91. Happy-ending version in *The House of Connelly and Other Plays* (1931) (contains music to songs); unhappy version in *Five Plays of the South* (1963).

10 December, 1931. Claire and Paul Sifton, *1931—* (1931). Strasberg. 12.

9 March, 1932. Maxwell Anderson. *Night Over Taos*. Strasberg. 13. In *Eleven Verse Plays* (1939).

26 September, 1932. John Howard Lawson. *Success Story* (1932). Strasberg. 121.

17 January, 1933. Dawn Powell. *Big Night*. Crawford. 7. Unpublished.

26 September, 1933. Sidney Kingsley. *Men in White* (1933). Strasberg. 351.

22 March, 1934. John Howard Lawson. *Gentlewoman*. Strasberg. 12. In *With a Reckless Preface* (1934).

28 November, 1934. Melvin Levy. *Gold Eagle Guy* (1935). Strasberg. 65.

19 February, 1935. Clifford Odets. *Awake and Sing!* Clurman. 185. In *Six Plays* (1939).

26 March, 1935. Clifford Odets. Double Bill. 136. *Waiting for Lefty*. Sanford Meisner & Odets. Complete version in *Representative Modern Plays, American*, ed. R. Warnock (1952); short version in *Six Plays*. *Till the Day I Die*. Crawford. In *Six Plays*.

30 November, 1935. Nellise Child. *Weep for the Virgins*. Crawford. 9. Unpublished.

9 December, 1935. Clifford Odets. *Paradise Lost*. Clurman. 73. In *Six Plays*.

13 March, 1936. Erwin Piscator and Lena Goldschmidt. *The Case of Clyde Griffiths*. Translated, Louise Campbell. Strasberg. 19. MS., Theatre Collection, New York Public Library.

19 November, 1936. Paul Green. *Johnny Johnson*. Music, Kurt Weill. Strasberg. 68. In *Five Plays of the South*. Record: Heliodor H25024.

4 November, 1937. Clifford Odets. *Golden Boy*. Clurman. 250. In *Six Plays*.

19 February, 1938. Robert Ardrey. *Casey Jones*. Elia Kazan. 25. Unpublished.

24 November, 1938. Clifford Odets. *Rocket to the Moon*. Clurman. 131. In *Six Plays*.

5 January, 1939. Irwin Shaw. *The Gentle People* (1939). Clurman. 141.

13 April, 1939. William Saroyan. *My Heart's in the Highlands* (1939). Robert Lewis. 44.

14 November, 1939. Robert Ardrey. *Thunder Rock* (1941). Kazan. 23.

22 February, 1940. Clifford Odets. *Night Music* (1940). Clurman. 20.

17 December, 1940. Irwin Shaw. *Retreat to Pleasure*. Clurman. 23. Unpublished.

History and Criticism. Harold Clurman's *The Fervent Years* (1957) is indispensable. Mordecai Gorelik, *New Theatres for Old* (1962) reproduces a few set designs

IV

The Group Theatre and its Plays

GERALD WEALES

★

HAROLD CLURMAN'S *The Fervent Years* may not be 'the' story of the Group Theatre, as the book's subtitle says, but it is so compelling an account that anyone who attempts to write about the Group cannot help using and being used by the story as Clurman tells it. His book is not an apologia for himself or for the Group. It is a kind of success story which describes one disaster after another, for surely the Group Theatre is the most successful failure in the history of American theatre. The nearest English equivalent is probably the Barker-Vedrenne seasons at the Court Theatre. There is no sustained objective account of the Group Theatre—not even so subjective an objective account as Desmond MacCarthy's little book on the Court—so one must go to Clurman for information about organization and production. Information, however, is the least important thing that Clurman communicates about the Group. The remarkable thing about *The Fervent Years* is that it moves so rapidly from practical matters (financing, casting) to aesthetic theory, from social commentary to anecdotal gossip, from pocket criticism to autobiography and that with all the shifts it manages so often—particularly in the early sections—to be moving. Twenty years after the book was written, thirty-five years after the Group was formed, the reader who is romantic or sentimental or idealistic about the theatre finds himself wishing that he could catch a bus for Brookfield Center, Connecticut, to be part of that first summer of rehearsal and preparation. It was the most important beginning for the Group, and the Group seems always to have been beginning.

---

of Group productions. Odets, *Clash by Night* (1942) and 'A Scene from *The Silent Partner*', *New Theatre and Film* (1937), pp. 5–9, are relevant non-Group plays.

There were two Group Theatres actually—the organization and the idea. Neither is very easy to pin down. Statistically, the Group Theatre began on 28 September, 1931, when Paul Green's *The House of Connelly* opened at the Martin Beck Theatre, and ended on 4 January, 1941, when Irwin Shaw's *Retreat to Pleasure* closed at the Belasco. But the decade of the Group's history is really more open-ended than that sounds. It presumably began, as Clurman says it did, in a general sense of disaffection with the Broadway theatre, even that of the Theatre Guild, for which the Group's organizing directors worked, and in conversations between him and Lee Strasberg. Important points in the Group's pre-history were the private production of Padraic Colum's *Balloon* (1928) by a group of actors who had gathered around Clurman and Strasberg; the Guild-sponsored production of *Red Rust* (1929), which brought Clurman and Cheryl Crawford together; the weekly meetings of interested actors, directors and well-wishers which continued from November 1930 to May 1931. By that time the Group had a play (the Guild had released *The House of Connelly* to them), a little money and twenty-eight actors; the summer at Brookfield Center began in June. The Group was—they should excuse me—in business.

The Group Theatre was first of all a producing organization. In the ten seasons that it existed, it was able to get twenty-two new productions on stage. There were occasional revivals (*Awake and Sing!* in 1939), tours, second companies (of *Golden Boy*, at least) and experimental evenings, but the main job which each Spring brought was how to get what on stage to keep the Group alive for another season. This meant that the Group was in competition with regular commercial managements for scripts, for theatres and, most important, for money. Except for a couple of years towards the end, after the success of *Golden Boy*, the Group was a hand-to-mouth operation. Beginning with its first production, 'under the auspices of the Theatre Guild', it is surprising how many Group productions are 'in association with'. It depended for much of its life on hand-outs from friends who believed in what the Group was trying to do, often from ex-Groupers who had been lured away to Hollywood.

This kind of operation is less fun in fact than it is in farce—in *Room Service*, say, or *The Butter and Egg Man*. It is certainly uncongenial to a group of men and women who believed, as the pre-opening announcement put it, that 'This theatre is an organization of actors and directors formed with the ultimate aim of creating a permanent acting company to maintain regular New York seasons.' The Group Theatre, then, was a community of artists. What that means, of course, is that for all the communal aims and the mutual admiration, there were continual dissension, misunderstanding, hurt feelings, wounded egos. The three directors—Clurman, Crawford and Strasberg—found themselves variously in isolation, in temporary alliances, banded together either for or against their actors. Even after the 1937 split, when Crawford and Strasberg left the Group, Clurman, as sole director, had the actors' Council to contend with. By this time, the idea of the permanent company was already in danger because it had become impractical to pay salaries to all members, acting or not, whenever there was a show running. The actors were still drawing up plans and preparations in the summer of 1940 when *Retreat to Pleasure*, the last play to bear the Group's name, was clearly an independent Clurman production using only a few Group actors. Aside from the friction between member and leader, and between member and member, which one would expect in any organization in which all voices have the right to be heard, there was a special problem that was the product of the political moment. There was a nucleus of Communists within the Group, as the Congressional testimony of Elia Kazan and Clifford Odets later indicated, which attempted—with no success—to take over the organization, to convert it into a democratic collective free of the directors' control to dictate the choice of plays. Clurman's book softens this aspect of the discord because he accepts that the Group as a whole, whatever the specific political allegiance of individual members, shared social as well as artistic attitudes. The disruptive forces within the Group, as Clurman's anecdotes so clearly indicate, were as often psychological as they were ideational.

Living in uneasy conjunction with the producing organization and the collection of combustible individuals—and sustaining both—was the Group Theatre as idea. There is an edge of self-mockery in Clurman's book as he describes how often he rose out of the shambles of an argument over practical matters to re-invoke the vision. By the time he wrote *The Fervent Years*, he understood why the dream failed, but that understanding never disowned the dream. The Group could not succeed because it 'held to a collective ideal in a competitive society' (p. 134) and because it 'aimed to cultivate the individual through a collective discipline . . . and America's culture is fundamentally individualistic' (p. 269). Although the Group smashed on the twin rocks of social context and individualism, the idea never died. A few years ago I asked the director Robert Lewis why he enjoyed lecturing at universities; his answer was that anyone who had ever been in the Group could not be satisfied on Broadway, not even with Broadway success; that he had to keep reaching out for that other theatre. To say that the Group's goal was to sustain a permanent acting company (that is, to provide guaranteed employment) is to over-simplify. The idea was not the company itself, but what it stood for—a place to stand, a community of fellow artists (and/or workers), a job that had both artistic and social validity. Clurman, speaking of the sense of purpose and community of that first summer, says, 'Here was companionship, security, work, and dreams' (p. 41). He quotes Margaret Barker's answer to a prospective employer who wanted to know how long she thought her engagement would last, 'If our play is a success—twenty years. If not—twenty years' (p. 50). The possibility of something as permanent as a theatre in so transient a world as that of American show business was an idea of home. Those who stayed with the Group kept trying to patch it, to shore it up, to make it a real shelter. Many of those who left it remembered it, as childhood homes are so often remembered, as tighter, cleaner, more secure than it really was. Franchot Tone is probably the best example of these. Never really comfortable within the Group, as Clurman indicates, he finally broke with them to find success in Hollywood; out there, he yearned for the ideal home he left, he sent money to help sustain it, finally he returned in 1939 to play Goff in Irwin Shaw's *The Gentle People* only to discover how right Thomas Wolfe had been.

It is impossible, as I said at the beginning of this essay, to talk about the Group Theatre without being infected by what Clurman has written about it, to be touched by the mystique of someone who was part of the experiment. Still, if the Group had meaning only for those who worked with it, there would be no point in talking about it at all—except in biographies. From the outside, too, the Group was important both as organization and idea. For ten years, merely by existing, the Group held out the possibility that serious theatre could be self-sustaining in the United States: it is an ideal as old as the pre-World War I little theatres in Boston and Chicago, as new as the festival theatres that are popping up like mushrooms out of the damp and expectant earth of the 1960's. As idea, then, the Group is part of a continual, a never quite smothered sense of possibility. On a more practical level, its contribution to American theatre is visible on bill-boards and in theatre programmes, on stage and on screen, in anthologies and in class rooms, and has been for twenty-five years. It is impossible to imagine what American theatre and film would have been like in the 1940's, 1950's and 1960's without the alumni of the Group Theatre. The Group gave a first chance to direct not only to Strasberg, Crawford and Clurman, but to Elia Kazan and Robert Lewis. It started or boosted the careers of such actors as Franchot Tone, Morris Carnovsky, Lee J. Cobb, John Garfield, Luther Adler. It used designers such as Mordecai Gorelik, Donald Oenslager, Boris Aronson. It carried the infant Odets in its womb until he was born, a full-grown playwright, with *Awake and Sing!* It introduced Sidney Kingsley, William Saroyan and Robert Ardrey as playwrights and helped along the career of Irwin Shaw. I do not pretend to admire the work of all these artists, but no one can deny their influence. Take a single but potent example: without the classes that Strasberg gave for the Group actors, beginning in 1931, it is hard to believe that there would have been an Actors Studio to change the face of American acting in the 1950's. The legacy of the Group Theatre is more tangible than an idea.

⋆　　⋆　　⋆

It is perhaps a little misleading to talk of the Group Theatre in terms of what it wanted to be or of what its members went on to do. It was not only a quest and an incubator, it was a body of plays. A reading of the extant plays produced by the Group may not give 'the' story any more than Clurman's book does, but it will certainly give one face of the Group and a better likeness probably than one would get from a look at the plays done by even so idiosyncratic a commercial producer as Jed Harris.

There is a family resemblance among the Group plays which can be detected through the surface dissimilarities. It is both ideational and aesthetic. To understand why this is so, it is necessary to recognize how the playwright was supposed to fit into the acting community and what the artistic aims of that community were. Clurman has an ancedote (p. 42) about how, during the first summer, some of the actors played an elaborate, card-stacking joke on the youngest, most naïve performer. 'I turned to Strasberg and asked: "Shall we interfere in this?" His eyes blazed. "We should interfere in everything." ' Strasberg's answer might have served the Group as an artistic motto as well as an organizing principle. Every member—actor, director, designer, playwright—was presumably working towards a unified statement of some kind. The production was designed not to give flesh to an author's play, but to embody an idea, a truth implicit in the story the playwright was trying to tell. If an actor who had played the lead in one play was asked to do a walk-on in the next, surely a playwright must understand that what he had written was only the beginning of what his play had to say. Playwrights or possible playwrights were often part of the rehearsal summers in the country; their plays, it was assumed, could find their proper shape by being exposed to the Group as a whole, by undergoing performance and suffering discussion.

On the face of it, this sounds like the familiar business of rewriting which, in a commercial context, is called management meddling and, in an institutional context, is called learning by experience. It is more complicated than that because the Group's aims were social as well as artistic. They did not think of themselves as an enclosed community, working to perfect an artistic product which could then be offered, take it or leave it, to a world outside. They saw themselves as a social unit working within (and sometimes against) society as a whole, and the product they offered had to be something more than a unified, an artistic whole. It had to say something significant and useful to and about society. There were great differences within the Group over what really was socially significant, but in general a kind of amorphous Leftist orientation prevailed. The Group was never a doctrinaire political theatre; it only occasionally produced a straight propaganda play with a specific political or social goal in mind. Although the Group took over the New Theatre League production of *Waiting for Lefty*, as though to say this playwright is ours, it was not the agitprop Odets who was the Group playwright; it was the author of *Awake and Sing!* If some members of the Group were politically impatient, like Odets and the actors whose production of *Lefty* kicked off the new Popular-Front organization, the Group as a whole (judging from their plays) shared a conviction that the economic system was faulty and the middle class (from which most of them came) was trapped in its own myths. Beyond that, and most important, they assumed that something could be done; they accepted the ritual optimism of the political Left. In retrospect that optimism seems a little naïve, but certainly no more so than the automatic existential despair that has characterized the last fifteen years. Whatever the social utility of optimism for that time, it was often in conflict with the subject matter or the form of a particular play or the prevailing inclination of a particular playwright. For that reason, the social plays of the 1930's, particularly those of the Group, whatever vitality they retain, often seem like crippled creatures.

A caveat: I am aware that in talking about the Group, their plays and the decade in such neat generalizations I am imposing order where there was a great deal of accident. Even though the Group was full of theorizers, of whom Clurman was probably the most prolific, there was no neat political-philosophical line that the plays were forced to walk. Even if there had been, the plays the Group did would not have filled that abstract bill, for the circumstances under which they were chosen varied greatly. In some cases, the playwright worked closely with the Group in preparing his script; in some cases, one director liked a play very much and, since the others were indifferent, it was taken; sometimes an outsider brought a script and a little money and the Group, with nothing else to produce, went along; sometimes a play was a desperate choice when there were no other possibilities in sight.

Having made my obeisance to accident, I can return to the generalizations and consider how the prevailing attitudes within the Group affected the choice of plays. If they were to say something of immediate significance to society, the plays needed to be new ones. For this reason the Group was not to be a museum theatre. In the summer of 1939, scriptless and spiritless, Clurman did put *The Three Sisters* into rehearsal, but when fall came Chekhov had given way to Robert Ardrey. Since it was American society of which the Group was to be a functioning part, the plays needed to be American. Only one European play was put on by the Group and it was based, however distantly, on an American novel. That was *The Case of Clyde Griffiths*, the adaptation by Erwin Piscator and Lena Goldschmidt of Theodore Dreiser's *An American Tragedy*; ironically, the most doctrinaire Marxist play put on by the Group, it was brought to them by Milton Shubert, one of *the* Shuberts. Aside from *Clyde Griffiths*, which exists in manuscript in the New York Public Library, four of the Group plays— Dawn Powell's *Big Night*, Nellise Child's *Weep for the Virgins*, Ardrey's *Casey Jones* and Shaw's *Retreat to Pleasure*—have not been published. Although certain things can be assumed about them from the conflicting descriptions of what they were like (read Burns Mantle's plot summaries alongside Clurman's comments), it is the other eighteen plays that show us what the Group thought a play should do. Something can be learned, too, from the two most famous Group rejections: Maxwell Anderson's *Winterset* (1935) and William Saroyan's *The Time of Your Life* (1939). Although Clurman says many cogent things about both plays in explaining his initial reaction against them, it is difficult to escape the suspicion that *Winterset* was rejected because Mio and Miriamne chose to die rather than to live in a corrupt world and *The Time of Your Life* because it was the peripheral Kit Carson and not the central Joe who was capable of action.

To see optimism as a thematic organizing (or disorganizing) principle, consider the three plays that the Group did during their first season: *The House of Connelly*, Claire and Paul Sifton's *1931*— and Anderson's *Night over Taos*. In only the Siftons' play does the action comfortably contain the ideational point. One of the first of the Depression plays, one of the most explicit calls for revolutionary action, *1931*— still seems one of the most effective plays of its kind. Although it ran for less than two weeks and played only to small audiences, it was a play on which later social playwrights built; Odets, who acted in *1931*—, must have found in the scene in which Adam and The Girl decide they cannot marry the basis for Episode III in *Waiting for Lefty*— 'The Young Hack and His Girl'. The Siftons use two streams of action, neither realistic, which merge in the final flamboyant scene in which the crowd keeps marching, Adam among them, into the sound of machine guns and singing offstage: 'The song is not the Internationale, it is that and more, a wordless battle hymn of ferocious desperation.' The scenes, cartoon-like in their simplicity, tell the story of Adam, a self-confident workingman, who sinks beneath the burden of unemployment, hunger, illness, humiliating charity into a will-less cipher until that moment of back-to-the-wall anger when he throws a table through the window of the restaurant where he works and finds his place in the crowd. 'That's beans, that's ham-and. That's women, that's gasoline. That's *everything*,' he says in scene i, flexing his muscles. 'I got it. I can lift more boxes, more iron, more sacks, load 'em faster, check 'em better, make more trips, do more work . . .' The scenes that follow are designed to show how the collapsing economic situation turns such apparently admirable dependence on self into a selfishness that plays into the hands of the oppressors, at first with Adam as observer, at last as participant; in scene xiii, an angry boy quits his job, in a quarrel which recalls Adam's in scene i, and Adam takes his place at a lower wage. At irregular intervals among the scenes there are interludes which take place in front of a factory gate in which a growing body of the unemployed is met with a few jobs, no jobs, locked gates, plant guards, police, the militia. The rising intensity of these mass scenes is such that the audience expects an explosion, one which will arrest the descending action of the Adam scenes and carry the play's Everyman-hero with it. *1931—* can be judged only as a propaganda play, a reaction to the economic situation which helped create it. Much that is dramatically naïve about it (the villainous caricatures, for instance) are implicit in the genre. In one sense, however, it is more sophisticated than some of the plays that follow; its call for collective action is not purely verbal, a lightly motivated last-scene speech from the hero; it is built into the play itself by means of mass movement techniques borrowed from the German Expressionists.

There is no marching in the streets at the end of *The House of Connelly* or *Night over Taos*, but in both plays the curtain comes down on a young couple confidently facing a difficult future. Leftist optimism under such circumstances looks very like the conventional happy ending, but, ironically, in neither play does the dramatist make the ending as acceptable as the Siftons do their revolution. The reason in the case of *The House of Connelly* is obvious; the play the Group did was not the one Paul Green originally wrote. Since both versions have been published, it is a simple matter to check the effect of the hopeful ending. The play was apparently conceived as a kind of allegorical statement about the inevitable destruction of the remnants of the old South; certainly the Connellys and their plantation are intended to stand for more than a single family. Their gentility and their aristocratic snobbishness are revealed as covers for years of sin, crime and cruelty. Their decay is implicit in the barren state of the spinster daughters and the unprofitable plantation, it is embodied in the physical weakness of Mrs. Connelly and the psychological weakness of Will and it is visible to the eye of the audience in the shabby splendour of sets and costumes. Big Sis and Big Sue, two Negro women who are at once characters, chorus and fates, provide the key to the meaning and the action of the play. It is they who introduce the story of the old General and his condemning to death of his bastard, the Negro Purvis, an incident which is at once a social parable (the inescapable ties of guilt and blood relation which join the Negro to the Southern white), a continuing metaphor (the sentence of death which lies on the house of Connelly) and a motivation for their action. It is they who kill Patsy, the white tenant's daughter, who represents a new spirit in the South, which must not be allowed, through marriage to Will, to re-inspirit the Connellys. From the beginning they predict her death ('Death gwine take her church-wedding bound') and in the last scene they smother her in their tow sack.

Dismissing Big Sis and Big Sue as literary borrowings, 'a stock device to round off a rather somber play', Clurman, using the communal *we* of the Group, tells in *The Fervent Years* how Green was persuaded to provide another ending. 'The vacillating hero . . . had to be given his chance to redeem his land and his life with the aid of the tenant girl, who loved him' (p. 44). The play ends, then, not by completing the action begun in the first scene and insisted on throughout the play, but by side-stepping into a cliché of kitchen comedy, by bringing down the curtain on Patsy, rich with practicality and love, preparing supper for her Will. Since the revisions apparently involved changing only the last scene, the audience is carefully prepared for an ending which the Group, foundered in affirmation, will not let them have. In the original version the dramatic function of Big Sis and Big Sue gives them a dignity which they do not have in the Group version in which they become the batty old women Patsy thinks them. In the original, Big Sis easily disarms Patsy, who tries to defend herself with a poker; in the revision, in which they, as Clurman tells us, 'had to be overcome by Patsy's firmness' (p. 44), she shakes the poker at them and they scurry off to the kitchen like handkerchief-head stereotypes straight off a Hollywood lot. Green is a literary dramatist by Clurman's definition, a playwright who makes conscious use of devices borrowed from the past, but to recognize that without seeing that the dramatic embodiment of his theme lay in his manipulation of those devices was to use ideology to convert a possible artistic statement into an impossible social one.

The contradictions in *Night over Taos* are probably Anderson's own. There is no indication that the play was altered to fit any Group preconceptions—in fact the Group accepted the play reluctantly—but since Anderson was actively interested in their work from the time of the pre-organization meetings it is possible that he brought to the play an uneasy mixture of Group optimism and his own romantic pessimism. If *Night over Taos* were a conventional Anderson play, we could expect the young lovers, Felipe and Diana, to choose death (which they seem quite willing to do in Act I) rather than to compromise with an imperfect world. The innocent and the idealistic are consistently defeated by the political, the economic, the mundane in the Anderson plays of the 1930's: *Elizabeth the Queen, Mary of Scotland, Winterset, High Tor, The Masque of Kings, Key Largo.* If Washington is not completely swamped in *Valley Forge*, it is because that play, like *Night over Taos*, is going in two directions at once. In *Taos*, which is set in 1847 when the United States was enforcing its claims to New Mexico, Pablo Montoya, the most powerful of the *ricos*, who has ruled his land like a king, is forced to relinquish his power over his peons and his family, to make way for democracy and his son. The play is a kind of bush-league *Götterdämmerung* which fails dramatically for two reasons. First Montoya, who promises heroic defiance, chooses a Sydney-Carton exit, having been talked rather than forced into it. Second, since the characters are never more than vehicles for ideas, Felipe (freedom) takes from Montoya (tyranny) whatever audience sympathy there is, and surely in such a play the dying god ought to remain the centre of audience concern. 'This is what death's for——' declaims Montoya, having taken poison, 'To rid the earth of old fashions.' This is a good, solid 1930's sentiment, a positive statement from the Left, but it is ambiguous in Anderson, for whom (see *High Tor*) it is usually negative, a necessary regret. The hopeful ending is further complicated by the fact that throughout the play the United States represents a double threat to Montoya; the North not only stands for freedom, but for accommodation, compromise. It is true that Federico, the son who represents that part of the impending change, is killed by Montoya, but it is difficult to accept that Felipe's freedom is riding in with clean hands. Anderson's anger at American society and government, which became increasingly bitter as the decade went on, can already be heard in Montoya's 'no laws, no loyalty . . . traders . . . whatever/They have they'll sell . . . behind each other's backs.' In this play, as in *Valley Forge*, Anderson uses the life-and-liberty rhetoric of American history, but his own disillusionment with that dream keeps the words from being inspirited with conviction.

In the plays that followed, heroes and heroines, sometimes together, sometimes apart, faced the future with determination, ready to battle their own worst instincts and the society that produced them because of 'Our own sense of the perfectibility of man', to use Clurman's words. Sidney Kingsley lets embolism kill off Barbara in *Men in White* so that a chastened but strengthened George can continue his medical career, now immune to the blandishments of wealth. Gwyn and Rudy in John Howard Lawson's *Gentlewoman* go their separate ways 'towards a red horizon', ending their preoccupation with their own small egos and their love affair, ready to 'fight hunger and death' instead of 'our own shadows', although it seems to be Lawson's desire that they escape rather than anything in the play that frees them from the moribund class to which they belong. The Paul Green-Kurt Weill musical *Johnny Johnson* borrows the Chaplin fade-out, as its hero, momentarily defeated, goes off whistling 'a little more clearly now, a little more bravely' or (on the record) singing 'We'll never lose our faith and hope and trust in all mankind'; Green's characterization of Johnny (half American rube, half the fool in Christ) and the melody Weill provides prepare the audience for an ending which, if it does not hope, at least refuses to despair. The two old men in *The Gentle People*, Irwin Shaw's parable about dictatorship, murder the gangster because 'if you want peace and gentleness, you got to take violence out of the hands of people like Goff and you got to take it in your own hands and use it like a club'. In Robert Ardrey's *Thunder Rock*, the characters whom Charleston invents in an attempt to escape the world teach him that there is neither escape nor necessity for it, that 'one after another—obstacles to civilization do get smashed'. There are a few Group plays in which the hero accepts as true the myth of American success and is destroyed by it, through suicide (Lawson's *Success Story*), madness (Melvin Levy's *Gold Eagle Guy*) or execution (*The Case of Clyde Griffiths*). Even these plays, which might be taken as diagnostic, are not negative because each of them suggests the possibility of another choice: the Marxism that Sol deserts in *Success Story* and to which Sarah may be returning; the revolutionary undertones which attract the artist Lon Firth before Gold Eagle Guy Button corrupts him; the allegiance to class which Clyde Griffiths cannot sustain, a failure which, since this is a teaching play, he voices for himself at the end: 'there is no greater sin than the sin of indecision'. Of all the Group plays, only William Saroyan's *My Heart's in the Highlands* fails to strike an optimistic note, for it shows that only through death can Mr. MacGregor reach his highlands and that even the buoyant Johnny must discover that 'I'm not mentioning any names, Pa, but something's wrong somewhere.'

I have left Odets out of this general accounting not because his work is ideationally inappropriate, but because he presents so perfect an example of a split-vision playwright that he needs a few pages to him-self. Beyond that, he is *the* Group Theatre playwright in a way that none of the others are. He was a member of the company from the beginning, an actor in many of the early productions. When, after years of trying, he convinced the directors that he was a playwright, his name became almost synonymous with the Group. They produced six of his plays (seven if we count *Lefty*), where no other playwright had more than two done, but even that figure is misleading unless one recognizes that, beginning with the production of *Awake and Sing!* in 1935, half the Group productions were of Odets plays. Of these plays, *Waiting for Lefty* and *Till the Day I Die* are special cases. *Lefty* is a positive play in the sense that *1931—* is, a direct call for action, Odets's only overt propaganda play. *Till the Day I Die* is an unsuccessful mélange, praised ordinarily only because it was an early anti-Nazi play; of course, that un-revolutionary playwright, S. N. Behrman, had already written *Rain from Heaven*. Odets uses a highly romantic curtain (Ernst Tausig's suicide recalls that of Anderson's Montoya) in a context that calls for a death as cold-blooded as the one in Bertolt Brecht's *Die Massnahme*; for Odets's play, like Brecht's, is essentially an examination of Party discipline, an ends-and-means exercise to show that the individual must be willing to sacrifice himself to the cause. The difference is that where Brecht's irony, probably unintentionally, infects his cold reason, Odets's lump in the throat affirms a temporary inhumanity for a presumed brighter future. It is in the other five plays that Odets can be seen at his best and most characteristic.

Describing the pre-playwright as he was in the difficult winter or 1932–3, Clurman says,

> Odets seemed to share a peculiar sense of gloomy fatality, one might almost say an appetite for the broken and rundown, together with a bursting love for the beauty immanent in people, a burning belief in the day when this beauty would actually shape the external world.
>
> (p. 109)

Later, he says that Odets's work is 'profoundly of the lower middle class with all its vacillation, dual allegiance, fears, groping, self-distrust, dejection, spurts of energy, hosannas, vows of conversion, and prayers for release' (p. 141). The products of this double nature are plays giving vivid and often humorous portraits of men and women trapped by the 'gloomy fatality' but decked out in the belief, burning not quite so brightly as Clurman suggests, that something positive (if unspecific) can be done. As Detective Rosenberger says in *Night Music*, 'I am in love with the possibilities, the human possibilities.'

It is significant that *Awake and Sing!* was originally called *I Got the Blues*, for the least likely thing about the play is Ralphie's conversion at the end. The play's strength lies in the Berger family. They are presented as if in a redoubt, conducting, under the generalship of Bessie, a holding operation against enveloping poverty. Bessie is supposed to be a kind of accidental villainess, the creature of circumstance, who fights the wrong battle bravely—to succeed within the society not to change it—and cripples the family even as she protects them. Her reward is that they all want to get away, actually or vicariously: Jacob plays 'O Paradiso' on his victrola and dreams of the revolution he never made; Myron yearns back to the pre-World War days of Teddy Roosevelt and hopes to get rich by chance—a sweepstake ticket or a long-shot; Ralph listens to the Boston mail plane pass over and regrets that he never had the tap-dancing lessons that would have made him a headliner; Moe (in the family if not of it) sings about 'the land of Yama Yama' and wants to get back to that island where oranges drop into your mouth. In the end, the brittle but soft-hearted Hennie makes her escape with Moe, and with Ralph's blessing, while he stays behind to do what Jacob failed to do: 'fix it so life won't be printed on dollar bills'. We can accept Hennie's action because she, like Bessie, is shown as a strong character, but Ralph is so convincingly weak for two acts, so much Myron's son and Jacob's grandson, that one might expect that 'masochistically pessimistic' ending which Clurman says the play had in its first version. Jacob's suicide (once again, suicide as a positive action) is supposed to have released Ralph from his helplessness, but his last speech is not convincing psychologically or philosophically:

> 'Awake and sing,' he said. Right here he stood and said it. The night he died, I saw it like a thunderbolt! I saw he was dead and I was born! I swear to God, I'm one week old! I want the whole city to hear it—fresh blood, arms. We got 'em. We're glad we're living.

How much more believable he is when he whines, 'It's crazy—all my life I want a pair of black and white shoes and can't get them.' The ironic thing about *Awake and Sing!* is that thirty years after it was written it is still a play of great vitality, but the life in it has nothing to do with Ralph's affirmation. It is the Bergers with their arguments and their cruelty, their sudden evidences of kindness and affection, the web of aimless conversation that holds them together that embody life. There is more vitality, more hope if you like, but not in the 1930's sense, in the scene in which Bessie turns on Schlosser, defending her father and her dog, than there is in Ralph as a tentative socialistic phoenix.

The family in *Paradise Lost* sound like the Bergers, but they have a stronger resemblance to the Connellys. The play charts the decline of the Gordons, and, as in the Paul Green play, the characters here are insistently symbolic: Ben, the athlete with the bad heart, the golden boy who will run no more; Julie, who plays the market in his head, as we watch his physical collapse on stage; Sam Katz, who is sexually impotent. As these characters decay physically, the Gordon business goes to pieces, the unions succumb to gangsterism, starved men lie on garbage dumps, the 'blue-gutted Yankee Doodle bastards' promise another war; as Leo Gordon, the protagonist, says: 'The world has a profound dislocation.' One can almost read Leo's character in that line alone. He is an intellectual, an artist if you like (he designs the ladies' bags and leaves the selling to Katz), gentle, rueful, slightly self-mocking. He cannot act to save his business because he does not believe in the kinds of action which he would have to perform: he cannot oppose the demands of his workers because he sympathizes with them; he cannot set a fire for the insurance because he is conventionally honest. Not that these lines of action would work; the impotent Katz is their advocate. Leo's problem is not to decide to do this or to do that, but to recognize that he is in a new world where old solutions, old comforts are dead. In the last act, with Ben dead (killed in his gangland debut) and the family dispossessed, Leo calls in some homeless men from the street and gives them the blood money that the dead Ben has earned. One of these, more rhetorical than practical, refuses the gift, makes the paradise-lost speech and accuses Leo of having learned nothing. At which point, with a swiftness that makes a teacher's mouth water, Leo absorbs his lesson and converts the negative message to a positive one: 'That was the past, but there is a future. Now we know.' He makes a long speech which ends, 'Ohhh, darling, the world is in its morning ... and *no man fights alone!*'; he opens the window and a fanfare (a block party is about to begin) is heard outside. Act III, which was finished while the play was in rehearsal, offers about as likely a solution to the problems posed early in the play as the end of *The House of Connelly*. It would be dramatically acceptable only if it could be read as ironic (like the end of *Uncle Vanya*), but Odets means us to take it straight; he would rather deliver the message than the dramatic goods.

In the revelations of Ralph and Leo there is the suggestion that collective action will change society, make it a place where love and life are possible. In the later plays—*Rocket to the Moon, Night Music*—the leading characters make similar discoveries but the possible embodiment of their hope is even more amorphous. Society is still the chief cause of the personal distress—Steve in *Night Music* recalls Jacob's life-on-dollar-bills line when he cries, '*Make this America for us!*'—but the solution (more properly, the first steps towards solution) are more clearly personal. In *Rocket*, Cleo goes out in search of love and Ben, having seen the world as it is, returns to his wife to make a new beginning. In *Night Music*, the bitter Steve, 'an angry Pierrot', as Clurman calls him, spends an enchanted thirty-six hours with a practical princess, a nice little girl from Philadelphia, and a dying fairy godfather, and learns from Rosenberger: 'Where there is life there is hope, in my humble opinion. Only the living can cry out against life. You are both alive and I love it.' In his description of *Clash by Night*, the first post-Group Odets play, Clurman says of Joe and Peggy, the young people who step out into the familiar Odetsian future, 'their presence represented a kind of ideological afterthought rather than the creative center of the play, which, no doubt about it, was pessimistic' (pp. 260–261). Perhaps Clurman, who had directed the earlier plays, could see *Clash* clearly because he was not involved in it. His criticism, however, suits the whole Odets canon. Leo's 'The world has a profound dislocation' is a better epigraph for the Odets plays that Ralph's 'We're glad we're living.' The genuinely positive element in Odets's work, his eye and ear for the humorous and painful details of daily living, which gives *Awake and Sing!* its power and which can be found intermittently in the later plays—a line here, a scene there, sometimes a whole character—was put in jeopardy by the positive philosophy that the plays insisted upon. At his most awkward, Odets lets his ideology violate character, disrupt mood and ignore the apparent direction in which his play is moving. Among Odets's Group plays, the most successful one dramatically—the slickest one, some critics said—is *Golden Boy*. The reason is that this is a play like Lawson's *Success Story*, the tale of an unfortunate fall, of a young man who trades his violin for boxing gloves, who buys the American myth of success and finds the taste of ashes in his mouth. His suicide is a consequence of the choice he makes early in the play. The alternate possibility, the action for change, is embodied in the peripheral figure of Frank, the union-organizing brother; he is a 1930's cliché, of course, but that is his function in the play, and it is better, for the play's sake, that he should fill that role than that Joe Bonaparte should assume it at the last minute.

In discussing the Group plays in terms of ideology I may seem to have put too great an emphasis on content rather than form. I think not, however, for it has been impossible to discuss the plays without showing how the ideas dictated the form or, too often, violated an implicit one. What may not be as immediately apparent is the strong stylistic resemblance among the Group plays. *The House of Connelly* is a combination Greek tragedy and regional folk play. *Night over Taos* is a verse drama in an historical setting. *1931—* and *Waiting for Lefty* are made up of naturalistic cameos in non-realistic frames. The Behrman-like *Gentlewoman* is a drawing-room play of ideas. *Gold Eagle Guy* is a chronicle play. *Johnny Johnson* is a musical satire. *The Case of Clyde Griffiths* is a lecture-demonstration. *Thunder Rock* is fantasy. *My Heart's in the Highlands* and *Night Music* are sweet, sad-eyed fables. Most of the rest of the plays, particularly those of Odets, have some claim on the realistic tradition. A label that might encompass such apparently divergent plays is the one that Mordecai Gorelik uses in *New Theatres for Old*—Left-wing symbolism. In borrowing his term, I have no intention of taking over his definition, although ours touch in many places. The affirmation in the Group plays, which came out of con-viction or desire rather than out of the material of the plays, dictated an artificial style. It was not simply that the plays tended to be parables, but that all the elements that went into them moved towards stylization. 'Even plays as close to traditional realism as *The House of Connelly* and *Awake and Sing!* were, in the Group's view, poetic plays and stylized as such, though accepted as "realism" by the majority of the audience and theatre commentators.' Clurman is here speaking (p. 235) in terms of production, but the same stylization is evident in the writing. I am not speaking of things as obvious as Maxwell Anderson's verse or the Siftons's use of abstract labels. A similar artificiality can be found in the characters and the dialogue of the plays that are more nearly realistic.

A character like Guy Button in *Gold Eagle Guy* is unusual among Group heroes because he suggests a psychological complexity to which most of the characters in these plays lay no claim. He is trapped finally by what the play has to say about the economic system; the variety of his motives are finally subsumed under demonic possession. Even so, Levy's play, for all its awkwardness, suggests the possibility of richness, even inexplicability in characterization. Compare Guy with Sol in *Success Story* or Gwyn in *Gentlewoman*. Lawson, who was moving towards doctrinaire Communism when these plays were written, was so mesmerized by economic determinism, by class as an identifying label, that he cut away most of the potential complexity in these characters so that they would not get in the way of the play's direct statements. For the most part, Group playwrights used stereotypes by choice. I intend the term not as pejorative, but as descriptive. There are two basic kinds of stock characters at work in these plays; they can be seen best in Odets's work, if only because we have more plays to consider in his case. The first type can be identified by dramatic function. Most of the Odets plays have, as hero, the young man on the edge of life, about to make his discovery (right or wrong) about where he is going. Ralph in *Awake and Sing!* and Steve in *Night Music* are remarkably alike because they perform similar functions in similar actions; Joe Bonaparte resembles them to some extent because he is the same character, although *Golden Boy* imposes a different action on him. Cleo in *Rocket to the Moon* is a feminine variation. The second type is on the periphery of the action, the one whose function is largely thematic. The great gallery of Odets figures who shape the mood of his plays, the soldiers in the trenches in Green's *Johnny Johnson*, the disillusioned emigrants in Ardrey's *Thunder Rock* are all characters of this kind. They are figures who can be identified by a recurring mannerism, a single preoccupation, a repeated line. Myron's recollection of the old days in *Awake and Sing!* not only strengthens the sense of a trap from which they all want to escape, but it serves to differentiate him from the other characters. Although such a character is obviously artificial, he gives an actor a firm hook on which to hang a performance and, since we customarily see other people in a single dimension, the result—unless the stylization is emphasized—is that the character looks realistic. Where Odets has it all over any other Group playwright who tries to draw such types is that—particularly in the early plays—he has a sense of vivid and often funny detail that makes his minor characters successful comic (or pathetic) turns.

The dialogue, like the characters, is also artificiality that seems realistic. When *Waiting for Lefty* was first produced, so the story goes, the audience was surprised and then delighted to hear their own language coming at them from across the footlights. As with most dramatic firsts, this one is a little suspect. Odets had presumably replaced ordinary stage English and literary dialogue with the vernacular of the Bronx. In fact, what he had done was to approximate a particular urban rhythm and utilize a tough, oblique way of speaking, a hard-boiled mask for sentiment, which was already used in American farce. Like a clever cartoonist, he exaggerated subtly, came down heavily on milieu-oriented metaphor ('I wouldn't trade you for two pitchers and an outfielder'), used a great deal of repetition, sprinkled his lines with the clichés of ordinary speech ('So go fight City Hall'); the result was a literary language which sounded like the real thing, a stage speech that avoided conventional poeticism, bland assumptions that realism meant flatness and the ludicrous overstatement of dialect comedians. The mannerisms were so marked, however, that Odets was soon parodying himself and any sharp-eared playgoer could identify an Odets speech, whoever wrote it. Here are three examples:

1. So that's what you think? That's what our love amounts to? Why don't you set that to music?
2. You might take a lesson from the lowly banana, Mrs. Finch—stick to your bunch or you'll get skinned!
3. Poverty's cracked her like a nutcracker cracks a nut.

The first is from *Success Story*, which was written three years before *Lefty* found a stage; the second from *The Silent Partner*, an Odets play that was never produced; the third from *The Gentle People*. Except when a playwright used an earlier convention (verse, a non-urban regional dialect, drawing-room articularity), all the Group playwrights wrote what came to be known as Odets dialogue, a conventional language which can still be heard coming out of our TV sets, and as likely as not out of the mouths of Lee Strasberg's students.

The plays produced by the Group Theatre all bear the marks of the organization that put them on stage. None of them is flawless and, as often as not, their flaws are the product of their own best intentions. Most of them have become period pieces, inoperative outside the social context that produced them. The best of them—*Awake and Sing!* and *Golden Boy*, for instance—transcend that context, and the worst of them have qualities—a provocative idea, perhaps, or a neat turn of phrase—that hold our attention. For the most part, the plays, like the Group itself, are successful failures.

Note

Biographies. Edward Estlin Cummings (1894–1964) was born in Cambridge, Mass., and studied at Harvard before serving in the Ambulance Corps in World War I, and suffering a period in a detention camp. After the war he lived in New York and Paris; he wrote a travel book, a ballet scenario and many poems, as well as two plays; he also painted.

Robert Lowell was born in 1917 in Boston, Mass.; his mother was descended from Edward Winslow, a Pilgrim Father, and his father from a family of poets, teachers and clergymen. He was an undergraduate at Harvard and then studied at Kenyon College, Ohio. In 1940 he married the novelist Jean Stafford and was converted to Roman Catholicism. When called up during the world war he declared himself a conscientious objector. In recent years he has remarried, to Elizabeth Hardwick.

Archibald MacLeish was born in 1892 in Glencoe, Ill. He was prominent in the 1930's as a poet and writer of radio plays like *The Fall of the City* (1937). In 1939 he was appointed Librarian of Congress. His play, *J.B.* was a Broadway success in 1958, in a spectacular production by Elia Kazan, and won a Pulitzer Prize.

William Carlos Williams (1883–1963) was born in Rutherford, New Jersey, and, after training in New York and visiting Europe, practised as a doctor in his home-town. His first volumes were *Poems* (1909) and *The Tempers* (1913); he published two novels, an autobiography, essays, letters, many poems and a volume of plays. His play *Many Loves* ran for nearly a year off-Broadway in a production by Julian Beck with Judith Malina in the lead.

Dramatic Works. e. e. cummings, *Santa Claus* (1946) and *Him* (1928/57); the first is in *Religious Drama 3* (1959) and *Him* in *From the Modern Repertoire, i* (1952) ed. E. Bentley (from which quotations are here made). *i: six nonlectures* was published in 1953.

Lowell's version of *Phaedra* (1961) is available in an English edition (1963). The English edition of *The Old Glory* was published in 1966; the text of *My Kinsman, Major Molineux* was printed in *Partisan Review* (1964) and is quoted here from that version.

MacLeish's plays include *Nobodaddy* (1926), *Panic* (1936), *This Music Crept By Me Upon the Waters* (1953); *J.B.* (1958) also appeared in an English edition (1959).

Williams's plays are *The First President* (1936), *A Dream of Love* (1949), *Tituba's Children* (1950); *Many Loves* (1959) and *The Cure* (1960; written 1952); all appear in *Many Loves and other plays* (1961), from which this chapter quotes.

Criticism. There is little dramatic criticism of the poets outside periodicals and reviews. MacLeish and cummings are considered by D. Donoghue in *The Third Voice* (1959) and there are relevant passages in, among other general works, C. Brooks, *Modern Poetry and the Tradition* (1948); J. Chiari, *Landmarks of Contemporary Drama* (1965); F. Fergusson, *The Idea of a Theater* (1949); and M. D. Zabell, *Literary Opinion in America* (rev. ed., 1951).

E. Bentley's *In Search of Theater* (1953) includes illustrations from his production of *Him*; an analysis of the play in terms of ritual patterns defined by F. M.

V

The Poets in the American Theatre

KATHARINE J. WORTH

★

THE dramatic achievement of modern poets has received much critical attention in the last two decades, Yeats and Eliot inevitably drawing the lion's share and inspiring interest in even the minor work produced within their ambience.

The special contributions of the American poets to the theatre have been less widely discussed, and are, indeed, outside America, barely known. e. e. cummings's *Him*, first produced in New York in 1928, was not seen by English audiences until 1965, while the plays of William Carlos Williams and Robert Lowell have had no English productions. Even Archibald MacLeish, better known as a playwright than the others, owes his dramatic reputation to the radio rather than the theatre, and the critical consideration he has attracted is partly due to the similarities between his situation and Eliot's.

Yet the dramatic experiments of the American poets deserve close attention, both for what they are in themselves and for the new theatrical directions they indicate. That the American theatre has found room for them only with difficulty is due less to imperfections in the work than to an inhibiting modern situation. At a time when the expression 'poetic drama' has come to have for most people 'a distinctly effete and pejorative meaning which, in most cases, automatically disqualifies it from competing on equal terms with other forms of drama' (J. Chiari, p. 81), any efforts to accommodate the poets must be

---

Cornford in *Origins of Attic Comedy* (1914) is found in *From the Modern Repertoire*, i (1952), ed. E. Bentley. The March, 1936, issue of *The Stage* is of special interest for cummings's essay, 'Burlesque, I Love it'.

H. Machiz tells the story of one côterie theatre in *Artist's Theatre*, 2 vols. (1960), and J. Beck and Judith Malina of another in *Tulane Drama Review* (1964).

counted for virtue and neglect of them seem only too understandable.

The American poets have had to depend upon the enterprise of the côterie theatre and, in so doing, to accept its limitations, not least of which is the special attitude it generates in audiences, actors and reviewers.[1] The disadvantages of this situation certainly show in their work; it exhibits technical defects of the kind to which playwrights unexercised in the popular theatre are prone. Yet from the weakness of their position the poets have drawn some of their dramatic strength. Indeed, one of the most interesting aspects of their drama is the use to which they have put the frustrations they have experienced in the theatre.

Their very sense of isolation, by providing them with a theme, has drawn them into the main stream of modern drama. They may exist, for practical purposes, on the extreme fringe of the American theatre, but their subject matter is central, the isolation of the individual in the world of his imagination, the desperation of his attempts at communication. Their attempts to reach a wider audience have led them into some fruitful experiments with dramatic form and language. They have explored the possibilities in popular theatrical forms, in colloquial speech, in non-verbal modes of expression, in a synthesis of prose, verse and music. Preoccupation with the idea of their audiences has stimulated formal experiment of striking originality. In its dramatic virtues, as in its weaknesses, the drama of the poets clearly reflects their peculiar situation in the modern theatre and their awareness of all that this involves.

★   ★   ★

Our attention is, then, limited to the poets who have made their names as poets outside the theatre, and, who, in coming into the theatre, have usually been regarded as attempting or making a second reputation. The four poets considered, though only one of them, Archibald MacLeish is normally sure of inclusion in theatrical works of reference, have all penetrated so far into the theatre as to have had New York

---

[1] The poets' dependence upon the côterie theatre, perpetuating as it does the distinction between 'poet' and 'playwright' which has bedevilled the twentieth-century theatre, involves them in a vicious circle. They are cut off from popular audiences who suspect 'poetic drama' when presented as such, though they may be prepared to respond to 'poetry of the theatre' when it seems to occur as an accidental by-product.

productions of their plays: it is therefore possible to consider their work in the context of the professional theatre. MacLeish has had a resounding Broadway success, with *J.B.*: the other three, Robert Lowell, William Carlos Williams and e. e. cummings have had the benefit of professional direction for their plays in off-Broadway theatres. All four have, in different ways, extended the frontiers of drama. Their achievement is their own, but the special problems they have as poets in the theatre are representative.[2]

The plays of Lowell and Williams achieved professional production late in their poetic careers, although Williams had been associated with amateur companies, both as actor and playwright, for years before *Many Loves*, written in 1940, was produced at the Living Theatre in New York in 1959. The sensitivity of the poets to their special position in the theatre is shown in their fondness for a dramatic structure which allows for a dialogue of attack and defence between stage author and stage audience or critic, rather in the style of Shaw's *Fanny's First Play*. Act II of e. e. cummings *Him* consists of a 'play within a play', presented, in a theatre of the mind, to an audience of one. She, being in love with the poet, is predisposed to sympathize, yet still finds it difficult; her suggestions that he should write something 'popular' draw from him sardonic comments on the gulf stretching between the only sort of play he can write and the theatre as Broadway understands it:

> I might add that it's sure of a long run: provided, of course, we receive the proper advertising—you know what I mean—'Broadway is enjoying a novel treat in one of the wittiest and most highly original products of American genius, entitled "How Dyuh Get That Way" by the authors of "Nuf Ced" . . . the subject of this rollicking farce is the 18th Amendment.' (p. 196)

Thirty years later, we find William Carlos Williams employing a similar technique, having an inner play in rehearsal before the author and the potential backer. Hubert, the poet-playwright, taunts Peter, the backer, with the ironical line: 'We don't like verse in plays'. The dialogue continues:

[2] Much interesting dramatic work by poets lies outside the province of this study. They range from very slight, minor dramatic efforts, like Wallace Stevens's *Three Travellers Watch a Sunrise* (1916) to the more considerable, *The Visionary Farms* (1953) of Richard Eberhart and the masques of Robert Frost, performed at the Kresge Little Theatre, 30 May, 1962, under the title, *The Theatre of Robert Frost*.

PETER. No, we don't.

HUBERT. I know that. But I know more. There is no verse, no new verse to write a play in. That's why. Invent it.

PETER. And you'll invent it. This is the usual avant-garde décor. Isn't it, Hubert: So far in front it's dragging at tomorrow's tail.

HUBERT. No. You'll see.   (p. 16)

What kind of audience they are writing for, if, indeed they have an audience at all, is a question much discussed by the poets. Williams has made the most pessimistic pronouncement: 'I don't really believe a "serious" play can be produced in the U.S. in our time; there is no audience for it' (*Collected Plays*, p. 434). MacLeish, the only poet to have had a Broadway success, in *J.B.*, is, naturally enough, more sanguine, although in 1953, in the preface to *This Music Crept By Me Upon the Waters*, he was dubious about the damaging compromises a poet might have to make to draw the Broadway audiences. 'Does Mr. Eliot's resounding success on Broadway offer a hint to those, if there are any, capable of receiving it', he asks, 'or was the prosodic price he paid too high?' At the time he wrote this, *This Music Crept By Me Upon the Waters* was about to be presented by the Poets' Theatre, Cambridge, and it seemed to MacLeish that the future might, after all, lie with the little theatre and a chamber drama in the style of the later Yeats. As well he might, he queried whether such a drama assumed 'conditions which do not exist in the United States', but concluded that, in the collapse of radio theatre under pressure of commercialism, 'Small, identifiable audiences may create in time a more enduring public for poetry than the large anonymous audiences radio could have reached.'

Whether this hope will be realized remains an open question, but the history of the little theatres in the last thirty years has not been of the sort to inspire confidence in their capacity to create 'a more enduring public'. 'Enduring' is, indeed, the least appropriate of words for these theatres. Their life expectation is usually short, seldom much more than the three years for which the Artists' Theatre, in its director's phrase, 'existed (and that is literally the word) in New York between 1953 and 1956' (p. 7). The Poets' Theatre, Cambridge, has been exceptional in staying power for an amateur group dedicated to the production of new scripts. In 1960, Herbert Machiz, director of the Artists' Theatre, could name only two theatres, since his own had expired in 1957, producing 'plays by creative writers who were primarily poets and serious thinkers' (p. 7). Three years later the Living Theatre, which opened in 1951, had collapsed in appropriately dramatic and stormy circumstances and by 1965 the Poets' Theatre had ceased to exist and a new experimental group, Theatre Company of Boston, was, according to the reviewer for *Best Plays of 1963 and 1964* 'still clinging to a beach-head in the 15-seat Hotel Bostonian Playhouse, fighting for support and survival'. The hopeful aspect of this otherwise depressing situation is the speed with which new companies spring up to replace the casualties. Since the expiry of the Living Theatre, the American Place Theatre, New York, has presented Lowell's *The Old Glory* (1 March, 1964) and announced its intention of providing 'a place, a staff and a broad program of practical work to American writers of stature: our poets, novelists and philosophers who wish to use the dramatic form, and to serious new playwrights'. The process seems likely to continue, with new groups thrusting up as the insolvent close down, theatres being contrived out of hotel rooms and church halls, but the character of the audience remaining much the same, the 'fit audience though few', towards which Yeats moved in his chamber drama and from which Eliot sought to move away.

★   ★   ★

The pull of the two different concepts of theatre has received much attention in MacLeish's critical writing on drama.* Like Eliot, to whom he is the closest of the American poet-playwrights, he craves a more popular, representative audience than the côterie theatre can provide, encouraged to hope for this, no doubt, by the success he enjoyed as a writer of verse drama for radio before commercial developments, as he says, 'remitted' the poets to 'the status *quo ante*—to the stage in the four-walled room' (Preface to *This Music Crept By Me Upon the Waters*). MacLeish always has his audience very much in mind, though he by no means manages consistently to adapt his style to the different requirements of radio and stage drama. Indeed, he often seems to be attempting a mixed form, appropriate to either kind of performance. The history of its production suggests that *This Music Crept By Me Upon the Waters* was so designed, being first produced as a radio play on the Third Programme of the B.B.C. in June, 1953, presented on the stage of the Poets' Theatre, Cambridge, in the autumn and then produced again,

---

* Unfortunately it has not been possible to quote directly from the works of Archibald MacLeish in the following account; when the editors learnt of this it was too late to redraft.

later in the year, by the B.B.C. Radio plays, such as *The Fall of the City* (1937) and *Air Raid* (1938) demonstrate his command of a technique adapted to a listening audience, but when, in a play such as *Panic* (1936), a seeing audience is indicated by the use of devices like the electric news bulletin, 'moving words in lighted letters', he is still inclined to rely upon the impact of sound for dramatic emphasis. The function of the illuminated words, for instance, is little more than to provide opportunities for choral verse from the crowds who read them aloud 'at a regular lagging beat as the machine forms them'. They also question the news, with a similar beat. A special effect is aimed at here, an impression of mounting agitation and panic, but the technique still suggests a radio dramatist dealing with the limitations of his medium. Dramatic tension depends upon contrasted patterns of sound and silence, focusing on the ticker tape inside McGafferty's office and the chorus outside. The climax, McGafferty's suicide, is conveyed with gradually diminishing sound, and calls for very close listening as 'the ticker, sounding more and more slowly in the silence, becomes almost inaudible: a vibration of air'.

Vibrations of air, patterns of sound, these are the characteristic effects of much of MacLeish's drama, whether written specifically for radio or not. Typically, in his very early play about the Garden of Eden, *Nobodaddy* (1926), the Tempter remains invisible and the audience is required to listen, with Adam, for some considerable time, to a 'thin, very musical voice, without apparent origin', a radio voice indeed. There is, certainly, a thematic reason for the disembodied voice, as the quotation from Blake which serves as motto to the published text indicates:

> Why art thou silent and invisible,
> Father of Jealousy?
> Why dost thou hide thyself in clouds—

but the explanation does not do away with the dramatic awkwardness of the prolonged listening. When, in a later play, *J.B.*, MacLeish handled a similar theme, with a popular audience in mind, he established the idea of 'invisibility' in more effective dramatic terms.

Already apparent in *Nobodaddy* is MacLeish's preference for rhetorical statement over implicit revelation of character. Situations are blurred and slowed down by discussion of the event before and after it; the climactic scene, the taking of the apple, has none of the dramatic excitement attaching to it in Shaw's *Back to Methuselah*, or, for that matter, in *Paradise Lost*. The characters are not held in a state of dramatic tension. Adam and Eve may keep us interested, up to a point, in what they say, less in what they do. When Adam disappears before the last Act, he is hardly missed, for with his share in the argument, now taken over by Cain and Abel, goes his dramatic function.

Yet despite the emphasis he puts on the abstract, representative elements in his subject matter, MacLeish is preoccupied with the search for a verse form based upon the particular and colloquial. As early as 1936, in the critical preface to *Panic*, he was explaining his rejection of the blank verse used in *Nobodaddy*, pointing out that for the rhythms of contemporary American speech which were 'nervous, not muscular; excited, not deliberate; vivid, not proud;' an accentual, short lined verse form would be more appropriate than either blank verse or 'relaxed forms of iambic composition'. Much of the poetic energy in the plays since *Panic* has gone into the creation of a verse form adapted to the rhythms of the spoken language.

The similarity of his technical interests to Eliot's is marked, nowhere more than in *This Music Crept By Me Upon the Waters*, where he attempts to fashion a verse flexible enough to express experiences ranging from the superficial encounters of a 'cocktail party' world to the mystical apprehension of the timeless moment. The situation, which recalls the opening and closing sequences of *The Cocktail Party*, is slight. Some leisured Americans sit in a moonlit garden in the Antilles, waiting for dilatory guests: when the guests arrive, romantic passages take place, but lead to nothing; eventually they all go in to dinner.

The situation does not 'give' us the characters. They come to us through their conversation which is built up round images drawn from the night, the sea and the island, where, as the title indicates, a 'sea change' is to be expected. The 'change' is worked out, however, in Eliot-like rather than Shakespearian terms. Two of the characters, Elizabeth and Peter, experience in a 'blinding instant' a revelation which separates them from their less perceptive friends and lovers. The dramatic pattern is designed to bring out the contrast between the different modes of sensibility, and the verse emphasizes it, adapting well to colloquial effects and to parodies of the lyrical mode. The small change of ordinary conversation is well handled, the heavily accented verse keeping the tune of commonplace speech while subtly exaggerating its mechanical quality. Imagery and rhythm also convey with delicacy the nuances of feeling, the moments of insight which form the central dramatic experience. But there is a tendency for character-ization to become blurred by a too free distribution of lyrical passages, a 'breach of decorum' which Denis Donoghue notes as a characteristic of 'mood plays', among which he includes *This Music Crept By Me Upon the Waters* (pp. 195–205). And when the time comes to show the outcome of the conversations in terms of action, the 'revelation' experi-enced by Elizabeth and Peter leads into an admission of mutual passion and a frustrated attempt at a liaison, which remains commonplace. The poetry has promised more than the action can perform, an unhappily common situation in the drama of poets.

The temptation to a relaxed, wordy form is one of the hazards of writing for radio or the over-indulgent côterie theatre. MacLeish's wish for the stimulus of a mixed, popular audience, is reflected in, and has helped to form, the much tighter, more expressive structure of the play which won him the Pulitzer Prize, *J.B.* (1958). Visual effects are vital in this play. The audience are not invited to listen from a distance to people talking, the radio method, but are made to feel themselves inside a stage theatre, the circus tent, in which they share with the actors the business of creating a play. In a sense they also share with the author, for though the circus employees, Mr. Zuss and Nickles, who stage the play, are not the authors of the Book of Job, they undoubtedly call the re-enactment of the story into being, Mr. Zuss's initial hesitation suggesting that he has a fearful knowledge of a creator. Like the poet himself, the play's two presenters are highly conscious of their audience: they bemoan a growing indifference to their wares, the popcorn and balloons, they address the audience directly, draw them into a special 'knowing' relationship, offering a privileged God's eye view of the action. That they stand for God and Satan their names indicate before they put on their masks, but they are not allegorical figures; in fact the skill with which MacLeish keeps the symbolism balanced this side of allegory is one of the most impressive features of the play. The actors remain human, knowing more than Job, able to direct his story, but in their turn directed by the voice speaking through the masks. When this voice is first heard, in the sonorous cadences of the Authorized Version, audience and actors are involved in the same shock and bewilderment. All are in it together, in the battered old tent, with the blurred signs of the zodiac just visible, realizing, in a moment of terror, that inspiration exists, clinging hopefully to rational explanations.

When the inner play begins, the dual roles of Mr. Zuss and Nickles, as actors and stage audience, nicely symbolize the uncertainty of their relationship with the unseen director. Mr. Zuss thinks he knows 'the Book': he insists on keeping to the well rehearsed pattern, rebuking Nickles's attempts at overturning it. Finally, when J.B. departs from the book, the actors are dispossessed; they leave their traditional acting areas, stage Heaven and stage Hell, to take up new positions on the same level as their fellow, who now directs his own play. Mr. Zuss had doubted at the outset whether J.B. knew he was 'in the play' at all; by the end it is his own role which seems equivocal. J.B. accepts his part, since, like Mr. Zuss and Nickles, he can do no other, but imposes his own interpretation, rejecting the old 'pro's.' reading of the book.

The inner play itself is less satisfactory, mainly because of uncertainty in the presentation of J.B.'s character. Is he meant to be in fact the 'perfect and upright man' for whom suffering is an opportunity to affirm faith? Or is he, as the early scenes suggest, a self-satisfied tycoon who needs to suffer to be enlightened? His first incredulity in the face of disaster, his conviction that God has been with him from the first silver dollar to the last controlling interest, point to the second interpretation, but this, if the correct one, cuts across the central argument which depends upon the idea of suffering as total mystery.

J.B.'s naïveté is, therefore, a dramatic liability. When he is required only to feel, he convinces. When required to enter into philosophical discussion he is inadequate, and we begin to feel doubtful about the effect intended in the contrasts of verse; whether we are meant to observe, as in fact we must, the difference in tone between the dignified biblical questioning and J.B.'s childlike version of it.

If the characterization is hazy, however, the action is much more effectively organized than in earlier plays.[3] The working out of the acting metaphor is impressive, bringing metaphysical speculation into the action in a fully theatrical way, and allowing for symbolic extension of character and event without undermining concrete realities. The circus tent may symbolize the universe, but it is never less than a real place where a performance is being given. MacLeish's need to be involved with an audience has here had fruitful results.

[3] That O'Neill may have provided a model for the structural outline is suggested by the resemblances between *J.B.* and *Days Without End* (1933), where we have a morality hero, a tempter in a mask, and an action following a pattern laid down in the book John Loving is writing.

★   ★   ★

The metaphor of a play only imperfectly understood by its audience
is also implicit in the structure of Robert Lowell's play, *My Kinsman,
Major Molineux*.[4] This 'political cartoon', one of three episodes in *The
Old Glory*, presented at the American Place Theatre in 1964, dramatizes
historical event as it appears to the eye of 'innocent' observers, who are
'in the play' without knowing it. Riddling dialogue, cryptic ballads,
'show' the event, the Boston Tea Party, as it strikes Robin and his
brother, the innocents abroad:

> Your aunt's the lord high sheriff,
> your uncle is King George;
> if you can't pay the tariff,
> the house will let you charge.

The expression of violent action through verse with the austere, formal
quality of ballad produces an interesting double effect: the events seem
distanced, completed and yet immediate. This effect is reinforced in the
stage setting which represents miniature houses 'in the style of a primitive New England sampler': through man-size doors characters emerge,
as it were from history, into the orbit of the stage light to play their
parts, receding again into Lilliputian remoteness. The balance between
far and near is pointed by the Ferryman who rows Robin and the Boy
to the scene of the action. He belongs to the play, indeed it is he who
finally kills Major Molineux, but he has an antique air, his costume
'half suggests that he is Charon', and he tells his passengers:

> People go round in circles here.
> This is the city of the dead.

before altering the sense to:

> I said this city's Boston,
> No one begs here. Are you deaf?

As the rustic characters seek through the city for their powerful
kinsman, Major Molineux, who has always just left the places at which
they arrive, they are in effect seeking the meaning of events around
them. Their bewilderment at what they see forces an ironical interpretation of these events. Violence and corruption are presented in
forms so oblique that the observers' naïve admiration of the city is not

[4] The account which follows, being based upon an early version of the play,
is intended only to give an impression of Lowell's dramatic style.

disturbed. We see them drawn into the historical process without recognizing what is happening and the result of this 'innocence' is shown at the end when Robin 'unconsciously' carrying the rattlesnake flag which has been thrust on him, throws dirt, again 'unconsciously' at the tarred and feathered body of his 'poor' kinsman.

The symbolism works brilliantly on two levels. Its first function is to reveal gradually to Robin the historical interpretation of the action, the replacement of the lion and unicorn by the rattlesnake. But beyond this it conveys to the audience a view of the historical action as a symbol of fatality. The full interpretation depends upon a symbolic pun, a play upon the word 'colour'. The change from the 'colour' or flag of King George to the colonists' 'colour', the rattlesnake flag, involves a taking over by the new power of the colour associated with the old, the colour of the 'lobster' or redcoat,

> horny, boiled and red,
> It is the Major's spitting image.

This blood-red colour gradually spreads across the stage as the transference of power is effected: the face of the Man in the Mask changes from grey to fiery red, an 'image of the times'; the homosexual asserts his patriotic orthodoxy by seeking out the red-skirted prostitute; the scarlet uniform, 'red coat blazing like the sunrise', is appropriated by the new order. Finally, what the symbolic colour represents, and what this implies for later history, is shown by the violent killing, on stage, of Major Molineux, with his kinsman standing by.

Lowell achieves an effect both intellectually sophisticated and theatrical, if somewhat monotonous, or, as a reviewer of the New York production saw it, 'stiff and forbidding', having 'precisely the limitations of a cartoon'.[5] His use of ballad and symbol results in a style very unlike, in its irony and ambiguity, the explicit rhetoric of MacLeish. These poets have in common, however, a preoccupation with verse as the standard dramatic measure. William Carlos Williams has set himself a different task; he attempts to integrate verse into a prose texture for special effects of contrast and illumination.

*   *   *

The technique is seen at its most spectacular in *Tituba's Children*, a play about the Salem witch trials and the investigations of the 1950's

[5] G. Rogoff, *Plays and Players* (January, 1965).

into 'un-American activities'.[6] The two trials are linked by the device
of a 'play within a play', the Salem episodes being reconstructed in a
Washington night club as an 'entertainment' for an audience of
Senators and State officials taking time off from their own witch
hunting. As the 'act' proceeds, it is invaded by ghostly figures who take
over the parts, replacing the jazzed-up, cynical prose idiom of the
modern version with the dignified, tragic cadences of the seventeenth
century. A fine sense of nemesis is produced by the helplessness of the
twentieth-century actors to avert the doom re-enacted by their
ancestors. Past and present merge: the modern courtroom fills with
Puritans who take their cues with ease in a familiar situation, objecting
'A papist! An idolator!' when a character defends herself against a
charge of Communism with the plea, 'I am a good Catholic'. The
persistence of Salem bigotry is pointed by the repetition of the old
grievances in a new idiom. The Senators watching the Salem play are
unaware of the parallelism in the situations but their casual reactions to
the actors demonstrate its reality. An Italian Master of Ceremonies or,
comically, an antelope-headed demon, ghostly visitant from the 'real'
Salem, draw from them such revealing comments as:

> 'What do we let 'em in for? Any of 'em? Grease balls',
> 'Who the hell was the little guy in red? I don't trust these
> foreigners'.
>> The dominant theme is the
>> three-hundred-year-old curse
>> that has been the scourge of our country.
>>> (p. 282)

It demands a style of tragic dignity to which modern prose idiom is
notoriously inimical. Williams solves the problem by using speech and
ballad from the Salem period to express the passions of a less articulate
people. The play is, indeed, a 'great swirling congeries of themes built
upon the Giles Cory ballad':

> Come all New England men
> And harken unto me.
> And I will tell you what did befall
> Upon ye gallows tree.

[6] *Tituba's Children* was written by 1950, preceding Lyon Phelps's *The
Gospel Witch* (produced by the Poets' Theatre, 22 May, 1952), and Arthur
Miller's *The Crucible* (1953). It differs from both plays in its emphasis on the
historical rather than the personal aspects of the Salem trials.

From this ballad emerges a key image, 'pressing to death', the fate of the eighty-year-old Giles Cory who refused to answer the charges against him. In the image, past and present meet. The psychological pressure exerted on the modern victims, shown in scenes of badgering by the press, harrying in court, comes into tragic perspective when related to the barbarous pressure of history. The point is made in a magnificent climax: the singing of the Giles Cory ballad during the ghostly re-enactment of the Salem trial is interrupted by a terrible, half muffled cry off stage, 'More weight! More weight!' and the scene dissolves into a modern courtroom, with the voice of Senator Yokell demanding, 'Mr. McDee, have you ever been a member of the Communist party?'

Here is a poetic imagination working in dramatic terms. Williams seems to be fully extended dramatically when he attempts this kind of tension between verse and prose, writing at a lower level of intensity in verse alone, as in *The First President*,[7] or in prose alone, in *The Cure*. In *Many Loves* the division of verse and prose serves to emphasize the contrast between an outer and an inner action. The inner play reflects the outer in the disguised shapes which life assumes in artistic form: verse is used for 'life', prose for 'art'.

Dramatic interest centres in the connections between the two actions. In each, the theme is the difficulty of knowing people and of loving. The protagonists in the outer play are Hubert, Peter who 'loves' him, Alise, his leading lady, whom he 'loves'. As the rehearsal of Hubert's play proceeds we gradually recognize that the three apparently disconnected[8] episodes which make up the whole are in fact what he describes them as:

> Three short sketches on
> a general theme, of which each is a facet
> casting its own aspect of the light.
>
> (p. 11)

[7] This is a special case, being conceived as a libretto for an opera cum ballet.

[8] The effect remained disconnected for some reviewers of the Living Theatre production, a review in *The Times Literary Supplement* (re-printed in *The American Imagination*, 1960, p. 95) describing the play as 'some quick disconnected insights into the private lives of New Yorkers, the whole smothered in a Pirandellian dressing'. Williams's own account of the play's genesis rather encourages such views: he tells how the idea of combining three one-Act plays

In the first episode, a young married woman, shaken by the pregnancy test which her lover has forced upon her, withdraws from another offer of love: in the second, romantic, adolescent love is turned by family opposition into a strange channel: in the third, a middle-aged doctor and young married patient attempt unsuccessfully to find release from tension and inadequacy in sexual love. Each episode, in fact, presents failures in love and indicates, through the painful separateness of the characters, the impossibility of knowing 'what actually the creature in the next bin is doing or feeling'. The theme is underlined by oblique indications of sexual deviation. The adolescent girl is drawn into the orbit of a young woman with implied Lesbian tendencies: the pregnancy test fails when the rabbit used is found to be a hermaphrodite. All is unfathomable, indeterminate, even the sex of a rabbit.

Peter's reactions to the play reveal its function as a mirror of the mind. He professes not to understand it, protesting after the first episode, 'I can't see the point. Is it related to something I should know about?' Later he answers his own question. To Hubert's, 'The mind's the scene', he retorts, 'Whose mind?' (p. 45) and he responds to seemingly innocuous passages such as Miss Breen's enquiry, 'Any young people?' with revealing violence:

> This from you! Since when have you
> become so courageous, my little sparrow?
> (p. 57)

The counterpointing of 'stage' dialogue in prose with 'real' comment in verse brings about the kind of revelation which Hubert associates with dramatic verse:

> That is what says
> what I am saying beyond the words.
> (p. 32)

Hubert's own words, in his dialogues with Peter and Alise, indicate an assertive personality, sure of himself as playwright and lover. The play reveals a more complex, divided self, by no means so certain of his sexual nature as the outer action suggests. Alise perceives this only at the end, when he accepts the humiliating stage wedding forced on them

---

he had written in 1940 came to him from seeing a group of three such plays by Noel Coward on Broadway: 'Why not take my own three plays and combine them under one title?' (*Collected Plays*, p. 431).

by Peter. 'He's too strong for you', she says, 'You poor boy.' The conclusion of the outer action, in masquerade and uncertainty, has in fact already been anticipated in what Peter calls the 'unresolved floating' action of the inner play, the characters left 'flapping their wings, like wounded birds'. Hubert is a wounded bird in his personal relations; in his imaginative transmutation of them he is supremely confident. At the end, as in the beginning, he remains certain of only one thing, his vocation as poet: 'There is only one thing that I intend to do—it is to learn to write a play in verse.'

Williams's fondness for the technique of the 'play within a play' demonstrates the genuinely dramatic quality of his imagination. He is drawn to 'act out' psychological processes. Even in a play like *A Dream of Love* (1949), where the subject, the relation between different manifestations of the creative impulse, might seem likely to prove intractable to dramatic treatment, he succeeds in finding a highly theatrical means of expression.

He casts the theme in the form of a marital struggle to arrive at a stage of mutual acceptance. The wife of the Doctor, who is also a poet —the resemblance between the author and his character is even clearer here than in *Many Loves*—tries to come to terms with his creative energy which results in both poetry and romantic infidelities. He loves her, but needs other women, so he claims, in the same way as he needs poetry: he reads her a poem which contains the experience; she half listens, falls asleep, cannot follow him. Up to this point the action, built up as it is round a discussion of poetic images, seems, though interesting, unlikely to offer a full dramatic experience. An over-leisurely development of the preparatory action is perhaps Williams's most pronounced dramatic weakness. With the Doctor's death in a hotel room during an act of infidelity 'the character of the play suddenly shifts to tragedy, with the wife occupying the central role' (*Collected Plays*, p. 433). The action tightens; what seemed earlier like casually selected objects of reference, acquire a new significance. The room in which Myra last saw her husband becomes a prison from which she cannot walk out. She makes a huge effort of the imagination, expressed in terms of a surrealist[9] reconstruction of day to day experience, the Milkman

[9] The stage directions calling for an expressionist distortion of the room recall O'Neill's directions for *All God's Chillun Got Wings*: in both plays lighting is used to change the height of the ceiling, create significant shadows and suggest the change of view experienced by an obsessed character.

producing bottles of blood-red liquid, the Butcher Boy, joining him as audience to the 'performance' by the Doctor and his mistress of the fatal scene in the hotel room. In the blaze of expressionistic fireworks with which the 'dream' ends, on the exultant repetition of the word 'Yes!', a consummation is reached. Myra regains her feeling for her husband, recaptures the dream they shared. When she wakes, and is at last able to make the decisive step out of the room, the forcefulness of the simple climax shows how surely the ideas with which the play began have been drawn into the substance of the action.

★   ★   ★

There are pronounced similarities between *Many Loves, A Dream of Love* and e. e. cummings's *Him* (1927), an exceptionally rich, seminal play, which reflects or anticipates many characteristic preoccupations of the poets in the theatre. Avant-garde in 1928 when it was first produced at the Provincetown Theatre, New York, *Him* was still avant-garde in 1965, when Eric Bentley produced it at the Salzburg Festival. In 1965, when the British première took place at the Harlow Arts Festival, Essex, audience and reviewers were struck by the play's fresh, contemporary quality, by suggestions of Pinter's rooms in the room of Him and Me, and the likeness of cummings's expressionist and music hall techniques to those of Osborne, Arden and the Brechtian school. The theme of *Him* is the working and effects of the creative imagination. Only two characters are 'real', the poet, Him, and Me, who is giving birth to his child, and in whose consciousness, distorted by anaesthetic, the poet's 'child', his play, is recreated. Me is at once protagonist and audience; Him protagonist, author and director.

The room of the mind, which in *A Dream of Love* frames only the closing scenes, here contains the whole action. Its imprisoning quality is conveyed by brilliantly placed emphasis upon the stage itself, the enclosing walls of the box set. The door, window and mirror, set in the three walls, change position in relation to each other as the action progresses, a device which not only establishes the disorientation of the protagonists, but draws attention to the illusory solidity of the fourth wall. The stage thus serves the function of precipitating metaphysical enquiry through the question: 'Does the fourth wall exist, and, if so, in what sense?'

Each wall opens up a different line of speculation. The window, which might be expected to give on to an open prospect, in fact turns

Him and Me in upon themselves: all they see through it is driving snow, which haunts them: 'O think of the snow coming down beautifully and beautifully frightening ourselves and turning dying and love and the world and me and you into five toys' (III. i; p. 230).

The snow increases the sense of claustrophobia but also of cosiness, security, as in the child's glass snow scene, with the tiny, enclosed figures, which the image suggests.

If the window, ironically, offers no outlook, the mirror gives a confused view, throwing back a series of distorted reflections. In the mirror, Him sees his other self, Mr. O'Him, the intruder and censor, the self he projects into his play as the Doctor. Me sees only a reflection of her physical self: she lives in a simpler world of feeling. Him's isolation, in his efforts to realize himself as man and artist, is well conveyed in such scenes as that when he kneels, praying, to his mirror image,[10] while Me unconcernedly primps her hair at the same glass. The mirror image is central: the dramatic action is organized around it. Him is writing a play about 'The sort of a man—who is writing a play about a man who is writing a sort of a play.' Inner play reflects outer play, one scene reflects another, in a seemingly endless vista.

In the third wall is a door. Me never goes through it, though at the very end she seems to be about to. That the possibility exists for Him is indicated by the dramatic emphasis given to his battered old hat: when he puts it on, he steps out of the room into the imaginative world whose continuing existence is shown in the presence on the side of the stage, throughout the action, of the 'so-to-speak Chorus' (*six nonlectures*, p. 81), the trio of Weird Sisters who knit the pattern of the play. Escape from the room comes only through the imagination. One of the most impressive aspects of the play is the splendidly physical sense of release which cummings achieves in the scenes of the inner play, and in the surrealist sequences of Paris and the circus which represent the imaginative experience before it is organized into formal patterns. The close, intense quality of the room scenes gives way to the rumbustiousness of burlesque, and the poetic spirit begins to work in Aristophanic style. Alone among the poets under discussion, cummings has the power to make us laugh. He puts it to good effect. In the inner play we are not

[10] O'Neill had dramatized the conflict between a man and his 'other self' through masks, in *The Great God Brown* (1926), and was later to deal with the same subject, in *Days Without End* (1933), with a technique similar to that of cummings in *Him*.

asked to reflect upon, we experience physically, in our laughter, the freedom of the work of art.

Farce is the dominant element of the inner play. Him's abortive attempt at suicide in front of the mirror is translated into splendid knockabout sequences between Will and Bill, business partners so mixed up that Bill is arrested for the murder of Will who killed himself thinking that he was shooting the Intruder, who finally turns out to be Will, after all. The painful self-analysis of the room takes on, in the burlesque, the ludicrous form of an Englishman, in New York, bowed under the weight of a huge trunk, marked 'Fragile'. To the policeman who demands what he has in it he confides that it is not a trunk, but his unconscious:

> Don't pretend you haven't heard of them in America. Why, my dear boy, I was given to understand that a large percentage of them originated in the States. (p. 210)

The inhibiting mirror self is swept from one scene into another, to be mocked, talked down, knocked down. In the Frankie and Johnnie sequence, where he figures as President of the Society for the Contraception of Vice, he jumps, screaming, off the stage as Frankie in person waves a phallic emblem in his face, drum taps substitute for the forbidden word and the jazz chorus chants triumphantly:

> Best Part of the Man
> Who Done Me Wrong.

Finally, in the one sombre episode, of the ruined city, which leads back into the room scene, he is overwhelmed by an angry, writhing mob, 'revolving furiously within itself and rumbling, choking, roaring'. He gives way before a physical pressure so strong that it is felt by the audience, kneels down, as snow begins to fall,[11] takes his clothes off and prepares to be reborn. The cathartic function of the inner play is nowhere clearer than in this scene.

The special effect of the burlesque episodes springs from the expression of interior conflict in terms of satire on the contemporary scene. We get a breath of the outside world, even though it can only penetrate

---

[11] A fine sense of continuity was achieved in the Harlow production of *Him* by having the snow effect of the city scene continue into the room scene; in a darkness lit only by a dazzle of snowy light, the voice of Me was heard:
> Where I am I think it must be getting dark:
> I feel that everything is moving and mixing, with everything else.

the 'room' in eccentric, phantasmagoric forms; respectable American tourists solemnly exploding each others' balloons; Mussolini swigging castor oil cocktails, surrounded by admiring 'fairies'. The Mussolini episode, and Bill's curious change of sex at the end of the Will and Bill affair are pointing to a degree of sexual ambivalence in Him, but the scenes function in terms of social satire, whether we recognize this or not.

cummings goes a stage further than Williams in charting the courses of the creative imagination. He takes us below the work of art to the 'foul rag and bone shop' from which it springs. In the surrealist sequence of the circus, the resurrected Doctor, as Barker, parades before an audience of reflections the freaks they in their turn reflect. Images of sexuality, formerly subdued at least to the decorum of the burlesque, figure here in gross, comical forms, the Six Hundred Pounds of Passionate Pulchritude; the King of Borneo, swallowing light bulbs with an inhuman rapacity which causes even Mussolini's fairies to faint.

The scene functions at the level of the heart beat, symbolized by the drum taps which Me, but not Him, has heard at intervals through the play. She is drawn by the drum into Him's circus world, appearing for the first time as a being realized by his imagination. She is realized in uncertain terms, being introduced by the Barker as a sex goddess, the Princess Anankay, but appearing, to Him's terror, as a mother holding a newborn baby. Yet she has penetrated into his imaginative life, while he has come to some kind of terms with his own image. This is a happy ending, of sorts.

The handling of images in the circus scene is theatrical in the noisiest, brassiest traditions of the theatre. The range of which cummings is capable is shown in the contrast between this and the final scene, back in the quiet room which is the source of all the violent creative activity.

In a climax of great power, cummings is able to leave the images to speak for themselves, the poet still confronting the invisible wall:

HIM. And may I ask what you are thinking?
. . . .
     Is it something about the window?
ME. No.
HIM. About what's behind you?
ME. Not exactly. No.
HIM. But you're thinking something about this room, aren't you?
. . . No, I can't guess.

ME. It has only three walls.

. . . .

HIM. I wish I could believe this.
ME. You can't.
HIM. Why?
ME. Because this is true.

Beside the vitality and rich texture of *Him*, cummings's verse play, *Santa Claus* (1946) seems slight and thin.[12] Like Williams, he seems to find dramatic outlet for his poetic force more easily in prose than in verse, and to draw strength from a complex structure depending upon the interaction of inner and outer plays. When structural pressure relaxes, the verbal flow is inclined to become undisciplined: the room scenes of *Him* become fully dramatic only with judicious cutting. Yet, despite occasional prolixity, the achievement remains impressive; indeed, cummings is one of the very few modern playwrights to have found a satisfying dramatic form for the 'stream of consciousness', rendering the complexity of the subject without forfeiting theatrical light and shade.

★   ★   ★

Does the evidence of the plays here considered support the common view of modern 'poetic drama' as a distinct, and inferior, dramatic kind, or have the poets made a real contribution to the theatre? We can see from certain features of their style—a tendency to verbal self-indulgence most marked in MacLeish and cummings, Lowell's monotony of tone, Williams's relaxed structure—that lack of contact with live audiences sometimes prevents the poetic impulse from becoming fully dramatic. Yet, paradoxically, their consciousness of absent or critical audiences has stimulated the poets to make original dramatic forms based upon their own situation, their need to find means of communication. Their poetic energy has done more than vitalize stage dialogue; it has invested the structure of their plays with symbolic force, even, in a play like *Him*, causing the stage itself to speak. The movement towards prose, colloquial usage, folk and music hall elements is an expression of their deep involvement in the contemporary scene. They are not least involved when they turn the spotlight on their own minds, taking for their material the creative process itself.

[12] Though Donoghue finds it 'spare and chaste' (p. 72).

Their concern with cummings's 'image', the 'image which appears not so much in the mirror of sleep as in a still deeper mirror', is also the concern of the age. The theatre should not ask whether it can afford to risk plays by the poets. It cannot afford to be without them.

Note

See prefatory notes for Chapters I and III for general books on American Theatre.

John O'Hara's comments on Broadway are in his *Five Plays* (1951) and William Gibson's account of the production of *Two for the Seesaw* in his *The Seesaw Log* (1959).

L. Abel's *Metatheatre* referred to in this chapter was published in 1963.

VI

Success and the American Dramatist

MORRIS FREEDMAN

★

THE dramatist has always clearly had a problem different from that of the poet or of the writer of fiction. Poets and novelists may survive for long periods on *succès d'estime* only, meaningful critical or editorial response that encourages continued work. Playwrights must have popular success as well; they obviously must work in a large social situation, with actors, directors, critics and audiences. What this has come to mean is that few serious American writers who have cared to succeed in the theatre have felt that they could afford the 'luxury' more common to the poet or novelist, that of ultimately pleasing themselves. (Not that pleasing oneself always leads to worthy results: one may have low ambitions; but *deliberately* not doing so can rarely lead to anything worth very much.)

The piquant account is relevant here of Saul Bellow's failure with his first play, *The Last Analysis*, in 1964, at the same time that his novel, *Herzog*, was achieving great critical and popular success. Bellow reported that he allowed director, producer and actors to keep changing the text of the play since he wanted to make a killing and was ready to heed any advice of experienced persons that might conceivably help. On the other hand, he felt certain that his novel would not satisfy a large audience and so he strictly resisted editorial changes: if few were going to read his novel anyway, at least it would remain exactly as he wrote it.

Obviously accommodation to professional demands need not be fatal to Broadway success: William Gibson recorded at length how his play *Two for the Seesaw* was tailored to satisfy production specialists of various sorts; it was a satisfactory commercial success. Gibson wrote about his experience:

Fifteen years earlier, when my work consisted of unpublished poems and a magazine asked me to change a word in one, I would not change the word; the poem went unpublished; it was a far cry to the present spate of rewriting to please.   (p. 94)

Such shaping has become one of the background specialties in the American theatre; witness the profession of 'play doctoring', especially for musical comedies, the technique of bringing in some expert, in dialogue or in building a situation, to resuscitate an ailing work on out-of-town try-outs.

For many American writers the theatre has come to be the main arena to achieve the fullest measure of literary success, perhaps precisely because of its more social character. But the theatre, while it has attracted writers who were first novelists, seems at the same time to have inhibited and intimidated them, very possibly because of the expectations the theatre establishes. Henry James's efforts to write a successful play were as strenuous as they were futile; Hemingway, a master of dialogue, brought off the remarkable feat of embodying probably his worst writing in a play, *The Fifth Column*; William Faulkner buried a closet drama in a novel, *Requiem for a Nun*, later to be made into a successful work for the French theatre by Albert Camus.

John O'Hara has written ingenuously about his own wish to write plays. He has become famous and wealthy through his novels, short stories, and film scripts; he has been taken seriously enough, in academic and in respectable literary circles, particularly for his short fiction, to have evoked scholarly and critical study and to have received esteemed literary acclaim. In the introduction to his collection of *Five Plays*, none of them ever commercially produced, he speaks here and there of the profit motive in writing, and what is most revealing about his comments is the intimation that a director's help *would* be welcome if it somehow 'guaranteed' a hit. It's the hit that matters; and, indeed, in *The Champagne Pool*, one of the five plays in the volume, a successful playwright does indicate gratitude to a knowing director. O'Hara makes evident, however indirectly, that 'success', a hit, cancels out any ugliness of compromise.

American drama has for so long been Broadway drama, that is, financially successful drama, that no writer can think of a 'hit', with all it implies of the importance of drama critics' reviews, long runs, large audiences, theatre parties, Hollywood bids for the movie rights, without having in mind those financial aspects of success that sometimes

blur or obliterate the other aspects of achievement. From the Provincetown Playhouse of around 1920 to the San Francisco Actors Workshop
of the 1960's, artistically ambitious and successful American drama has
led directly to Broadway. Provincetown 'fulfilled its promise' and its
efforts with the Theatre Guild and Eugene O'Neill; the directors of the
serious, energetic, ambitious San Francisco group, Herbert Blau and
Jules Irving, have gone to the Lincoln Repertory Theatre in New York,
only a step or two from Broadway (where, hopefully, they will
sustain and fulfil the promise of the Workshop). The costs of putting
on a Broadway play have increased so fantastically since the end of
World War II that only a Croesus could afford to ignore financial
considerations. Two contrasts, cited by Eric Bentley:[1] *Life With
Father* (1939) cost $23,000 to produce; *Life With Mother* (1948),
$85,000. A pre-war Saroyan play cost $5,000; a post-war Williams
play, $115,000.

During the great economic depression of the 'thirties, 'success' as
measured simply by money became somewhat meaningless. Serious
drama and serious workers in the theatre would have suffered virtual
extinction of their careers but for the formation of government
sponsored groups like the Federal Theatre, especially the Mercury
players under Orson Welles, and of private ones, like the Group
Theatre. Freed from the pressures to be conventionally 'successful',
these groups were free to work with repertory or with experiments (a
jazz version of *Macbeth*; a fascist-uniformed *Julius Caesar*; the 'living
newspaper' documentaries, like *One Third of a Nation*; the social
realism of Odets). A small number of individual playwrights with
organized leftist support could find backing for plays on something like
the plight of the Scottsboro boys, the young southern Negroes who
would have been judicially lynched but for the intervention of northern
lawyers supported by the Party. In short, in the 'thirties an American
drama seemed to be developing not governed mainly by 'success'.

But the subsequent careers of the various personages connected with
these ventures emphasizes the determining force of 'success'. As the
United States climbed out of the Depression, almost without exception,
everyone—from Odets, the writer, through Franchot Tone and John
Garfield, the actors, to the directors and producers of the Federal
Theatre, the Group Theatre, and the privately sponsored productions—
moved on, more or less permanently, to Hollywood and the massive

[1] *American Drama and Its Critics*, p. 188; *The Dramatic Event*, p. 244.

salaries of the films. Perhaps Harold Clurman alone was the most significant figure who remained working principally in the theatre, as director and critic.

This pragmatic measure for the American dramatist has had various results over the years. It has meant, for one thing, that, with the glaring exception of O'Neill, we have had no writer who has continued to produce for the stage a body of work that approaches in substance and variety the work of contemporaries in Europe, Brecht, Pirandello, Lorca, Anouilh. The successful American playwright is honoured by being given every chance not to write plays again, much as in the academic world the 'successful' professor is taken out of the classroom altogether. Clifford Odets is our most famous instance of the dramatist diverted from the theatre by Hollywood and television contracts (where he turned out workmanlike but not memorable scripts); more recently, Paddy Chayefsky, whose Broadway plays had not even had a chance yet to add up to the promise, let alone the fulfilment of Odets, has left the theatre; and others. Perhaps there is a sense of 'reward' here for work well done on Broadway by the offer of the passport to Hollywood, the chance to retire to Stratford to live like a gentleman with a veritable coat of arms. Frederick Loewe, the composer of the music for *My Fair Lady*, *Camelot* and some lesser known but equally estimable works before these, has announced from his yacht in the Mediterranean more than once, as if to reassure himself, that he would never write a note again since he was now wealthy enough never to have to do so. After success, what?

But it is likely that writing for the theatre has always been determined by matters of market, of competition (rivalries between theatrical groups, for example, in Elizabethan and Restoration England), of pressures of various sorts, even aesthetic ones, to pick up the idiom of the new fiction, say, or of films, or of television. In the United States, the pressure of 'success' has dominated over other pressures, even to the shaping of the text, to the determining (sometimes unconsciously) of subject matter.

Edward Albee's main talent, for instance, probably still lies, as does Ionesco's, and perhaps Pinter's, in short, tight, one-act plays. But Broadway has never been hospitable to the one-acter. After his success off-Broadway with *The American Dream*, *The Zoo Story*, *The Sand-box*, *The Death of Bessie Smith*, all tightly vignetted one-act plays, Albee moved on to Broadway with his sprawling, enormous work, *Who's*

Afraid of Virginia Woolf? It has been hugely successful in the usual American terms: much money, several road companies, film rights, fame, the accompanying revival of interest in his earlier short plays. The point is that, whether or not we think *Virginia Woolf* a good play, I doubt that we would have had it at all but for its length, a prerequisite for Broadway investment and production.

The recent brief career of Kopit, who went from a long play (*Oh Dad, Poor Dad, Mama's Hung You in the Closet and I'm Feeling So Sad*) to short ones (e.g. *The Day the Whores Stormed the Tennis Court*), may reinforce this point: he has thus far, in the mid-'sixties, failed to fulfil his promise, as the phrase goes, in Broadway terms. He might have been better off to have started with the short plays.

★   ★   ★

From the 'twenties, when the theatre in America first began to have a stature comparable to that of the theatre in Europe, the theme of success has permeated the subject matter of our most important playwrights. Themselves so rigorously controlled by success, they often seemed obsessed by the power, both creative and destructive, of success in the larger American landscape. George Kelly's *The Show Off* is about a common American type, the grown man who always boasts of imaginary achievements beyond his capacity or his understanding. His *Craig's Wife* is about a woman whose notion of marriage—indeed, of life—is to present the façade of perfection and to maintain it, to offer to the neighbours, her audience, a fixed landscape of success, in her sterile marriage, in the frozen finality of her household interior.

In the 'thirties, successful serious drama was politically oriented, specifically leftist. But, even when success was realistically a most distant chimera, a play like *Awake and Sing!* recorded as the major ambition of the characters their longing for the middle-class images of success: a decent income with the perquisites that flow from it (marriage, a home)—almost simply that and little more. The title would seem to call for more than a mere ascension from poverty and defeat, 'Arise and *Sing*,' a reaching for some private, ecstatic, human fulfilment, but the text modestly limits itself to 'success' alone. Good enough, certainly, as a start for singing, but it is the end, the climax. In Arthur Miller's *Death of a Salesman*, all that Willy Loman wants is the middle-class apotheosis of success: a mortgage paid-off, a car clear of debt, a

H

properly working modern refrigerator, an occasional mistress, sons 'well-liked' if uneducated and aimless. Willy Loman is Babbitt, twenty years later.

The plays of Tennessee Williams are dominated by an atmosphere of un-success and anti-success, which may be part of their total perverseness, a denial of the main American impulses of ambition and fulfilment. Tom Wingfield in *The Glass Menagerie* and his sister and mother are impotent in making their way in the larger world, from which they escape to their several private refuges. His mother dreams of her youthful successes as a Southern belle, distant conquests that live ideally in the memory only, with no blemishes of reality or of fact. Stanley Kowalski in *A Streetcar Named Desire* scorns the substance and the surface of clean, properly spoken, middle-class American success, scorns the pride that comes with family lineage. Himself proud only of his greasy, dirty proletarian work and appearance and speech, his whole bearing a defiance of the usual accoutrements of success, he systematically sets out to destroy the barely flickering spark of family pride, perhaps the only success she has ever known, which sustains Blanche Dubois, his sister-in-law. Williams's later works frequently include as critical incidents the physical decay or a physical assault and consequent maiming, directly or indirectly sexual, of successful, even heroic figures.

Our serious playwrights, while they remain in the theatre, sooner or later get down to the matter of success in something of its ambiguities and perplexities. Odets in *Paradise Lost*, one of his later plays, relates success to bankruptcy, death, disease. The hero, sums up Malcolm Goldstein, 'has lost the paradise of the middle class, but has found a better life among the homeless proletariat' (*American Drama and Its Critics*, p. 139). Odets, ironically, anticipated Williams, in finding 'success' through rejecting middle-class ways and values.

Miller in *After the Fall* provides an uncomfortably clinical dissection of several aspects of American success, which we know, as we come to the play, he has achieved himself in plenitude: that fame that allows the 'successful' intellectual, the archetypal hero of the intelligentsia for the fashionable moment, to carry off into marriage the archetypal American beauty queen; the fame that provides, through money and self-confidence, ready escape by divorce from early and unglamorous marriage; that enables one, through the excuse of the demands of worldly importance, to neglect the ordinary fidelities asserted by family; to neglect, as convenient, one's other identities, the force of friendships, or of being Jewish: success raises one to a level of social functioning where the routine mortal amenities are beside or below the point. *After the Fall* is 'clinical' because, in spite of its patent wish to find absolution, it is relentless in its exposure.

Guilt accompanies success in America; some of our best writers are driven to excesses of apologia, destructive self-examinations under the pressures of success, denying it, explaining it away, even mutilating it. Ambition and the fulfilment of ambition are still to be apologized for, a satisfactory climax after energy expended still to be denied or explained away, no time to relax with the pleasure of work or play well done, our vestigial Puritanism asserting its domination. Arnold Weinstein in *The Red Eye of Love* (1962) burlesques the American lust for success (the main character is an indefatigable inventor, neglecting wife and child, developing a doll that would get sick, run a temperature, and eventually die so that he can then market a flood of medical and funeral toys to sell with the doll) at the same time that he offers in his dramaturgy an anthology of successful vaudeville, burlesque-house and movie techniques: slapstick routines, quick shifts of scene, silly word-play, top-banana and straight-man skits.

O'Neill's power derived in good measure from his capacity to go his own way, which was to try one way after another. He remained a dramatist, not simply because he could afford to, but because he had to: it is ludicrous to imagine an O'Neill in Hollywood or working for television. (Faulkner, of course, did go to Hollywood, but he never accommodated comfortably. He became a Hollywood legend rather than a film writer; he had no significant screen credits to himself.) Although O'Neill in his adult work was perhaps less conditioned than other writers of his generation by the usual pressures of American success, the initial conditioning had already worked its effects. O'Neill's career of working with various forms and themes culminated in the mighty *Long Day's Journey Into Night*, published and produced post-humously, which is the lucid and bitter record of how O'Neill's actor-father sowed the seeds of Gene's physical and perhaps psychological ill-health and general wretchedness in a life-long compulsive drive to amass and keep a fortune. O'Neill understood and forgave, not just his father but himself. But even O'Neill, at least in his earlier years, kept providing American audiences what they seemed to want at one time or another, the portentousness of *Strange Interlude* or of *Mourning*

Becomes Electra, the somewhat strained domestic comedy of *Ah Wilderness!*—scarcely among his better plays.

★   ★   ★

The very fact that American drama has had to satisfy particular large audiences at particular times has meant that in some way successful plays have articulated, however obliquely, social needs or responses of various depths. A long running play like *Abie's Irish Rose,* which began its career in the 'twenties, like the dialect vaudeville comedians of the time, with their Yiddish, German, Irish and Italian accents, surely had something to do with the coming to maturity of the children of immigrants of various backgrounds. Indeed, the play recorded a particularly dreadful union in reality, an Orthodox Jewish and an Irish Catholic pairing: the memories of pogroms were still vivid among Jewish immigrants from East Europe; the Christian peasant's superstitious dread of secret Jewish blood rituals was equally vivid. Yet the text was trivial, sentimental, straining after comic effect, mixing accents, making the most out of the obvious incongruities and ironies. Blackface minstrel shows, seemingly innocent and vastly popular American entertainment throughout the untutored areas of the country that Mencken once described as a cultural Sahara, had their roots in slavery; they lurk behind the sinister surface of T. S. Eliot's *Sweeney Agonistes.* American drama brings up from the depths hidden, repressed, suppressed pre-occupations and terrors, but then renders them innocuous in the interest of 'success'.

Two of the most successful plays of the 'twenties, Maxwell Anderson and Laurence Stalling's *What Price Glory?* and Ben Hecht and Charles MacArthur's *The Front Page,* recorded the adolescent camaraderie of masculine *milieux,* the war front, a newspaper office, where women were demeaned or excluded. They are innocent enough records of that unconscious homosexuality in American life that Norman Mailer makes such a fuss about 'exposing'. And Mrs. Craig systematically tried to impose her vengeful sterility on her male dominated world. We can too easily over-simplify the complexities of the context in which these plays appeared, but, without saying more, it may be enough for the moment to note that in the 'twenties women were beginning to enter and make their way in the full American scene.

Odets recorded the bitterness of resignation during the 'thirties of a straining middle class to achieve some significant measure of American 'success'. That the families he depicted were primarily Jewish and matriarchal reflected a larger American pre-occupation, hinted at in the matriarchal family of John Steinbeck's *The Grapes of Wrath*, more clearly enunciated in the wide popularity of Jewish themes in the 'fifties and 'sixties. Jewish ambitions and situations (in Odets, Miller, Kopit and Albee), so deeply Puritanical and family oriented, were crystallized distillates of larger American sensitivities. The over-protective, emasculating Jewish mother (Bessie Berger in *Awake and Sing!*) found her counterpart in the greater American mother (Mom of *The American Dream*). Jewish 'momism' anticipated the larger national Momism uncovered by such different observers as Philip Wylie and Geoffrey Gorer. (Gorer went so far as to relate the American fascination with bare bosoms in advertisements, the movies, musical comedies, burlesque houses and magazines to a continual need throughout adulthood for maternal nurturing.)

Arthur Miller's largest success has resided possibly in his uncanny talent to keep attuned simultaneously to both the loud and the subdued melodies of American life. *All My Sons*, a play about a businessman's greed during World War II, was written, as Miller tells us in the introduction to his collected plays, to examine the area of widespread moral ambivalence towards the sacrifices everyone was supposed to be making: trivial and large cheating was commonplace. The suggestion was that business success during war could somehow only have been immoral and criminal; the suggestion received a wide welcome. *The Crucible* caught the country's sense of bewilderment and fright during the McCarthy era.

Death of a Salesman, still probably Miller's best play, is built around more subtle, more amorphous themes, and consequently more significant ones: the surviving sense of insecurity even after the New Deal among the middle classes whose fathers still had to sell themselves. Willy Loman, desperately wanting an 'American' identity (to be well-liked, to have a football hero for a son), cannot accept himself (apparently Jewish, he never alludes to the substantive implications of this fact), cannot see that veneer alone wears down and vanishes (he does nothing to give his sons those roots in education, for example, which, the play makes clear through the career of Bernard, their cousin, are necessary to a real American success). Willy never blames himself for anything; and he is compelling enough to offer anyone ready to grab at the chance a rationalization for any private failures of his own: destruction comes from out there and is always unjust.

For many in the audiences of the late 'forties and early 'fifties, the period of greatest success of the play, Willy Loman's groping for stability and status mirrored their own attempts to establish a rooted identity in the uncertain post-Depression and post-war landscape.

Miller was early obsessed by the role 'success' plays in moulding destiny in America. In his introduction, he writes about a 'desk-drawer' play, later to be produced for four nights, *The Man Who Had All the Luck*, which he describes as a failure:

> This play was an investigation to discover what exact part a man played in his own fate. It deals with a young man in a small town who, by the time he is in his mid-'twenties, owns several growing businesses, has married the girl he loves, is the father of a child he has always wanted, and is daily becoming convinced that as his desires are gratified he is causing to accumulate around his own head an invisible but nearly palpable fund, so to speak, of retribution. The law of life, as he observes life around him, is that people are always frustrated in some important regard; and he conceives that he must be too, and the play is built around his conviction of impending disaster. The disaster never comes, even when, in effect, he tries to bring it on in order to survive it and find peace. Instead, he comes to believe in his remarkable ability to succeed.
>
> (*Collected Plays*, pp. 13–14)

Miller concludes his résumé of *The Man Who Had All the Luck* by remarking that it is now possible for him 'to see that far from being a waste and a failure this play was a preparation, and possibly a necessary one, for those that followed, especially *All My Sons* and *Death of a Salesman.....*' (p. 14). The first records the destruction that comes to the successful man in America, for success came to him only through criminality; the second records the destruction that comes to the unsuccessful man who has dedicated himself to pursuing only the appearances of American success.

★   ★   ★

Early in the century William Dean Howells, the American novelist, critic and editor, suggested that British drama differed from American in being concerned with larger, social contexts rather than with smaller, domestic ones (*American Drama and Its Critics*, p. 10). Surely, this is an oversimplification, and one that has gone through many modulations over the decades, but it may still be somewhere near the heart of the mystery accounting for success in the American theatre. Theatre-going in America has always been a somewhat different sociological phenomenon from that in other countries. The earnings of our jolly musicals alone would demonstrate that American theatre is before anything else a form of entertainment, in the company, say, of the circus, state fairs and athletic contests. Critics have argued that American drama cannot be 'literature' because it has, first, to be 'likable', to 'please', and pleasure is here served best by sentimental evasions, the appearances of boldness and independence, opportunities for the audience to identify itself with characters and causes but in no disturbing sense. 'As a consequence,' Robert Brustein has written, 'American drama often seems to be the most mindless form of legitimate culture since eighteenth-century sentimental comedy, a form to which it bears more than a little resemblance' (*American Drama and Its Critics*, p. 252).

Thus, it is easier for American audiences in the 'sixties to confront the Negro question, North or South, through the familial pleasantness of Lorraine Hansberry's *A Raisin in the Sun*, rather than through the socially sweeping and brutal James Baldwin's *Blues for Mr. Charlie* or the sustained insult of LeRoi Jones's *Dutchman* (in which a white girl, after flirting with a Negro young man on the New York subway, stabs him to death when he asserts his 'independence' to be whatever he wants to be, including an imitation of a white contemporary). According to this view, the fact that *A Raisin in the Sun* is a cleaner and more coherent piece of craftsmanship than the other two works (all by Negro writers) has less to do with its success than its attractive surface. William Saroyan's *The Time of Your Life* gets through to us better than Eugene O'Neill's *The Iceman Cometh*, with which it has thematic and dramaturgic relations, because of its greater sentimentality and warmth. It is certainly true that O'Neill's work strives for a larger, symbolic mysteriousness than the momentary, boozy divertissements of a saloon hospitable to assorted odd characters. Elmer Rice's domestic epic, *Street Scene*, is more memorable than his *Adding Machine*, a comment on the mechanization of modern man. William Inge's husbands, wives and children are far less abrasive than Edward Albee's or Tennessee Williams's families; Inge has 'delighted' more audiences than Albee and Williams.

There is a continuum in American 'dramatic' entertainment from the most popular forms (vaudeville and burlesque dialogues, radio and television's thin melodramas, Hollywood slapstick or domestic comedies and westerns, staged bad-guy-versus-good-guy wrestling matches, rock-'n-roll singing, even circuses and cowboy rodeos) to the more cultivated, less popular ones (opera and theatre). There have been many attempts, indeed, to link the two extremes; the choreography of a number of semi-operatic musicals has been based on the movements of cowboys, baseball players, or of Mack Sennett's Keystone Cops. It seems to me unresponsive to actuality to insist that popular forms have only blunted the effectiveness of our more serious forms. Indeed, it may be that we can sometimes examine the point and character of success in our serious drama by considering appropriately our frivolous entertainment.

O'Neill, for example, has long posed a problem to serious American critics. Indeed, one has written a famous essay, 'Trying to Like O'Neill'. O'Neill is certainly anything but ingratiating. He requires effort. Why? I suggest that it is precisely because of his intensity of concentration on an issue, on a form, on a text—almost without regard to the relation of the work to an audience, to its performance as a *theatrical* experience. It may well be that his great, fumbling inarticulateness, or, at best, fuzzy articulateness, has something to do with a greater American inchoateness, a greater American incapacity to come down in some traditional manner to tight and sharp fundamentals, a groping for self-justifying transcendental formulations; but I think it is his conscious, willed, controlled unawareness of, indifference to, audiences that accounts for the extravagance of his effects, both the successes and the failures.

In actuality, America is a collection of audiences, ranging enormously in its preparation for certain entertainments (New York dudes are as baffled by rodeos as cowboy primitives might be by opera), but in essence more linked than any two excessively divergent groups are likely to concede. Consider a rodeo audience somewhere out west as opposed to a small group in Greenwich Village viewing Jack Gelber's avant-garde *The Connection*, a play showing a group of addicts, including a jazz combo, waiting to make connection with their supplier of heroin. Both are involved, as Lionel Abel put it in his essay on the play in *Metatheatre* (1963), in making a 'connection', in becoming involved in the activities going on, in finding a moment of special meaning to themselves. Americans 'participate' with a remarkable suspension of disbelief; they identify with and, not infrequently, themselves join the action. It was during a New York performance of Osborne's *Look Back in Anger* that a lady in the audience rushed on-stage to belabour Jimmy Porter with an umbrella for his ugly treatment of his wife.

American drama may be especially difficult, for native or foreign critics, to grasp in anything like its entirety because the tendency is to neglect or ignore or disdain certain obscure areas. Eric Bentley has commented about American critics that though 'they know something of literature . . ., they are anti-literary; they are pro-theatrical but know little of acting' (*American Drama and Its Critics*, p. 192). Not only do American students of the drama frequently fail to connect the theatrical with the literary, but in emphasizing the literary so exclusively, they frequently fail to see the drama in its larger social context. One example of neglect is the career of Gertrude Berg, who, in the 'twenties, was the leading actress and, from time to time, one of the writers of the radio and television serial, *The Rise of the Goldbergs*, that went on almost as long as *Amos 'n Andy*, another 'ethnic' entertainment, about Negroes. Mrs. Berg has in recent years gone through one popular matinée drama after another on Broadway, one of them with Sir Cedric Hardwicke, in which he played a Japanese gentleman and she an Orthodox Jewish widow from the Bronx who marries him. Her continued popularity, especially with the Jewish middle-class matrons of New York and the surrounding areas, who largely make up the matinée audiences of Broadway, suggests that there is a significant element of identification of audiences with her, and with the characters she portrays, involved in her success. It may also tell us something about the folksiness requisite to a larger theatrical success in this country, the meeting of expectations that may be simple and conscious (to hear a funny story, to see a pleasing turn) or complex and unconscious (to have worked out relationships that are nearly anthropological in their remoteness from the familiar surfaces).

The ritual aspect of American theatre has been emphasized in some recent discussions about Edward Albee, in order to account for his success, which has been especially galling to a number of observers, including a divine, Tom F. Driver, from Union Theological Seminary. He concludes an essay called 'What's the Matter with Edward Albee?' as follows:

This accounts, I believe, for the so-called 'involvement' of the audience at *Who's Afraid of Virginia Woolf?* Since the situation and the characters are false, the play provides an occasion for the display of pseudo-emotions: mock anger, mock hatred, mock envy, and finally mock love. These are provided on stage by the actors, with whom the audience enters into complicity. Thus the audience achieves, at no expense to its real emotions, a mock catharsis.

In addition, there is reason to suppose that the very roughness and the gaucheries that mar Albee's plays contribute to his success. Most of the values that operate in our society are drawn from the bourgeois ideal of domestic harmony, necessary for the smooth functioning of the machine. Yet we know that there are subconscious desires fundamentally in conflict with the harmonious ideal. Albee satisfies at once the ideal and the hidden protest against it. In his badly written plays he jabs away at life with blunt instruments. If his jabbing hit the mark, that would be another matter. But it doesn't, no more than does the child in the nursery when he tears up his toys. That is why Albee is the pet of the audience, this little man who looks as if he dreamed of evil but is actually mild as a dove and wants to be loved. In him America has found its very own playwright. He's a dream.   (*American Drama and Its Critics*, p. 244)

'Ritual' of one sort or another does seem to characterize the most recent off-Broadway successes and failures of any importance. The ritual aspect of *The Connection*—the formalized waiting—has been remarked on. Another work of The Living Theatre, which originally staged *The Connection* and *The Red Eye of Love*, was *The Brig*, a deadpan, unplotted, theatrically unmodulated depiction of a day in a U.S. Marine stockade for its own prisoners. The work was shattering to the ear-drums and the nerves of audiences as the actors performed the fixed, dance-like, rigidly disciplined routines of Marine prisoners, as they woke up in formation, went to wash in formation, and called out for orders in loud, mechanical voices, using a prescribed vocabulary.

A number of works are closely related to the highly topical and satirical, frequently improvised sketches prepared for supper and night clubs. Weinstein's *The Red Eye of Love* has been mentioned; he has not yet received the critical appraisal his work calls for (although his play has been published by Grove Press); he continues to write sketches for club performances. Mike Nichols, who began his career as an improvising night club satirist with Elaine May, has gone on to directing Broadway successes, *Barefoot in the Park*, *The Odd Couple* and *Luv*, and the movie version of *Who's Afraid of Virginia Woolf?* His impulsive spontaneity has seemed to work most effectively, it has turned out, in the context of fixed, even ritualistic drama.

'Happenings' have been the theatrical equivalent of anti-representational 'action painting' or of the anti-music of John Cage. These are productions, staged now in various cities throughout the country, which do not follow any scenario or script, are simply set into motion by an idea, the actors responding to one another and to the audience, with lighting and music similarly determined ad lib. LeRoi Jones's *Dutchman*, perhaps most notably, displays both the virtues and defects of a happening, in its discursive lengthiness and in its seeming spontaneousness. Paradoxically, Lionel Abel's most recent domestic experiment has been reported to be a highly formal, even ritualized, dialogue on a Greek theme, in which the characters are fixed as in some of Beckett's plays. But then Kopit's *Oh Dad, Poor Dad*, however jazzed up with ballet-like absurdities (Jerome Robbins, the choreographer, directed) and gag-lines and gimmicks, was a highly schematized rendition of a classical Oedipal situation.

$$\star \qquad \star \qquad \star$$

American drama since the end of World War II has shown bursts of energy suggesting that a renascence is going on similar to the one that followed World War I, and possibly greater. The current equivalent of the Provincetown Players, founded just after World War I, has been not only the San Francisco Actors Workshop but the several other attempts throughout the country, most notably the Lincoln Repertory Theatre in New York and Sir Tyrone Guthrie's playhouse in Minneapolis, to found companies that would produce both the classics and the work of new playwrights. The Santa Fe Opera Company in New Mexico, has pioneered in producing for the first time in the U.S. avant-garde operatic works whose main emphasis is dramatic, Alban Berg's *Lulu* and Shostakovitch's *The Nose*, an 'absurd' text based on Gogol and proscribed in the Soviet Union. The Ford Foundation, in an experiment that lasted too short a time to show serious results just yet, sponsored the attachment to theatrical companies throughout the country of novelists and poets so that they might absorb some of the pleasures and crafts of the theatre. In the middle 'sixties, Murray Schisgall (*The Typists, The Tiger, Luv*) is emerging as a major talent.

Also, in New York, a group of serious younger novelists and poets, persons like Phillip Roth, Norman Mailer, Herbert Gold, James Purdy, Robert Lowell, are attempting works for the theatre. And Saul Bellow has not given up drama.

Important, too, in the renascence has been the recent work of a group of critics of American drama who are more than merely journalists or merely academicians; they combine a scholar's width and depth of perspective with the good critic's or philosopher's instinct for rearranging old formulations and introducing new ones: John Gassner and Robert Brustein at Yale; Eric Bentley at Columbia University; Allan S. Downer at Princeton; Henry Popkin, who has taught at Brandeis and New York Universities. The recent study of O'Neill by John Henry Raleigh, of the University of California at Berkeley, is a model for others to emulate in its seriousness and in its striking insights. The work of Lionel Abel in formulating a new dramatic theory, in *Metatheatre*, and in his highly experimental plays, has been invaluable in revealing new possibilities both in the analysis and the writing of plays.

The boldness of publishers, particularly Grove Press and Hill & Wang, in putting out interesting dramatic texts without regard to their popular success has made available throughout the country for study or just simple enlightening reading plays that hitherto could only be encountered in production.

Albee has perhaps built his success on distilling too immediately fashionable essences of the absurd theatre and of pop art, especially in *The American Dream*. (But then the title of this work may well justify any such distillation.) The point of Albee, however, as it was of Tennessee Williams, when he was the theatre's fair-haired young man, or of Arthur Miller, or of Clifford Odets (all of whom have gotten *their* lumps when riding high) is that he may be satisfying current and deep American needs that can only be satisfied in the American theatre at this time in this particular way. We may find in the history of the theatre, or in that of any art, that some periods and some peoples have allowed themselves to be satisfied with works that have turned out to have no redeeming aesthetic merit whatsoever, that could be justified and understood by later or different peoples only as sociological or anthropological phenomena. But I think we should pause to consider that some Restoration observers responded to Shakespeare patronizingly, and that it is generally easier to sneer than it is to catch strange idioms and learn and understand new ways. The American theatre probably suffers more from its uniqueness than others because success asserts such a powerfully shaping role in it, and, while Americans cannot live comfortably with success, they cannot live at all without it.

Note

Biography. Arthur Miller was born in New York City in 1915, the son of a manufacturer and shop-owner. He graduated from high school during the depression and was unable to go to a university; he worked in a warehouse and, like Bert in his *Memory of Two Mondays*, saved enough money to go to the University of Michigan for one semester; he completed his courses by working on a newspaper and by gaining prizes and other financial aid. He has been married three times, the second time to the film star Marilyn Monroe.

Works. Miller's plays are *The Man Who Had All the Luck* staged for four performances in 1944 and published that year in *Cross-section, 1944*, ed. E. Seaver; *All My Sons* (1947); *Death of a Salesman* (1949), which was directed by Elia Kazan; *The Crucible* (1953); *A Memory of Two Mondays* and *A View from the Bridge* (1955)—these five plays are in *Collected Plays* (1957; English edition, 1958), from which all quotations in this chapter are taken. His adaptation of Ibsen's *An Enemy of the People* (1950/1) is reprinted in *Four Plays of Our Time* (1960).

Later works are the film-script *The Misfits* (1961) and two plays, *After the Fall* (1964) and *Incident at Vichy* (1965).

Miller's articles include 'The Family in Modern Drama', *Atlantic Monthly* (April, 1956); 'The Shadows of the Gods', *Harper's Magazine* (August, 1958), reprinted in *American Playwrights on Drama*, ed. H. Frenz (1965); 'The Playwright and the Atomic World', *Tulane Drama Review* (June, 1961), reprinted in *Theatre in the Twentieth Century*, ed. R. Corrigan (1963); 'With Respect for Her Agony—But with Love', *Life* (7 February, 1964); 'Tragedy and the Common Man', *New York Times* (27 February, 1949), reprinted in Frenz, 'Conversation at St. Clerans', *Guardian* (25 February, 1960); and an interview with H. Brandon in *Sunday Times* (20 March, 1960), reprinted in *As We Are* (1961). A bibliography by M. T. Eissenstad is in *Modern Drama* (May, 1962).

Criticism. There are three books entitled *Arthur Miller:* by D. Welland (1962), R. Hogan (1964) and by S. Haftel, with the subtitle 'The Burning Glass' (1965). J. Goode tells *The Story of the Misfits* (1963). H. Clurman has an article in *The Nation* (25 October, 1965) called 'Plays and Politics'; others are by T. Coleman in *Guardian* (23 January, 1965); L. Fiedler in *Waiting for the End* (1964); Mary McCarthy in *Encounter* (May, 1957); H. Popkin in *Sewanee Review* (1960) and *American Drama and its Critics*, ed. A. S. Downer (1964); A. Seager in *Esquire* (January, 1960); and G. Weales in *Tulane Drama Review* and *American Drama since World War II* (1962). On the autobiographical element in *After the Fall*, see R. Gilman, *Book Week* (8 March, 1964) and H. Brandon, *Sunday Times* (19 January, 1964).

VII

Arthur Miller: the Development of a Political Dramatist in America

ERIC MOTTRAM

★

ALTHOUGH some of the stage sets for his plays may have suggested the contrary, Arthur Miller's theatre has never been experimentally avant-garde: from his beginnings he has aimed at a critical clarification of the already existent attitudes of liberal-minded American theatregoers. His plays are written for and largely from the point of view of a man whose attitudes are not radical and innovatory but puzzled, confused and absolutely resolved not to break with his fellow countrymen. He has maintained his theatre as nearly popular as an intellectual playwright may and still be tolerated on Broadway since the 1940's. Two of his plays were included in the opening season of the Lincoln Centre repertory company, the New York approximation to an initiatory national theatre, where he functioned as the official contemporary dramatist. *After the Fall* and *Incident at Vichy* seemed to satisfy no one at the time, and yet in these plays once again Miller dealt with his local themes of faith and meaning within the confused national and personal life of America, and dealt with them without abstractions which might call for a re-thinking of the Great Society.

Miller once remarked: 'I can't live apart from the world'. Yet his plays dramatize the ways in which a man alienates himself from his society and fights to get back into it. Until his most recent play, the structure of that society goes uncondemned and unanalysed, taken as if it were an unchangeable artefact. The weight of action falls cruelly on the individual within the fixed, powerful society which fails to support him at his moment of need and remains, as he falls, monolithically immovable. 'Evil' is those social pressures which conflict with an equally vaguely defined individual integrity in the hero or heroine. But critical though he is of American, perhaps Western, values, Miller finally has come to believe that 'evil' is really the natural cruelty of human nature seen, not as a product of historical social structures, but as inevitable data. The dilemma of his last two plays lies here in a nagging circularity which makes his work typical of frustrated American liberalism.

Part of the problem may well be the nature of Broadway where Miller has found success. Commenting on the high cost of seats in Broadway theatres and the influence this has on the composition of audiences, Harold Clurman ventured the opinion that this public is not genuinely concerned with politics: 'The ordinary American might define politics as something to do with elections and graft . . . something to which one lends oneself for a few minutes a day on TV, or can be disposed of by a cursory glance at the headlines and by gossip about "personalities". Politics is a sort of sport and no one except a politician needs to devote himself to it' (*The Nation*, 25 October, 1965). The implication is that Americans are not concerned with the means of change in their society. American theatre responded politically to the Depression and New Deal years but, after World War II, political theatre for the majority was the televised McCarthy trials. Today the cry is 'dissent!'; but as Clurman observes:

> we hardly know what to dissent from except such enormities as totalitarianism, the insults of individual powers, narcotics and teen-age killers. Dissent usually involves criticism of our country, than which there is none better on earth. Dissent, moreover, smacks of softness towards foreign ideologies. We had enough of that in the Thirties.

Clurman's irony yields, however, to nostalgia for the theatres of the 'thirties which brought forth a handful of decent plays that did not divorce entertainment from daily life. Arthur Miller began his career in the Federal Theatre, a state-aided post-Depression project created by the Roosevelt programme of national recovery. He joined this group just before its conclusion, but he has remained in the public arena of social theatre. In 1965 he was elected the first American international president of PEN, and the choice was supported by the Yugoslavs and popular with the Russians. The following November he refused an invitation to the White House in protest against President Johnson's

Vietnam policy. Now in his fiftieth year, Miller writes: 'When the guns boom, the arts die and this law of life is far stronger than any law man may devise': a woolly publicity statement, no doubt, but the protest was true enough and based concretely on the United States' rejection of Hanoi peace proposals. Yet, as part of the White House celebration of the signing of the Arts and Humanities Act, Mildred Dunnock read two passages from *Death of a Salesman*.

In his plays, Miller's restless social conscience moves towards the logical nihilism of *Incident at Vichy*—from the sociality of the 'thirties, through the confused liberalism of the 'forties, to the bewildered emptiness of the 'sixties. The plays are the barometer of his audience, measuring through his own sense of the pressures of the last quarter of a century. Before the House Un-American Activities Committee in June, 1956, he admitted that he protested against the outlawing of the Communist party, opposed the Smith Act (whereby it is an offence to advocate the overthrow of the U.S. government by force), and refused to name people he had seen at Communist writers' meetings seventeen years earlier. The Committee's attorney read a revue piece on which Miller had collaborated in 1939, which represented the Committee, already investigating un-American activities, as an insane Star Chamber, torturing its helpless victims:

ATTORNEY. Well, Mr. Miller?
MILLER. But that was *meant* to be a farce.

At this stage in his career, Miller met American establishment society head-on and won a tactical victory—and a dangerous position in the series of moves he began in his youth.

* * *

His father's image, as a man and an American, diminished for the boy when the Depression brought poverty to the family. The rich clothing manufacturer in decline became the youth's symbol of national experience. The middle-class young man drove trucks, unloaded cargo at the docks, waited at hotel tables and studied journalism at Michigan University by working at night on the *Michigan Daily* for an income that was supplemented from the National Youth Administration and a few prizes for writing (he gained three drama prizes before graduation in 1938). The Theatre Guild National Award of 1937 he shared with Tennessee Williams. Money came later from

I

radio scripts. Rejected by the army in the war (for unsteady knees), he worked as a fitter in the Brooklyn Navy Yard and then on the script for a training film, an experience written up in *Situation Normal* (1944). Hollywood did not attract him, and in 1944 he wrote *Focus*, a novel-study of anti-semitism. Miller's first play on Broadway concerned luck, a theme which haunts American literature since the Civil War because it involves deciding where the responsibility for success or disaster lies—with man, society or God, universal will, a determinist force in Nature or history.

There were difficulties: the American hero of such a fate drama could not be a king or a prince; and the idea of gods playing gloomy tricks with Americans contradicts the Constitution. But fate crept in by the back door, held open by liberal confusion. O'Neill said: 'I am not interested in the relations of man to man, but of man to God', and Miller quotes this in his article 'The Shadows of the Gods', refusing its implications: 'I too had a religion, however unwilling I was to be so backward. A religion with no gods but with godlike powers. The powers of economic crisis and political imperatives which had twisted, torn, eroded, and marked everything and everyone I laid eyes on.' He admires Tennessee Williams for his 'long reach and a genuinely dramatic imagination . . . his aesthetic valour, so to speak . . . his very evident determination to unveil and engage the widest range of causation conceivable to him. He is constantly pressing his own limit . . . He possesses the restless inconsolability with his solutions which is inevitable in a genuine writer.' Both writers know that analysis itself is short-measure: 'ultimately someone must take charge; this is the tragic dilemma.' We are trying ridiculously to create an Oedipus:

> whose catastrophe is private and unrelated to the survival of his people, an 'Oedipus' who cannot tear out his eyes because there will be no standards by which he can judge himself; an 'Oedipus', in a word, who on learning of his incestuous marriage, instead of tearing out his eyes, will merely wipe away his tears thus to declare his loneliness.

But somehow, for Miller, his characters must have a universalized validity. Leslie Fiedler comments on this problem with accuracy: he sees Miller as one of those Jewish American writers who 'creates crypto-Jewish characters, characters who are in habit, speech, and condition of life typically Jewish-American, but who are presented as something else—general-American say, as in *Death of a Salesman* . . .

Such pseudo-universalizing represents, however, a loss of artistic faith, a failure to remember that the inhabitants of Dante's Hell or Joyce's Dublin are more universal as they are more Florentine or Irish' (p. 91).

The Man Who Had All the Luck is too pat an exposure of a struggle for success in a Middle West town. The mechanism is too obvious. But the action does ask the typical Miller questions, here at the outset of his career: do men control their fate at all or are they 'jellyfish moving with the tide' (which is exactly Dreiser's initiatory query in his Cowperwood series)? Do men 'get what they desire' or are they helpless victims of some indifferent force, god or providential power? Already Miller's answers are 'yes' and 'no' together. The man who had all the luck believes that 'good luck' brought him business success, killed his girl friend's bullying father in an accident, and gave him a healthy son. His friends fail simply through 'bad luck'. Realization that fate rules indiscriminately threatens to drive him mad, and he is happier when he is made to understand that his own ability and careful action were involved. Miller equates caution with goodness and equivocates thoroughly over the central issues he raises.

All My Sons, based on a true story, presents Chris Keller, the returned army officer, rejecting Joe Keller's criminal irresponsibility, whether he is his father or not. The father shoots himself once the son knows the truth. He accepts his fate, but so does the son. In a position of wartime responsibility, Joe had allowed 120 cracked engine-heads to go from his factory into P40 aircraft, directly causing their pilots' deaths, the slaughter of his own son's comrades in battle. He allowed his subordinate and next-door neighbour, Deever, to be imprisoned and disgraced for his own criminality, but at the age of 61 he comes to realize that those pilots were 'all my sons', and commits suicide—but with nothing to say about Deever. Keller's life is a waste: he forfeits his son's love and his own good name for a public business ethic which is strictly unusable in private, family and neighbourhood life. The business ethic puts financial and social self-interest first, and social responsibility and purpose second. The war exposes the radical moral division: Joe's horror at his own crime is insignificant beside his larger irresponsibility to 'a universe of people'.

This plot is presented through unstylized conversation, with a minimum of stage devices, symbolism or heightened language. The terror emerges from the ordinariness of the scene in which moral sense is smothered and self-accusation follows enlightenment. Miller wants

Joe Keller to be innocent in so far as he is 'the uneducated man for whom there is still wonder in the many commonly known things, a man whose judgments must be dredged out of experience and a peasant-like common sense'. He is to be a Miller archetype, in fact. His son, Chris, is the other archetype Miller will constantly return to: the moral idealist taking his cue from the moral gyroscope of inner-direction, to use Riesman's term. He retains his capacity to love in spite of capitalist and war experience. The mother has Joe's 'talent for ignoring things': she is a fatalistic horoscope-reader who believes God is that 'certain things have to be, and certain things can never be'. The surrounding neighbourhood, the nucleus of society, thought Deever deserved his fate and that Keller was 'smart': up to a point, the social ethic condones things as they are. Ann—the sweetheart of Keller's other son, Larry (airpilot presumed dead in action)—will marry Chris, whom she resembles in moral idealism, but she is Deever's daughter. Her father's crime against humanity is simply an unforgivable act, father or not. Keller hypocritically puts a case for Deever based on the convention of the 'little man' alone and afraid, caught in the business machine. The past, in Miller's Ibsen manner, reaches into the present and overcomes the future. Chris tells Ann, 'we're going to live now!', and the play proceeds to destroy that confidence.

The example of responsibility is the men of Chris's company dying for each other, and this is opposed to the 'ratrace' exemplified by the Keller business. Miller's moral centre is a slightly old-fashioned expression of the notion that property is a crime:

> when you drive that [new car] you've got to know that it came out of the love man can have for a man, you've got to be a little better because of that. Otherwise what you have is really loot, and there's blood on it.

Like the Proctors, in the later Crucible, Chris and Ann have to have their love and respect tested in the fire of public events. A minor character criticizes Chris—'he wants people to be better than it's possible to be'—and insists that compromise is necessary. Keller believes that he betrayed the pilots for his family and, especially, for his son, 'my only accomplishment'. In Act II, in this struggle of fathers and sons, Deever's son George determines to apply the law to release his father by condemning Keller. He resists family softening and the Mother's accusation of hardness and self-destruction. Miller's point is

that the community ethic rests on moral chaos, and at the height of the
family cosiness he allows Keller to betray his faked life. The Mother is
made to blurt out her truth: Larry must be alive because if he is not,
Joe Keller killed him. As Chris's love for his father vanishes, possibly
too abruptly, Miller makes Keller give his central plea for justice:

> what could I do! I'm in business, a man is in business; a hundred and
> twenty cracked, you're out of business; you got a process, the process
> don't work you're out of business . . . what could I do, let them take
> forty years, let them take my life away? . . . Chris, I did it for you,
> it was a chance and I took it for you.   (p. 115)

This is the root of the action and Chris turns on his father:

> For me! Where do you live, where have you come from? . . . Is
> that as far as your mind can see, business? . . . Don't you have a
> country? Don't you live in the world? What the hell are you? You're
> not even an animal, no animal kills his own, what are you?

But Miller makes Keller say before his suicide only 'I'm his father and
he's my son, and if there's something bigger than that I'll put a bullet in
my head' (p. 120). He is therefore finally a martyr to a false ethic of
family and business sentimentality. Chris believes in a code of traditional honour older than America and capitalism. Keller can cry,
'a man can't be Jesus in this world!'; but the answer is that Chris only
wants people to be better and responsible, and the play concludes in a
suicide of shame and hopelessness without the slightest suggestion as to
how American society could be changed to prevent these circumstances
endlessly repeating.

★   ★   ★

Death of a Salesman takes up the battle of fathers and sons and removes
the argument from the clear-cut war case to the everyday case of
Willy Loman destroying himself for business and family. The long run
of this play on Broadway was remarkable considering its sombre
pathos which offers no release from tension and sadness. Basically it is
an expressionist play of degradation, and in spite of one feeble question
put to the audience, once again Miller leaves the conflict between a man
and his society hanging fire between suicide and an intolerably unchanging world. He scores his points, with undoubted success, through
a system of language which repeats ordinary catch-phrases and shared

jargon, manipulated to cover the facts. Where *All My Sons* concentrated its retributive action into fifteen hours, *Death of a Salesman* uses flashbacks within an expressionist set in order to present the contents of the sixty-year-old hero's mind as he draws towards suicide after self-perceived wasted life. Again, the waste is not countered with any suggestion of radical change in the society's ethic which caused it. We are offered only the wife's cry of warning to her two sons in Act I:

> I don't say he's a great man. Willy Loman never made a lot of money. His name was never in the paper. He's not the finest character that ever lived. But he's a human being, and a terrible thing is happening to him. So attention must be paid. He's not to be allowed to fall into his grave like an old dog. Attention, attention must finally be paid to such a person. You called him crazy . . . a lot of people think he's lost his—balance. But you don't have to be very smart to know what his trouble is. The man is exhausted . . . A small man can be just as exhausted as a great man. (pp. 162–3)

But what terrible thing has happened to Loman, what attention must be paid, what has exhausted him, and what kind of balance has he lost? He is not a murderer like Keller, but he too reaches the shocking realization that his life has been work and for nothing. Loman has been unable to learn that business ethics, the morality of his work-community, oppose the traditions he assumed were still in action: the personal ethic of honour, the patriarchal nature of a basically benevolent society and family, and neighbourhood relations. He speaks the very language of that acquisitive society, without hypocrisy, the terminology of the world which throws him off-balance.

Miller presents a fairly full context for the suicide, but he cannot show his hero attaining any profound understanding of his end. Loman's father made flutes and sold them himself throughout the States in the self-made businessman's manner. Loman's brother Ben is the next stage: the man self-made outside America: 'Why, boys, when I was seventeen I walked into the jungle, and when I was twenty-one I walked out. [*He laughs.*] And by God I was rich' (p. 157). In stage three, the jungle is New York, the American city, where a man stays, burdened by a house overtopped by skyscrapers, household payments on equipment with built-in obsolescence, mortgage and insurance worries, and a built-in belief that the competitive society is life itself at its best. As in *All My Sons*, the son penetrates some of the father's illusions. Biff Loman tried life on a Texas ranch but remained inhibited by his father's standards. In a flashback Miller presents the father–son relationship as a manic cult of youthful athletic prowess operated at the expense of maturity, with Dad as the great pal and Mother the source of binding love. Miller's criticism, as far as it goes, emerges from the conflict between youth and age, private and public life, optimism and suicidal despair. Like Keller, Loman perceives he has 'accomplished' nothing, but it is still 'the greatest country in the world' even if 'personal attractiveness' gets you nowhere. He perceives that 'the competition is maddening', but he refers here to the uncontrolled birthrate only. His second son, Happy, is also a salesman, already lost to booze and sex, obsessed with the empty word 'future', always on his lips.

But the boys are only in their thirties, and at least Biff knows he is still 'like a boy', as his father is, locked in the national myth of youthfulness. Once a Loman's energy is drained by his society he is thrown aside, in this case casually sacked by the son of the man who has been his boss for thirty-four years. He protests: 'You can't eat the orange and throw the peel away—a man is not a piece of fruit!' He is wrong, but Miller cannot find anyone to help him. The language itself blocks understanding: 'well-liked', 'create personal interest', making 'an appearance', 'knocking 'em cold'. The appalling hypnotic power of such repeated terms is the action of a deadly stifling of vitality in the name of optimism. Loman's exhaustion is the tiredness of empty buoyancy, of feeling 'kind of temporary' about himself. His wife provides loving despair; Biff knows he is a 'fake'.

Lost honour and comradeship permeate Miller's work. His men live on a vision they cannot make work. Loman lives in a world where his sons are Adonises, with Biff on the football field in a golden helmet 'like a young god—something like that. And the sun, the sun all around him.' But the boys' old school friend Bernard, who worked at his books, is now defending a case in the Supreme Court, and it is Charley, his father and Loman's old friend, who says outright that personal relations and codes of honour are meaningless now:

> Why must everybody like you? Who liked J. P. Morgan? Was he impressive? In a Turkish bath he'd look like a butcher. But with his pockets on he was very well liked.   (p. 192)

But Loman is beyond advice and change; in fact he is dead already, believing that, through his insurance, he is worth more, in cash, dead than alive, and this at least would atone for his cruelty to his wife and betrayal of his sons. It now comes out that Biff lost the will to live when he saw his father with a tart, and lost the will to pass his exams: 'we never told the truth for ten minutes in this house' (p. 216). They are all victims of a 'phoney dream' and it is the American dream.

Happy still believes his father was right, even after the suicide, and many of Miller's audience must have agreed in their hearts. But Loman is what happens to an ordinarily uneducated man in an unjust competitive society in which men are victimized by false gods. His fate is not tragic. There is nothing of the superhuman or providential or destined in this play. Everyone fails in a waste of misplaced energy. A travelling salesman is on record with a good criticism of the play: 'that damned New England territory never was any good'. But other men made another criticism (in the phone calls, letters and telegrams Miller received): 'I saw your play. I've just quit my job. What do I do now?' One man said, 'Why didn't Willy Loman go to the Household Finance Corporation and solve all his problems?' Two large corporations asked Miller to address their sales meetings. Earlier, *All My Sons* had been picketed by the Catholic Veterans and the American Legion. Times change. But Miller's message is ambiguous: Loman may be 'uneducated' and the victim of a 'vulgar idea of success', but the system which fails him is 'inevitable', as inevitable as the world of Dreiser's Clyde Griffith.

Miller presents *Death of a Salesman* and *All My Sons* in a spirit of puzzled, anguished analysis but does not suggest to his Broadway audience that anything so radical as revolutionary change in American terminal society might be necessary. In his essay, 'Tragedy and the Common Man', contemporary with *Death of a Salesman*, he repudiates the idea that 'the tragic mode is archaic' owing to the absence of socially elevated heroes and the advent of habits of scepticism and analysis. He vaguely refers to modern psychiatric uses of Oedipus and Orestes complexes which 'apply to everyone in similar emotional situations'. This acceptance of muddled notions of Greek tragedy and modern psychology leads him to plump for that old stand-by for the American liberal, 'the individual', once again comfortably unexamined:

> I think tragic feeling is evoked in us when we are in the presence
> of a character who is ready to lay down his life, if need be, to secure
> one thing—his sense of personal dignity. From Orestes to Hamlet,

Medea to Macbeth, the underlying struggle is that of the individual attempting to gain his 'rightful' position in his society.

But if the hero dies at his own hand, with the sense of waste and bewilderment still entire within him, who can now be interested in anything but the chance of changing the values of the society that brings him to that degradation? The hero's challenge today threatens the hierarchical determinations of the controllers of society and their representatives, the play's backers and audiences.

Tragedy is the consequence of a man's total compulsion to evaluate himself justly.

But if that evaluation must take place in a structure of injustice, of subservience as a wage-slave, of self-help within an economic structure which limits or denies the hero's self-fulfilment, and of an ideology which determines only that some men are more equal than others, then you have the dilemma of Miller's plays: not tragedies but plays of partial awakening to fate before a conclusion in suicidal waste. Miller believes that the tragic flaw (itself a misreading of classical theory) is not weakness but 'inherent unwillingness to remain passive'. The passive, therefore, are flawless and the majority are passive; Miller realizes accurately that the 'terror' of this kind of life lies in 'the total onslaught by an individual against the seemingly stable cosmos surrounding us . . . the "unchangeable" environment'. But surely the 'evil' lies in those who perpetuate this environment, passively or actively. If the plot is not to be simply a mocking of the non-passive man, it must show a real chance of heroism and change. This Miller fails to do. 'The thrust for freedom', he says, 'is the quality in tragedy which exalts. The revolutionary questioning of the stable environment is what terrifies. In no way is the common man debarred from such thoughts or such action.' But the common man is liable to arouse only pity as a poor fool in terror for his life unless he is allowed an understanding that his revolt is towards ends which have a specific chance of attainment. Otherwise the context is rigid sterility.

At least Miller does not degrade human life in the manner of Broadway psycho-drama which claims that self-analysis cures everything, or of the social melodrama which claims that economic change predicates total human change. He wants theatre to present 'a balanced concept of life' in which the hero's need is 'to wholly realize himself' without the questioning author preaching revolution. Consequently, when Loman is betrayed by the myths and ethic of his society, all we are given is his wife's pitiful cry: 'Attention, attention must finally be paid to such a person.'

★   ★   ★

Miller says *The Crucible*, his next play, concerns pure evil. He removes his action now to the seventeenth century and uses a language which forfeits the contemporary tensions of *Death of a Salesman* for the jargon of a theocracy. Related to contemporary McCarthy hysteria, *The Crucible* reconstructs the Salem witch trials of 1692, and therefore requires a lengthy exposition to establish the community's ethic, law and attitude towards non-conformity and truth-telling before the moral climaxes of Acts III and IV. The characters are figures in a morality play, as usual in Miller, but for the first time he shows insecure authority violently enacting its neurosis against the man who says 'No' to the law and'Yes' to his inner-directing conscience.

The action spreads from spring to autumn and needs the sense of accumulating time for its development. There are no flashbacks to dissipate suspense. The theme of masculine honour is there at the outset in the Reverend Parris' fear for his 'good name' and 'character' in the community he needs to win. But his daughter appears to be under a witch's spell and the old man fears for his reputation and power if his house is claimed to be devil-haunted. In fact the 'spell' is part of a clever fraud perpetrated by his seventeen-year-old niece, Abigail, who has intimidated a group of Salem girls, playing witchcraft in the woods, into denouncing John Proctor, a good man whom she seduces without much difficulty. The teenagers challenge these early adult Americans and neither side will admit their fraud and fear. Gradually girls and adults believe in the magic and act on their beliefs, even though they involve torturing, burning and hanging their neighbours and friends. The law becomes a tool of acquisitive power and fearful irresponsibility.

But even Abigail cries to her uncle, 'My name is good in the village! I will not have it said my name is soiled!' Part of her motivation is having seen her parents' heads battered in by Indians. She is in fact a delinquent, taking her morality from the world she knows. The centre of adult truth she attacks is John Proctor, a farmer in his middle 'thirties, and his wife Elizabeth, a development of Chris and Ann in *All My Sons*, idealists with their 'own vision of decent conduct' which is not the law of the trials.

Proctor has sinned with Abigail, to use the language of the play, and it is a simple and acknowledged sin of the flesh, punished by his wife's coldness, but not a violation of his inner self. He is not a bad man but he 'likes not the smell of this "authority" ' and he has factual evidence that Abigail's accusations of witchcraft are fraudulent. He is challenged by the Reverend Hale, an intellectual, proud of his specialized knowledge of the devil, a theorist whose blind ignorance of what 'authority' may do with his learning drags him weeping into degradation.

Miller's encompassing theme is man judging man, a theme present in his two previous plays and reaching through to *Incident at Vichy*. Proctor's stance of judgment annoys the community and especially its judges, Danforth and Hawthorne. Proctor's wife, Elizabeth, observes:

> I do not judge you. The magistrate sits in your heart that judges you. I never thought you but a good man, John—only somewhat bewildered. (p. 265)

It is exactly the relationship between Loman and Eddie Carbone and their wives; and, as with those characters, here too the community 'goes wild' around the Proctors, whose traditional conscience is exposed. John's inner-directed stability cries out against the witchcraft and injustice, in Act II:

> Is the accuser always holy now? Were they born this morning as clean as God's fingers? . . . Now the little crazy children are jangling the keys of the kingdom, and common vengeance writes the law! This is warrant's vengeance! I'll not give my wife to vengeance!

As Elizabeth is cried out for a witch, John feels himself exposed to more than society's criticism, to 'God's icy wind' of which the 1692 events, like the McCarthy trials, are taken as an example. Act III presents trials and denunciation in which, in spite of Proctor's clear proof of the girls' fraud, the judges and accusers go too far and Hale awakens to his responsibility: 'I have signed seventy-two death warrants; I am a minister of the Lord, and I dare not take a life without there be proof so immaculate no slightest qualm of conscience may doubt it' (p. 297). But he is over-ruled by another infallibility, that of law, and therefore Proctor is driven to attack law when he attacks the trials. In doing so he attacks authority. The trap begins to close on him and Miller comes as close as he can to supporting the individual against society without crying for revolution—which is just as well, since he himself had to appear before the House Un-American Activities Committee before long.

The play turns on a trick of authority by which Elizabeth is forced to lie for the truth. Proctor accuses Abigail of being a whore and claims his wife cannot lie. Elizabeth denies he is a lecher when he has already admitted his lechery. Now there is double proof that he has 'cast away his good name'. He cries out that Elizabeth 'only thought to save my name!', but the girls play their witch-game again to enable the judges to bring Proctor down, until, faced by the perversity of the events against him, he says 'God is dead', and damns himself finally. Hale, who has come to support him by now, rushes from the assembly denouncing the whole procedure his intellectuality had abetted. In Act IV he begs Elizabeth to make John confess and save his soul and perhaps his life. She replies 'I think that be the devil's argument', which is the point at which the play recognizes the central terror of its action—the complete reversal of 'good' and 'evil'. When John tries to make out a case for gaining his life for their joint future, she simply says: 'I cannot judge you, John'. Miller's point is that, since Proctor is a good man, it is vanity on his part not to recognize he is like all men whose wicked souls God sees and it is wicked not to leave his family provided for. So he may as well confess. But he switches the action here to focus fully on John's integrity: in a corrupt time, that alone is valuable. Elizabeth adamantly remarks: 'John, it comes to naught that I should forgive you, if you'll not forgive yourself' (p. 323).

The following scene is a moving recognition of mutual love, respect and charity, and one the finest Miller has written; it is the central, adult, positive humanity of the action. But what comes out of it is unconvincing. Proctor confesses (to regain his life) but will not accuse others—'I cannot judge another'. Realizing his own confession will be used as an instrument against them, he tears it up: 'You will not use me! It is no part of salvation that should use me!' The reason for these climactic words, which reverberate throughout American literature since the Declaration of Independence, Proctor makes into a proclamation for total integrity:

> Because it is my name! Because I cannot have another in my life! Because I lie and sign myself to lies! Because I am not worth the dust on the feet of them that hang! How may I live without my name? I have given you my soul; leave me my name!   (p. 328)

He exits to his execution, accepted so voluntarily that it has suicidal qualities of self-sacrifice, even though he is a victim of the system.

Proctor, unlike Keller and Loman, chooses his own fate more in the romantic lineage of promethean defiance of authority for personal honour, made secure by death. But the social structure, once again, remains intact, and it is exactly here that Jean-Paul Sartre's film script alters Miller's play.

Les Sorcières de Salem (1957), a film made to Sartre's script by Raymond Rouleau, focuses clearly from its beginning on Proctor's rebellion against the use of personal power which condemns people as sinfully corrupt by inevitable theory. Proctor's sensuality and his identification of Elizabeth with the God of prohibiting sex and the God of judgment is firmly established, and Sartre enters into a general criticism of the Protestant ethic and its relations with sex, money and power relationships. The clerics link the devil with lower-class rebelliousness against the rich and powerful—in fact the storekeeper, from whom Elizabeth wishes to buy her daughter a doll, remarks: 'there are no witches among the rich'. Sin is overtly sin against state authority, only made to seem sin against Jonathan Edwards' God. In such a theocracy, the borderline between actual 'possession' and playacting is uncertain and some of the women in the meeting house climax are as 'possessed' as the girls. An organization of 'sensible citizens', both bourgeois and workers, sends a deputation to the Governor, but the lower classes come to distrust their leaders and plan among themselves to attack the gallows to forestall Proctor's execution. Danforth hopes to foil this plan by setting up the gallows inside the prison and welcomes the rebellion as an opportunity to strike at the people without remorseful conscience.

Sartre also has Abigail come to Proctor secretly, to make him confess so that they can escape to New York where no one will know of his shame; and she tempts him by threatening to become a whore in Boston. His desire for her cannot stand the idea of her body used by other men and he writes his confession accordingly. This has the effect, in the film, of making Abigail a far more sympathetic figure of passion, even when Proctor negotiates the crucial change from passion for her and love for Elizabeth. But he is hanged finally as pre-revolutionary martyr. Abigail's cries for help arouse the rebels to break into the prison but they would hang her too, as a traitor. As the final funeral cortege begins, it is Elizabeth who saves her: she quietly observes that she herself, and all of them, are guilty of the murder of Proctor. Her last words are: 'Release her—she loved him', and Abigail stands shocked in a new understanding as the procession moves out of the village into the countryside.

Sartre has virtually filled out the sexual and historical details of Miller's play, which he treats as a sketch. But he also transforms Miller's characteristic despair and stress on a man's exemplary suicide into hope for social change through the murder of a hero. The film is more complex than the play, and more convincingly three-dimensional if rather more philosophically dogmatic. If the aim of such a historical drama is to analyse the present in order to change it, the deeper and wider the analysis the better. As Miller owned, *The Crucible* did not help to defeat McCarthy: 'No liberal did that. The army defeated McCarthy. He attacked a general, and that was a deadly mistake' (*Guardian*, 23 January, 1965). The play's success came later, played to small non-commercial audiences already prepared to accept the liberalism it embodies.

★   ★   ★

A View from the Bridge compromises between the remote moral history of seventeenth-century Salem and contemporary Brooklyn. Eddie Carbone, like Proctor, is fearful of losing his good name and arrives, not at the suicidal hopelessness of Keller and Loman, but at the most logical death in all Miller's plays. He is killed in self-defence by the representative of the ancient traditional law which, the dramatist insists, is deeper than state social law: it is the law of honour, perpetuated in Sicily. *A View from the Bridge* is a drama of the emigrant in the New World (Carbone and Marco are Sicilians), and of the uneducated man confused by different kinds of moral law and the ambiguity of his own sexual feelings. Eddie is confronted, as in classical tragedy, with a situation for which he is unprepared, like Antony and Othello, and like Solness the masterbuilder. But Miller's hero is a carefully delineated working man, a dock labourer, to whom once again attention must be paid, in the pathos of his self-discovery.

Miller says he wanted the play to be without suspense or theatricalized life (Introduction to *A View from the Bridge*, 1960); based on a true incident, as a number of his plays are, he did not wish his action to depend on 'psycho-sexual romanticism' or 'mere sympathy' for a 'misunderstood victim'. The feeling aroused must refer to 'concepts, to codes, and ideas of social and ethical importance'. Suspense is there only in so far as the audience knows only too well how events will turn out;

'the basic feeling would be the desire to stop this man and tell him what he was really doing to his life'. That is, to educate him, and therefore the audience is presumed to be able to educate Eddie Carbone, a disastrous assumption, to say the least.

Eddie, a worker indistinguishable from his neighbourhood type, depends for his good name on being at one with the community standard. His final 'I want my respect' is the heartbreaking cry of a man whose self-esteem had depended entirely on society, unlike Proctor's inner-direction. Eddie is other-directed: 'his value is created largely by his fidelity to the code of his culture'. That culture is European; not American but Sicilian. As in *Death of a Salesman*, the scene is Brooklyn, but here it is the dockland slum most of us only see from Brooklyn Bridge. The 'fatal violation of an ancient law' is presented in naturalistic language within an expressionist set, and the action is framed, made into a detached myth, by the choral character, Alfieri, an emigrant Sicilian lawyer who partakes of the action but also speaks directly to the audience. It is he who sees, helplessly, the inevitability of Eddie's defeat, and sees two laws in conflict—the ancient pre-Greek law, the natural law as it is called, and the state law, represented by the Immigration Bureau.

But since this is Red Hook and not Sicily, in the lawyer's words 'we settle for half, and I like it better. I no longer keep my pistol in my filing cabinet. And my practice is entirely unromantic' (p. 379). If you know what natural and state law are and that they conflict, and know yourself, you can work out a life. But Eddie does not know and the action takes its 'bloody course', and the key word is 'honour'. Eddie's niece Catherine, brought up as his daughter, and nearing womanhood, is chosen out of her typists' class for a good job. This is an honour to the family, and it is also an honour to shelter two illegally emigrant Sicilians, relatives of Eddie's wife Beatrice. Community law is exemplified in the story of Vinnie Bolzano, a kid of fourteen who snitched on his uncle to the Immigration Bureau and is then turned out by family, and community and never seen again. Eddie accepts the honour and the justice of this law entirely.

One of the newcomers, Marco, is an ordinary hardworking man planning to return to his family in Sicily; his brother Rudolpho is young and plans to become an American. He is a blond, handsome fellow who sings high tenor, spends his money on clothes, makes dresses for Catherine and seems totally unlike the image of normal masculinity acceptable to Eddie. Rudolpho and Catherine fall in love and intend an early marriage, and it is at this point that Eddie's repressed sexuality for his niece appears as tyrannical concern for her welfare, while his nervous sexual feeling for Rudolpho takes the form of bullying and teasing, staged excellently through a little sparring match which words could certainly not improve. Miller now shows the hand of what he calls 'destiny'—'who can ever know what will be discovered? Eddie Carbone had never expected to have a destiny'—and the term means a horribly typical fate, apparently.

Miller's presentation of Eddie's inarticulate life is brilliantly written as his terrifying bewilderment increases. Alfieri tries to explain to him what is happening, but Eddie is obsessed and has no notion of the complexity of love and of social understanding. What Miller does not mention in his play is the failure of this community to become American, the chronic failure of the new society to impose an equitable social law which might over-rule the primitivism of Sicily. When Eddie gets drunk and kisses Catherine, he responds to Rudolpho's challenge by pinning his arms and kissing him as well. Miller's stage direction makes clear what he requires here: *'They are like animals that have torn at one another and broken up without a decision, each waiting for the other's mood'* (p. 423). The scene is prepared for in two ways which show what Eddie's condition is: first, Beatrice saying to him, 'When am I going to be a wife again', and Eddie's refusal to discuss the matter; and secondly, his statement to Alfieri: 'I mean he looked so sweet there, like an angel—you could kiss him he was so sweet.' But he cannot stop the marriage, the process of natural law. Alfieri warns him:

> The law is nature. The law is only a word for what has a right to happen. When the law is wrong it's because it's unnatural, but in this case it's natural and a river will drown you if you buck it now . . . You won't have a friend in the world, Eddie! Even those who understand will turn against you, even the ones who feel the same will despise you! (p. 424)

But it is too late for such rationality to change an uneducated, passionate man like Eddie, and a man whose Americanism has not even begun. He betrays Marco and Rudolpho to the other law's representatives, the Immigration Bureau, in order to be rid of the threat to his masculinity; and immediately Sicilian law takes over, condemning his betrayal of honour. Eddie stands alone as a man who has lost his respect.

In betraying the brothers he betrays himself and his cry is futile, as his appalled wife knows and accepts. Alfieri counters Marco's sense of the dishonour in not killing Carbone with another law which denies it, but Marco's reply is easy: 'All the law is not in a book.' Alfieri counters again with the basis of law in America: 'Yes. In a book. There is no other law.' But Miller leaves the argument in the air with the lawyer saying, 'Only God makes justice': which justice, which law, Miller does not say. Americans must settle for half, which is civilization. But does God settle for half too? If that is the case, then tragedy is not destiny but a lack of education. The confusions are not sorted out and the play rushes on to death scenes. As he becomes the 'nothing and nobody' Catherine rejects, Eddie cries 'I want my name' and 'I want my respect', but the only way for him to get it now is a knife-fight. The argument ends in warfare.

The animals attack each other (it is Miller's image); the law of blood in Red Hook exerts itself; Marco turns Eddie's knife back into its owner; the logic of his death is exactly within the ancient law. Miller tries to recover from this display of destiny with a liberal gesture, with Alfieri's desperate assertions: Eddie was wrong, his death useless, but we are to respect something called 'himself purely' because 'he allowed himself to be wholly known'. So he is to be loved and mourned but 'with a certain . . . alarm'. That 'alarm' is like the 'attention' in *Death of a Salesman*, a gesture of liberal hesitation to go through with the needed radical criticism of the society which permitted and therefore encouraged this killing, this waste and this chaos. Miller's plays are a warning cry from his warm, uncertain heart detached from the economic and social implications which his head hesitates to act upon.

★   ★   ★

In February, 1960, Miller was saying that he did not in fact share Alfieri's views. He stated his dramatic aim in characteristically didactic terms: 'I try to unveil a truth already known but not recognized . . . [The theatre] can help to make man more human—that is, less alone' (*Guardian*, 25 February, 1960). It is the loneliness of his heroes which produces their measure of cathartic response in the audience: the continuity from father to son breaks down; the parent generation dies in the chaos the son inherits. In 1958, Miller worked on a film script which again took up this material, focused this time on delinquent youth in New York ('Bridge to a Savage World': *Esquire*, October,

1958). The conflict of laws in *A View from the Bridge* becomes the laws of the city streets of America: the gang codes are the codes of primitive societies or clans: 'When a Youth Board worker descends into the streets he is going back into human history a distance of thousands of years. Thus, it is fruitless merely to say that the delinquent must be given love and care—or the birch rod. What is involved here is a profound conflict of man's most subtle values.' These boys lack contact with 'civilized values' passed on from the father: 'social obligation, personal duty . . . rudimentary honour'. This kind of socially responsible analysis is present throughout Miller's career. He speaks of 'our hunger for purpose' (*Sunday Times*, 20 March, 1960), the need to unite psychology and politics in a theatre which will 'draw a whole world into one man, . . . bring a national experience to bear on an individual subject' (*Observer*, 14 October, 1956), and the failure of contemporary writers to make direct social comment in their work because of their 'failure of belief in the depth of alteration that will follow if you expose an injustice' (*Observer*, 8 September, 1957).

The kind of problem he has had with the moral and political content of his plays appears clearly in 'The Playwright and the Atomic World'. Speaking of the reception of his plays outside America, he notes that Europeans are 'more interested in the philosophic, moral and principled values of the play than we are', whereas Americans 'create methods of reaching the great mass of the people'. Majority acceptance pays fabulously, both financially and in terms of influence, and Miller accepts this himself, along with the criterion of judgment such a position must also hold: 'the most plain aspects of usefulness'. Miller wishes to write for a majority audience and his next venture was a film which concerns the transformation of popular American hero-types caused by the changes in industrial capitalist society. In *The Misfits*, the cowboy, the airman and the blonde female tamer of the West reappear divorced, alienated and bewildered, hunters of the old securities of the self at home in a society.

Miller relocates the figures of myth in economic and sexual reality. But the myth remains powerful, even in its new form. Roslyn, the anchoring symbol of sexual vitality, is part of another dream, too:

she is all that the Jew dreams: the *shiksa*, whom his grandmother forbade him as a mate . . . played by Marilyn Monroe [at that point Miller's wife and converted to Judaism], who, under the circumstances, was bound to triumph over the male Old West, the Gentile's

Saturday-matinée dream of violence and death, personified by Clark Gable, tamer of horses and women.   (Leslie Fiedler, pp. 87–8)

Not only Miller was personally involved in this film; as James Goode has shown, the director, John Huston, and three of the leading actors were all, in some sense, enacting their life-roles through Miller's script. The Gable, Clift and Monroe film-images were more than actor's roles for their creators, and were part of a national mythology of the last three decades. The film is set in Reno, Nevada, 'the last stop of the vanishing American innocent' (Goode, p. 92), the town of divorce and gambling, and the appropriate scene for a script concerning divorce, heroic action changed by the economic market, the evasion of society by men who wish to stay innocent, and the chances of defeat for the individual in a corrupting time. Miller's feeling for his misfitted— Keller, Loman, Proctor—reaches a curiously pure form in *The Misfits*. There are no villains, and not even society is a villain. The main characters are good but complex and unstable, and while they undergo tests of integrity, they have nothing in them of Hemingway's un-whimpering stoics. Miller's men do not have to kill by inner necessity and they are tender to women, whom they need as Hemingway's men do not. Gay Langland works at a trade which serves his identity. When he fears he is losing Roslyn 'he asserts his identity; he wants to call up his powers. When he is doing his work he feels most himself. He wants her to see the power within himself . . . the balance of disaster and hope in life is finally struck by both these people' (Goode, pp. 73 ff.).

Miller reaches, therefore, for a comedy of balance in which his main characters come to terms with each other and society; but at the end of the action Langland has still 'to find some means of coming to terms with a settled existence, and face the struggle between a personal code and social cooperation'. Roslyn 'comes to see that the violence in man, which is the violence in all of us, can exist side by side with love'. Miller explicitly wished to avoid the dominating theme of American literature since the Civil War, the victimization of a man by inhuman social forces, 'the documentation of defeat', accompanied by stoic 'personal lament' and concluded in meaninglessness. Instead of the proletarian hero who is not 'permitted to think by the literary tradi-tion', Miller wished to create a dramatic hero of 'felt knowledge', for the first time in his career.

The Misfits benefits greatly from film possibilities. The mountains on

the horizon contain the wild horses; the city contains the market,
divorce courts and temporary homes. Between them lie Guido's
home, built by the airman for his wife who died, the rodeo where
Perce Howland shows his skills at Dayton, and the arena of the sterile,
neutral lake, the alkali waste to which the horses are driven and on
which the men demonstrate their skill. Guido's wartime skill is used for
the peacetime rounding up of mustangs, but this in itself is a mechanization of the traditional pastoral skill of men pitted against animals on the
ground and hand to hoof. As the market for traditional skill retreats,
airman and cowboy individualism becomes isolated into lonely
bachelor games played to avoid commitment to a job for wages which
reduces men to personnel. The city of divorce and money opposes the
country of manhood trades and vitality; the hunters begin to search
for home.

Within these versions of American traditional themes the unchanging
factor is Roslyn's challenge to the three men who refuse to work for
wages. Perce remains fixed in endless boyish tests for manhood at
rodeos; Guido remains the liberal who 'can go just so far into clinches
and then just isn't there' (Goode, p. 215); only Gay achieves Roslyn's
love and will try for a balance between wages and individualism which
does not involve endless proving and competitiveness. This is Miller's
most detailed and ambitious work, and if the film was not a masterpiece, at least Huston and the actors never betrayed the seriousness of
the writer's demands. Miller's treatment, as it appears in book form, is
broad and symbolic, intended to be filled out by the visual images:

> The movie springs from the way we dream. The art of cutting
> follows the physiology of a dream. In the dream we accept because
> we see it . . . The movie hits you in a very primitive part of your
> psychological make-up. The play, on the other hand, is built on
> words . . . The greatest impact will come from the image. (p. 261)

The opening shots of *The Misfits* provide the initial context for
Miller's story of 'the professional man': Main Street, Reno; gambling
palaces; dislocated tourists and divorcees; a radio commentator boast-
ing Reno's 411 divorces this month against Las Vegas's 391 (sponsored
by Rizdale Coffee and Dream-E-Z tranquillizer); and the statue of a
pioneer family. Into this scene are projected Roslyn, awaiting divorce,
a girl still virtually a child in spite of her career of 'interpretive dancing'
in night-clubs, and the man this 'golden girl' will settle for, Gay
Langland, aged forty-nine:

he sets the rhythm for whoever he walks with because he cannot follow. And he has no desire to lead . . . Homeless, he is always at home inside his shoes and jeans and shirt, and interested.   (p. 13)

But this inner-direction has led to isolation, divorce and alienation from non-agrarian society. Roslyn's role is to indicate 'a path through the shapeless day', and Guido's house becomes a home between city and wilderness. Guido remains locked in fear and self-pity, but he can recognize Roslyn's 'gift of life'. Perce is nearer the Hemingway sportsman ideal; in his late 'twenties he has become a bucking horse rider, 'a resident of nowhere', a naïve and gentle boy whose sewn-up face of rodeo toughness conceals his eternally unfinished self, raw from his father's accidental death and his mother's re-marriage. He fits, in his honest lack of 'remorse or excuse', only into the town without police and law whose absurdity is 'so senseless as to rise to a logic, a law, a principle of destruction, as when one is knocked down by a bicycle and killed on the way to a wedding'.

Perce's 'pure lust for glory' is absurd, too, but it draws Roslyn's pity for his necessary trial and connects him to her own sense of glory, shown in the paddle-ball game, which, like the rodeo for Perce, resists its gambling context. Guido's 'elderly' plane also redeems the absurdity of his mechanized rounding-up of the mustangs. But Miller connects Roslyn's nature with the vulnerability of the rodeo and wilderness horses, as well as with Langland's bitch, and her open fear and sympathy is further linked with the vulnerability of Langland as he drunkenly searches for his children in the Dayton crowd and falls pathetically from the hood of the car. Roslyn is associated with wild nature in the tree in Guido's garden, with the moon, and with the sky and plants. Again it is Guido who articulates her position: 'You're really hooked in; whatever happens to anybody, it happens to you. That's a blessing.' The crucial speech, therefore, is Langland's explanation to Roslyn why he must sell the horses for dog-food: it is deeply connected with why he, like Carbone and Proctor, must assert his manhood:

When I started, they used a lot of them I caught. There was mustang blood pullin' all the plows in the West; they couldn't have settled here without somebody caught mustangs for them . . . It . . . just got changed around, see? I'm doin' the same thing I ever did. It's just that they . . . they changed it around.

The hesitations confirm the vagueness as to who 'they' might be: Miller refuses his hero much 'felt knowledge' here but gives him enough guilt to prepare for the final victory of Roslyn, her understanding that 'a kind man can kill'. This takes place in the film's finest scenes: the trapping and release of the mustangs, driven from the wilderness by plane and hunted on the 'prehistoric lake bed' which 'glistens like ice', 'a picture of the moon' or 'God's country'. Roslyn initially sees all three men as killers, and Gay turns on her as the female type itself, that 'puts the spurs to you—We ask them too much—and we tell them too little. I know—I got the marks!' But when Perce bids for Roslyn by attempting to free the trapped horses, it is Roslyn who cries out, after seeing Gay at his trade: 'Oh, Perce! I don't know!' This is the turning point of the work, leading to Gay's recapture of the mustang—nearly killing himself—and his symbolic freeing of it and, thereby, himself. His lament is paradoxically his victory:

> They changed it. Changed it all around. They smeared it all over with blood, turned it into shit and money just like everything else. You know that, I know that. It's just ropin' a dream now . . . Find some other way to know you're alive . . . if they got another way, any more.

Miller cannot say more than that. The end of the cowboy is not moved into the beginning of a new viable life in the West, and the end of the myths of manhood peter out in a feeble image of Roslyn and Gay driving home by a star. But Miller certainly has not, as Gerald Weales claims, 'abandoned tragedy and gone the way of Broadway and Hollywood' ('The Tame and Woolly West', *The Reporter*, 2 March, 1961). Nor is it simply a matter, as Robert Hogan has it, of an indictment of both society and the family, the one 'tawdry and valueless', the other 'disintegrated' (p. 38). Miller's comedy of balance is more complex: the relationships between the main characters explore the needs for American hero-types to change if they are not to be alienated from surviving as men. They have to 'settle for half', and refuse violence, love their women and hope for new work.

★   ★   ★

After the Fall, his next work, shows the need for this change in Miller's first intellectual professional man, a lawyer called upon to make complicated public and private decisions. In American culture and its literature, the lawyer is the central figure taming the frontier and the jungle of cities, the man whose tongue and head move America from lawlessness to the Constitution, the hero who stabilizes America in human rights based on the protection of property and the establishment of personal security.

But this play contains, notoriously, an analysis of the playwright's own recent public and private life. Shortly after shooting on *The Misfits* was completed, his wife, Marilyn Monroe, identified strongly with her role as Roslyn, announced her separation from Miller—on Armistice Day, to be precise. Clark Gable died shortly after making this, his last film, and Miss Monroe committed suicide a little later. Such events, inevitably for a playwright connected with Hollywood and Broadway, became public property, but Miller must have expected this trial. In a conversation with Huston he had defined the differences between American and English writers:

> The English writer sometimes doesn't wish to identify himself with what he's writing about. He wants to be superior to it. The American writer says, 'This is what I am.' It's self-revelation. Some English writers don't want to give themselves away. They're more modest. . . . Certain codes of behaviour can't be converted into money and are going by the board all over the world. People degenerate when they only respond to things because there's prospect of gain or usefulness. . . . Somebody's got to say things which are profitable are not necessarily right—and to make that statement is already treasonous.   (*Guardian*, 25 February, 1960)

After the Fall is Miller's self-revelation and treasonable comment on the nature of profit, necessity and American moral behaviour in mid-century, a re-working of *The Crucible* in contemporary terms into which he worked his own American confusions of public and private life. The play is also a comment on how sexuality had become 'a convention' in the theatre, 'a kind of shorthand through which we can appear to enter into the lives of people we're seeing'. He also intended to teach Americans, traditionally fancying themselves 'open-handed, on the side of justice, a little bit careless about what they buy, wasteful, but essentially good guys, optimistic', about their under-level, 'the level which confronts our bewilderment, our lonely naïveté, our hunger for purpose' (*Sunday Times*, 20 March, 1960). The play concerns also the difficulty of locating 'the forms of disintegration' in the personality striving for integrity. As in *The Crucible*, the analysis of the self and justice is central, but Miller is aware that since the 'forties that kind of analysis had become 'a device to exclude the world. Economics, politics, these are widely regarded as mere *gaucherie*. Thus self-pity and sentimentality rush in.' The leader is O'Neill once again: 'his self-pity, his tortured questing, his relentless doubt, overwhelm his often stagey solutions: the other writers too often were sealed up in their plays'. O'Neill exposed himself.

These ideas of self-reform as a dramatist produced Miller's first Expressionist, Strindbergian play, in which the action streams from the self-centre of the hero, and it is clear that part of the reason for this form is that Miller was 'perhaps less ready to believe than he once was that this gap [between man as he is and man as he could be] can be narrowed by the passage of wise laws, the election of competent officials, or any organized gestures whatever. He is thinking more closely on man's lack of any profound concern with his true nature and his consequent failure to recognize the true nature of his inevitable bonds with others' (Allan Seager).

So, instead of enriching the social and political context of his moral actions, Miller places the burden of guilt and decision increasingly on the individual, and in that direction lies the nihilism of his two most recent plays.

Quentin, the lawyer hero of *After the Fall*, tries to recover from a world 'they' changed around and from women who demanded too much. The plot takes in his Jewish family, domineering mother, Depression ruin, the McCarthy trials and their tests for personal loyalty, and the evidence of German concentration camps. Quentin cannot provide for his women because he cannot love for long, if at all, and his Jewish experience (at home and internationally, by implication) exacerbates his feeling of victimized indecision. The events and characters of this condition are presented as an autobiographical simultaneity exploring a present-tense crisis: Quentin seems to address an unseen Listener, the embodiment of the captive audience rather than an equivalent of Alfieri.

The tone is one of distressed need to confess, convince and expose, and it is hardly more interesting than the tired rehearsal of a trite series of common events, known to any American audience: the betrayals before the Congressional Investigating Committee, the disillusionment with 'thirties socialist ideology, and the broken marriages, including one to Maggie, a pop singer clearly modelled on Marilyn Monroe and a finely drawn portrait of a girl's distrust of a man with nothing but failed beliefs behind him. The failure of the play has also to do with the O'Neill type of language, a self-condemning rhetoric oscillating between the pseudo-poetic and the pseudo-analytic, all neurotic unfinished queries and platitudinously self-defeating counter-opinions. A comparison with Fellini's $8\frac{1}{2}$ is completely damaging to *After the Fall*. Miller intended to show the killing power of truth and the devastation of love by the quest for power. But, unlike Fellini, Miller indulged in theories of 'innocence', in the fashion of the American dream of evaded responsibility—Miller says 'by innocence I mean the blindness as to one's own motives, one's own actions', and the danger which follows. The resulting play is a cancelling dialectic of truth-telling and evasion, of power against love (as crude as that), and the way out this time is no star in the sky to drive by, but Holga, the European woman who no longer believes in innocence or fall from innocence, but only in the bravery to carry on. This is not a convincing version of the traditional marriage of American innocence and European experience: it is far too schematic a solution for the isolating arrogance of a hero who has the nerve to believe himself innocent as he makes mistaken decisions. Miller believes that Quentin learns in the end 'to summon courage to take life in his arms', but what can 'life' mean since the action shows at least that Quentin cannot be 'mature', a term defined by his first wife as 'knowing that another person exists'. That knowledge came through finally in *The Misfits*, but here it is merely asserted by a sterile lawyer surrounded by whispering ghosts of his past. The analogy between his betrayal of friends and wives and the planned Nazi extermination of the Jews is spurious. We are left with an American professional man's manic desire to confess exhibitionistically that he feels, really, and that he is therefore different from the callow mob of indifferents.

In reply to critics who disliked his use of Marilyn Monroe in the play, Miller wrote (*Life*, 7 February, 1964) that Maggie was not Marilyn but a symbol of 'the self-destructiveness which finally comes when one views oneself as pure victim . . . —of parents, of a Puritanical sexual code and of her exploitation as an entertainer'. Her suicide is the result of self-destructive forces which are externalized in the Depression, Auschwitz and McCarthyism. But the play only hints, insistently, at that kind of complexity and of the nature of guilt in America and the world in the 1960's. Quentin's effort to open Maggie's eyes to her complicity in her own destruction is intended to be 'an act of love' which emerges from his own relinquishing of false innocence. But this cannot appear in the play because everything is part of Quentin's vision of himself: the form is essentially self-congratulatory. The limbo-quality of the set itself maintains a false expressionism of 'no walls or substantial boundaries', symbolic 'eyes' in the concentration camp tower, and the 'neolithic' and 'lava-like' tri-level stage and sporadic lighting intended to be 'a mind questing over its own surfaces and into its depths'.

After the Fall has a limited interest for its Americanisms. Here is one more hero engaged in 'a series of proofs', the tests of capitalist democracy involving bravery and the conquest of the wise powerful father, dominant mother and loyal brother. Nearer to Moses Herzog than the hero of *Altona*, Quentin comes to his 'bit of decision' after realizing that he alone can offer himself 'justification' or 'condemnation'. He is 'hung up', cannot 'blame with confidence', indulges in fake imitation crucifixions in a hotel bedroom, and admires Holga because she decided for the Hitler assassination plot without striving for 'some goddamned . . . moral victory'. He throws aside expectations of 'saving grace' from love or socialism or patriarchal Jewishness. But the failure of nourishment in Fitzgerald's heroes has become an embarrassing arrogance in this lawyer's exhibitionism.

His fellow-travelling senior had lied in the 'forties about the blessings of Soviet law, and lied for the Party: what he now fears is the investigation not of his opinions but his lies. But Miller's comments are feeble: 'why is the world so treacherous?' and, with a silly glance at Yeats, 'why do I think of things falling apart?' Act I is the rehearsal of betrayals, faithlessness and lying, the timeless breaking of illusions and repetitive movement towards inevitable hopelessness, compounded by Oedipal guilts and sterile desires to be 'innocent' and to live 'a straightforward life' in times of international moral chaos. Quentin emerges as the man who tried to avoid moving either way until 'the web of connection between people' proves illusory during the McCarthy trials. As in all his plays, Miller wishes to fuse his public and social theme with his sexual material in order to show the failure of integrity the hero must commit. In this case, Quentin's first wife points to his basic failure: 'you want a woman to provide an—atmosphere, in which there are never any issues, and you'll fly around in a constant bath of praise'. A woman becomes his 'instrument' instead of 'a separate person', and this in turn is what he cannot bear for himself. He refuses to be identified as 'a Red Lawyer' or a particular man in love with a particular woman. At this point Miller begins to develop Maggie.

Initially she has a pleasantly dotty simplicity and literalness. Her lonely vulnerability, like Roslyn's, asks to be used by men. She acts a certain self-protective 'innocence' which covers her life as a woman of the world, a judge's mistress, an entertainer at conventions, and so on. She maintains a certain wholeness, symbolized by her 'unbroken' hair. Like Roslyn, we are told, she is 'just there', 'like a tree or a cat', but society transforms love for her into 'an issue'. Quentin confronts her wholeness as a divided man, ignorant of morality, guilty of irresponsible feeling for his lawyer friend's suicide, and associated (by the stage-set) with the German tower. Act I ends with his querying:

> Then how do you live? A workable lie? But that comes from a clear conscience! Or a dead one. Not to see one's own evil—there's power! And rightness too!—so kill conscience.

The O'Neill-style pattern of rhetoric is typical of the nihilistic movement of *After the Fall* which exhausts itself in Act II. This begins with Quentin's desire for power and decisive action, and 'the death of love' which that implies. But most of the action concerns the deterioration of the Maggie–Quentin relationship. His respect for her provided some of the courage she needed to become a star, but, like Quentin's, her professional success barely conceals an absence of self-knowledge and integrity. She clings to him as an image of manly security until she sees him as he actually is, a man who needs her to transform: 'she . . . gave me something! The power to change her!' But Maggie herself substitutes charity for love, and expects her whims about money and her extravagant ego to be taken solemnly. She temporarily becomes Quentin's Eliza Doolittle, 'a kind of proof, somehow, that can people can win' or be organized into self-sufficiency. But she also becomes an exploited entertainer, 'some kind of joke' in the public eye. To heal this dialectic of love and power, Quentin seeks to make his love operative in the world by guiding her career. But this 'power to transform somebody' ends in Maggie seeing him as protector, lawyer and promoter, and not that original man she needed, who simply 'believed in me'. It is towards this impasse of failure that *After the Fall* moves. Act II rushes with dreadful velocity towards Maggie's inevitable attempt at suicide and Quentin's total alienation from self and society. Maggie's cries—'I mean what is it? . . . I mean what do you want?'—remain unanswered. The ex-Party lawyer commits suicide calling Quentin's name and Quentin himself also refuses to be responsible for Maggie: 'I have to survive too, honey.'

The action is neither tragic nor comic but a melodrama of faithlessness. Once again, Miller drives his hero and heroine to breaking-point, as if he were obsessively tormented by the questions: how far can you trust people and at what point will they break and their faiths crumble? when is suicide the only exit? All Miller's plays concern suicide as the result of conflict between self and society; he is the significant American dramatist of alienation, the undertow of whose theatre is wilful self-destruction. *After the Fall* concludes in a paralytic tension between faith and will which destroys the cult of the individual. The agent of death is to be whisky-plus-tranquillizers, both, ironically, popular aids to living in America. Both Maggie and Quentin are obsessed with an equally popular original sin: the dominance of Mother. Quentin is the type of the modern American liberal: he seeks to condone for his sexual and moral irresponsibility by re-emphasizing the inevitability of failure and agonizing in public over his atoning self-pity. At least Miller suggests that only 'God' can provide that 'limitless love' which Quentin and Maggie demand of each other. Quentin's final cry is an echo from the whole of nineteenth- and twentieth-century American literature: 'Maggie, we . . . used one another!' The desire for 'innocence', limitless love and power are all based on this Unpardonable Sin, the theme of both Hawthorne and O'Neill: the inability to 'judge' another person or oneself once the stability of inherited moral law decays into the chaos of individualism.

Maggie survives, but Quentin survives blighted with the knowledge that he, like every man, harbours the desire to kill and the desire to 'cure' or save, the equal parts of egomania. It seems unlikely that Holga's minimal hope could rescue him from such a crushing belief.

*   *   *

This nihilistic despair controls the belief and emotion of Miller's most recent play, *Incident at Vichy*. Quentin was shown moving from 1940's Communism to 1960's despair, rather as Miller moved from the simplifying social structure of *All My Sons* to the belief in the hopelessness of human nature itself: 'the wish to kill is never killed, but with some gift of courage one may look into its face when it appears, and with a stroke of love—as to an idiot in the house—forgive it; again and again . . . forever?' The climax of *Incident at Vichy* is an act of courage and love within the context of nihilism.

It is a short play, an hour and three quarters in a 'place of detention' where nine men and a boy, picked off the streets as suspected Jews, ask themselves about their lives while awaiting interrogation and humiliation for some irrational purpose at the hands of 'experts'. The stage directions again try to universalize the local action into a representation of western attitudes in the post-war period—no less. Miller's treatment of the Occupation is too broad to be taken seriously, but, once again, as an American play with a European setting for its ideas, it is interesting. On the Left is Bayard, a Communist electrician, the artisan revolutionary, rather in the 1920's Russian film manner. Through him, Miller casts a nostalgic glance at his 'felt knowledge' ideology, but while he does allow that ideology may sustain courage, he condescends atrociously to Bayard. For the Communist worker, the meaning of suffering is not personal but historical, a matter of 'the economic and political forces' and of 'faith in the future; and the future is Socialist'. He believes a 'viewpoint' sustains a man under violent interrogation because he feels his symbolic nature as a resister against Big Business. His 'spirit' is the future.

Miller's treatment of this serious and far from uncommon position is a mockery that can comfort his Broadway audience and let them think that it need not be taken as a criticism of themselves. Next, he offers an artist's stance that only God knows what things 'mean'; a business man's confidence that he will be released (he is, and Miller is not interested in whether he is a Jew or not); and an aristocrat's belief that Nazism is not an ideology but 'an outburst of vulgarity' to which 'many cultivated people' succumbed—why, is not discussed. Monceau, the actor, believes that one plays a role to suit the circumstances. These are responses to the theme of victimization. The actor says, if you don't look like a victim and don't feel like one, you will escape; by 'creating one's own reality in this world', you win. If you feel valuable you can create the illusion that 'you are who your papers say you are'. Thus 'they' are defeated. These almost parodistical versions of Miller's obsessive themes are not discussed or acted out, although, Leduc the army psychiatrist admires the truth of role-playing and the courage to act it through. But to Monceau it is not courage but talent. Miller appears unaware that this kind of pseudo-philosophizing is an effrontery to millions who *were* victimized through Hitler's consciously planned ideological action. For reality he substitutes Bayard's role-playing as worker and Monceau's role-playing as victim. Across this polarity he places the aristocratic Von Berg's argument that a worker can be 'confused' into being a Nazi and that only 'a few individuals' can resist adoring Hitler—though what this 'individual' ability is, is not discussed.

'They', in fact, reduce a man to his nose, his papers and his penis in Vichy, and to the 'furnaces' in Poland, and these facts terrorize Leduc into contemplating a plan of escape, like Proctor before him. (Incidentally, women are not active in *Incident at Vichy*, only present as shadowy irritants behind the scenes.) Von Berg is the centre of Miller's argument that claims the 'furnaces' are believable simply because they are 'so inconceivably vile'. 'They' have the power to do the inconceivable: 'it paralyzes the rest of us'. But what 'inconceivable' means is not discussed: all we get is 'they are poets, they are striving for a new nobility of the totally vulgar . . . Their motives are musical, and people are merely sounds they play.' Moreover, this is the pattern of 'the future'. The dramatic effect of this speech is seriously to modify the effect of Von Berg's final gesture of love and courage until it becomes absurd as well as sacrificial. This is reinforced by the dialogue between the German major and the Professor from the Race Institute which exposes the irrationality of the penis test, since some Gentiles would not pass it. But the major is trapped by his position into carrying out these tests based on racial absurdity. This situation is in turn backed by Monceau's refusal to believe that his old German audiences could burn actors, while Von Berg tells how a fine young oboe player was arrested only after the police had listened to his rehearsal playing. Leduc challenges Monceau's idea of 'creating yourself' when 'they point to that spot between your legs'. Everything and everybody breaks in the power situation.

Gradually, Von Berg moves into the play's centre. He opposes Monceau's idea that race is a law of the human condition that has simply to be lived with; as Leduc observes accurately, in that case 'your heart is conquered territory'. But Leduc himself now breaks, Viennese psychology or not. In a dialogue with his fellow war veteran, the major, the psychologist challenges the German officer to prove his claim to be 'different' by releasing them: 'I will love you as long as I live'. But for the German 'nothing of that kind is left' and Miller cunningly allows him to support the earlier arguments of Von Berg and Monceau:

There are no persons any more, don't you see that? There will never be persons again. What do I care if you love me? Are you out of your mind? What am I, a dog that I must be loved? You—*turning to all of them*—goddamned Jews!

Miller has by now equated the despairs of the major, Von Berg and Monceau, got rid of his Communist and his capitalist, and left Leduc with his own absurdity of rejected love. Everything is finally, therefore, a game of power with ciphers. To the major's question 'why are you better than anybody else?' Leduc, like Quentin, has no reply, since in his terror he admitted that he would accept being released apart from his fellow prisoners. This checkmate of valuelessness enables Miller to dispose of every quality except ultimate selfishness, silence and the shot of a revolver: 'I have you at the end of this revolver', the major tells Leduc, 'he has me' (indicating the Professor)'—and somebody has somebody else'. Miller is playing with the trap or prison situation which haunts American writers in this century, the existential absolute of power control. But he is determined to go on from there. Von Berg and Leduc are left at last with the Old Jew and a vision of endless pointless suffering, repeated meaninglessness, 'total, absolute', unsharable waste, on their minds. Even Von Berg had discovered that the weight of his friends' murder or apathy 'seductive'; he had come near to experiencing the sexuality of power (Miller comes no nearer)—'I had dreams at night—Hitler in a great flowing cloak, almost like a gown, almost like a woman. He was beautiful.' This total impasse is 'the price of idealism'—surely, the most cynical remark that can be made about the twentieth century, even if it is currently fashionable in America.

Von Berg wants ideals he cannot imagine; meanwhile, like Quentin, he has nothing, and it is symbolized by the pathetic bundle of white feathers the Old Jew lets fall as he goes to his interrogation. Miller leaves Von Berg and Leduc in a relationship of cynicism and despair, but without the philosophical and literary details of the final confrontation in *The Representative*. Leduc believes every Gentile is anti-semitic; the Gentile Von Berg refuses to agree. The guilt of Quentin at being relieved of responsibility and love by the death of friends and relations, reappears here in Leduc's definition of 'Jew': 'the man whose death leaves you relieved that you are not him'. In this way Miller reduces the murder of three million Jews, for a particular reason and under particular circumstances, to a bit of philosophical reaction so dogmatic as to rebuff understanding. He makes half-concealed references to Ivan Karamazov and Sartre but cannot rise above mere assertion and counter-assertion in abstraction. The psychologist can only see a future in which men will accept their irrational, murderous nature and understand that their ideals are 'only the little tax they pay for the right to hate and kill with a clear conscience'. Von Berg counters this abject cynicism only with another assertion: there are still 'foolish people and ineffectual' with traditional moral standards. Leduc, like Quentin, believes change will come only when 'you face your own complicity' in killer-humanity. Von Berg denies this. And so on.

Out of such a contrived impasse only a sensational gesture could be dramatically tolerable. Miller can suggest no argument for the future based on social change, through economic legislation, education and sexual understanding. Von Berg's thought of suicide if Leduc is right— that Nazis 'in some small and frightful part' are doing his will—is irrelevant, and the answer to the question (which Quentin also asks at the end of *After the Fall*) 'what can ever save us?' is not another attempt to live (there are no Helgas possible in this play), but personal sacrifice of life, a kind of suicide for another man's life, a martyrdom. Leduc takes his pass to freedom from Von Berg, 'his eyes wide in awe and terror'. Although there is not, and could not be within the frame of dramatic reference, any discussion of this act of transcendence, what follows renders it an absurd gesture to avoid the impasse of power and meaninglessness. Von Berg and the major stand 'forever incomprehensible to one another' and four new prisoners are brought in.

The act of pure sacrifice takes place, therefore, in a vacuum of despair reached through a nihilistic argument based on a false dramatization of a polarity between individualism and idealism. Miller can only see the present repeated endlessly as the future. His nerve has failed, and it is due to his mistaken beliefs. Of *After the Fall* he said it concerned 'the human animal's unwillingness or inability to discover in himself the seeds of his own destruction'. Life is only possible after 'the recognition of the individual's part in the evil he sees and abhors'. How the transition, through the self's transformation to some new condition, is to be managed, we are not told. Miller holds to his belief in self-converted individualism rather than the interaction of personal and social change at many levels and in many different ways. The realization that one is involved in a killer-humanity may, after all, encourage one to kill without the burden of guilt. Miller is caught between a belief in a fixed 'human nature' and a desire to see it change. His anguish is distressing and devitalizing in its futility. The majority of the world strives forward for peaceful freedom from power situations and their de-humanizing violence, whether in peace or war. Miller, with honesty and persistence, and a degree of dramatic skill, remains fixed in a hell which he maintains cannot be outdated.

Miller repeatedly refers to his dramatic aims as 'a balanced concept of life', but fails to find the philosophy and the form to embody this apparently necessary goal. In 'The Family in Modern Drama' (1956) he asked a characteristically American question (the tradition is discussed in Harry Levin's *The Power of Blackness*, for example), which he related to a universal and timeless need reflected in the world's drama: 'How may a man make of the outside world a home?' He believed this infers a timeless conflict between the individual and the world beyond him, which is the essential dramatic conflict from *Prometheus Bound* to Kaiser's *Gas* and O'Neill's *The Hairy Ape*. The dramatist's 'mission' is to formulate this question:

> It is the everlastingly sought balance between order and the need of our souls for freedom; the relatedness between our vaguest longings, our inner questions, and private lives and the life of the generality of men which is our society and our world.

Again, at the conclusion to his introduction to the *Collected Plays* (1957), he stressed a balance which 'embraces both determinism and the paradox of will', towards which his plays work as to an 'unseen goal'. But the terms of this mission themselves destroy the hope of reaching balance: self and society are placed obstinately apart by the very set-up of the actions. Miller's obsessions with 'good name', law and authority, self and society, the Unpardonable Sin and the inevitability of suicide in extreme situations, overwhelm his arguments into simplified analyses, confusions and a final paralysis of desperate warnings. Perhaps the release from such an armour can come only from a more detailed understanding of that 'little tax' which is the mainspring of trust in human ability to learn and change.

Note

Biography. Thomas Lanier Williams was born on 26 March, 1911, in Columbus, Mississippi; his father was a commercial traveller for a shoe company, and his mother the daughter of an Episcopalian minister. His early childhood was spent in different parts of Mississippi and Tennessee (hence his nickname); from the age of eight onwards he lived in St. Louis, Missouri. He began writing at the age of fourteen; in 1928 he published his first story in *Weird Tales*. A course in journalism at the University of Missouri remained uncompleted. In 1938 he obtained a B.A. at the University of Iowa where he followed a course in playwriting.

He wrote several full-length plays for production by The Mummers, a semi-professional St. Louis theatre group, in the mid-'thirties. Strongly influenced by D. H. Lawrence, he also wrote a number of short plays. A production of *Battle of Angels* by the Theatre Guild in 1940 died before reaching Broadway because of a poor reception in Boston. But the New York success in 1945 of *The Glass Menagerie* established Tennessee Williams as a leading American playwright, a position confirmed by *A Streetcar Named Desire* which Kazan produced in 1947. Kazan also did the first production of *Camino Real* (1953) and *Cat on a Hot Tin Roof* (1955). Frequently violent or macabre in his plots, Williams turned to comedy in *The Rose Tattoo* (1951) and *Periods of Adjustment* (1960).

Since achieving success in the theatre, Tennessee Williams has spent a good deal of his time outside the United States.

Editions. The plays listed have been published in the same year as their first production. Others published are *American Blues: Five Short Plays* (1940), *You Touched Me!* (1942), *27 Wagons Full of Cotton and Other One-Act Plays* (1945), *Summer and Smoke* (1948), *I Rise in Flame, Cried the Phoenix* (1952), *Orpheus Descending* (1955), *Something Unspoken, Suddenly Last Summer* (1958), *Sweet Bird of Youth* (1959), *The Night of the Iguana* (1961), *The Milk Train Doesn't Stop Here Any More* (1963) and *The Eccentricities of a Nightingale, Slapstick Tragedy* (1965).

Penguin Plays have published paperback volumes of *Sweet Bird, A Streetcar* and *Menagerie*; *Cat*; *Tattoo* and *Camino Real*; *Orpheus, Something Unspoken* and *Suddenly Last Summer*, as well as the film script of *Baby Doll* (1957); the volumes of plays contain brief autobiographical notes by the author. References in this chapter are, wherever possible, to the Penguin texts.

Criticism. B. Nelson's *Tennessee Williams* (1961) is a useful interim summary of biographical and literary facts; it lists critical references to Williams's plays up to 1960. An interesting essay written subsequently is 'The Desperate Morality of the Plays of Tennessee Williams' by A. Ganz, reprinted in *American Drama and Its Critics*, ed. A. S. Downer (1965). Tennessee Williams 'interviewed himself' in *Observer* (7 April, 1957), under the title 'The World I Live In'. A bibliography is in *Modern Drama* (1958-9), and a more recent bibliography is appended to Gerald Weales' *Tennessee Williams* (1965).

VIII

Cinematic Structure in the Work of Tennessee Williams

GEORGE BRANDT

*

EVER since the introduction of sound made the all-talking movie a commercial *sine qua non*, the American film industry has been indebted to the theatre for a good deal of its raw material. The ready-made plot and dialogue of successful stage plays—and their equally ready-made publicity—were too good a bet for Hollywood to miss in its years of glory; and even in the latter years of decline the practice of making 'the film of the play' has continued. A long line of stage drama (often adapted merely in the rudimentary sense of being broken down into camera set-ups, with some establishing shots thrown in and some exterior sequences added to 'open up the action') stretches across the American screen all the way from *The Last of Mrs. Cheyney* and *Quality Street* to *The Moon is Blue*, from *Arsenic and Old Lace* and *Born Yesterday* to *Bus Stop*. Even the film musical (not primarily a literary form) as often as not began life on the stage: *Oklahoma!*, *West Side Story* and *South Pacific* are cases in point. Film theorists may frown on the practice, and it is true that it has contributed to keeping the American film dialogue-bound. But then, original film scripts have frequently been as guilty in this respect.

What in turn has the cinema given back to the American theatre? Not much. In view of the vast output of the American film industry (497 feature films were made in 1952, before the great decline set in) its impact upon the stage has been remarkably small. The general conception of plot structure, characterization and dialogue-writing has been coloured only to a minimal extent by the new techniques of dramatic story-telling opened up, at least potentially, by the younger medium. What are these new techniques? Ever since Griffith, the cinema has been known to enjoy the greatest freedom in time and space, largely as a result of the editing process, even though film-makers might often neglect these new opportunities. The film can make unexpected connections, reverse the flow of time, break down complex events into significant details, leap from China to Peru, or look at causality from a fresh angle. The formal changes brought about by the use of real locations, the big close-up, the inclusion of slices of life have made new dramatic structures possible. Thus, when Cassavetes made his actors in *Shadows* improvise entire scenes, it was natural for the plot to be loosely knit—indeed ostentatiously *not* well made.

In fact, the cinema has done more than merely tell the old stories in a new way. Placing man in his actual environment, it has been able to project unexplored, non-literary forms of drama. In *Nanook of the North*, the Eskimo hunter's enemies are hunger and cold, not any human rivals. Sucksdorff's *The Great Adventure* makes the tale of the farm boys with their pet otter attractive and interesting instead of mawkish precisely because they are *real* boys on a *real* farm with a *real* otter.

But if the American novel learnt its lesson at an early date (Dos Passos published *Manhattan Transfer* in 1925), the theatre has been slow to follow suit. Perhaps some of the freedom in Thornton Wilder's plays derives from the cinema; but plays like *The Long Christmas Dinner*, *Our Town* and *The Skin of Our Teeth* owe more to James Joyce and to Oriental theatre. *Death of a Salesman*, on the other hand, has some links with cinematic structure as well as the stream-of-consciousness of the modern novel. The original scheme of the play was even further removed from the ordinary space-time structure of drama than the version that finally reached the stage. Arthur Miller had this to say about it:

The first image that occurred to me which was to result in *Death of a Salesman* was of an enormous face the height of the proscenium arch which would appear and then open up, and we would see the inside of a man's head. In fact, *The Inside of His Head* was the first title . . . The *Salesman* image was from the beginning absorbed with the concept that nothing in life comes 'next' but that everything exists together and at the same time within us; that there is no past to be 'brought forward' in a human being, but that he is his past at every moment and that the present is merely that which his past is capable of noticing and smelling and reacting to.[1]

[1] *Collected Plays*, p. 23.

Such visual probing into the human mind had, of course, been a frequent pre-occupation of the cinema for decades—particularly the French and German cinema in the 'twenties. Pabst made his *Secrets of a Soul* in 1926, and the even earlier *Cabinet of Dr. Caligari* presented the world through a madman's eyes.

But it is Thomas Lanier Williams, better known as Tennessee Williams, who of all American playwrights has most effectively learnt the lessons in freedom that the cinema has to teach. He has been orientated towards the cinema for a very long time. A biographer of his tells us that the young Williams was a great movie addict while still at high school. 'During the years in St. Louis, out of loneliness and the desire to escape from home, he spent much of his leisure time in cinemas. The quality of the presentation did not often matter' (Nelson, p. 27). The imaginative hold that films had on him then is reflected clearly enough in Tom, the narrator in the transparently autobiographical *Glass Menagerie*. Frequently nagged at by his mother for spending so much of his time in the cinema, Tom replies, 'Adventure is something I don't have much of at work, so I go to the movies . . . I like a lot of adventure' (p. 155). Here the author is plainly speaking for himself as an adolescent.

Williams broke through as a writer not for the theatre but for the cinema to begin with: he was a contract script writer for M-G-M in 1943. It was not a particularly happy period of his career; his writing assignments turned out to be flops. His original screen play *The Gentleman Caller* was rejected by his somewhat short-sighted employers. However, the script proved to be capable of being adapted to the stage, the reverse of the customary procedure; and there, under the new name of *The Glass Menagerie*, it put its author in the front rank of American dramatists during its New York run in 1945.

Since gaining his (rarely uncontroversial) position of eminence in the American theatre, Williams has provided the cinema with a steady stream of script fodder. No fewer than ten of his plays have so far been adapted for the screen: *The Glass Menagerie* (1950), *A Streetcar Named Desire* (1951), *The Rose Tattoo* (1955), *Cat on a Hot Tin Roof* (1958), *Suddenly Last Summer* (1960), *The Fugitive Kind* (1960)—this is the screen version of the play *Orpheus Descending*—*Summer and Smoke* (1961), *Sweet Bird of Youth* (1962), *Period of Adjustment* (1962) and *The Night of the Iguana* (1964). His novel, *The Roman Spring of Mrs. Stone*, was made into a film in 1961. Williams himself worked on the adaptation of *Suddenly Last Summer* and *The Fugitive Kind*.[2] In them-selves these screen versions, which incidentally have varied considerably in terms of artistic and box-office success, do not necessarily prove any-thing much about the cinematic structure of the plays on which they are based. Some of these plays were in fact palpably unfilmic. The film adaptation of *Suddenly Last Summer* (even though it was done by Williams himself, in collaboration with Gore Vidal) lost much of the play's claustrophobic intensity by an opening up of the action in time and space.

But when we turn to the plays themselves, we see strong cinematic features in at any rate some of Williams's work. A characteristic quality of his drama is a degree of stylization imposed on more or less naturalistic material. This stylization, which rarely rises quite to the level of poetry in diction or concept, has variously caused Williams to be called an exponent of the 'Gothic' ('The gothic style deals with extremes of pain and joy and expresses them directly', writes Alan Downer),[3] of 'poetic naturalism' (John Gassner's description) or of plain 'expressionism'. Perhaps the latter term, which provides a, by modern standards, long theatrical ancestry for Williams's devices and intentions, fits best. It is the one that Williams has himself used and justified on essentially realistic grounds in these words:

> Expressionism and all other unconventional techniques in drama have only one valid aim, and that is a closer approach to truth. When a play employs unconventional techniques, it is not, or certainly shouldn't be, trying to escape its responsibility of dealing with reality, or interpreting experience, but is actually or should be attempting to find a closer approach, a more penetrating and vivid expression of things as they are. (Production Notes to *The Glass Menagerie*.)

This realistic aim, not actually always adhered to in some of his more Gothic moods, puts Williams's expressionism closer to a cinematic vision of reality than to the expressionism of the post-World War I period. (Even that school, with its emphasis on spotlighting, its mon-tage of short scenes and its expressive acting not unlike the histrionics of the silent screen, was arguably influenced by the cinema.)

*   *   *

[2] I am indebted for the full list of Tennessee Williams films to Brenda Davies, of the Information Department of the British Film Institute.

[3] *Recent American Drama* (1961), p. 32.

Tennessee Williams's cinematic qualities emerge most obviously perhaps not so much from the screen adaptations of his plays as from his original film script *Baby Doll*. This was written in 1955 for Elia Kazan to direct; although it was based on two early one-act plays (*27 Wagons Full of Cotton* and *The Long Stay Cut Short*), *Baby Doll* was conceived in wholly filmic terms. The film owed much of its success to Kazan's firm handling of the actors and to his visually exciting compositional sense; the exhibition of Carroll Baker in a brief nightie, curled up in a nursery cot, also made for spectator appeal. But the script itself has solid virtues as an example of crisply visualized screen writing, even though one may sense that the story of the Sicilian cotton-gin superintendent's getting back at a business-rival arsonist through the latter's virgin wife does not quite bring out the theme lurking somewhere underneath the surface.

The story sets the persons squarely within their specific environment which is invested with a characterizing as well as a wider symbolical function. The crumbling mansion the Meighans inhabit shows up the absurd gap between Archie's status-seeking and his actual financial situation. It also hints at the decay of the South's aristocratic way of life, as does Blanche Dubois's (never actually seen) plantation Belle Reve in *A Streetcar Named Desire*. The difference between the two is that Blanche *belongs* to Belle Reve whereas Archie Meighan is grotesquely out of place in this Palladian ruin. Baby Doll Meighan, associated from the opening sequence with the nursery in which she sleeps away from her husband-in-name-only, represents a vivid satire of a recognizable facet of the American sex war. Silva Vacarro, who stirs Baby Doll into adult awareness, is harder to anchor in reality. He is part of Williams's private myth of the Latin lover whose natural sensuality puts to shame the patently inadequate White Anglo-Saxon Protestant. (Lady Torrance, in *Orpheus Descending*, Rosa Gonzales, in *Summer and Smoke*, and Jacques Casanova, in *Camino Real*, all combine Latin blood with a passionate nature.) Vacarro's swiftly evolving relationship with Baby Doll is sketched out by briskly filmic means. Their encounter takes place on a hot afternoon—first in a rankly luxuriant yard full of tall seeding grass, then in the cool mysterious intimacy of the mansion. A casual emphasis is laid on significant properties; the overtones of actions trivial in themselves build up into a long courtship ritual like the mating dance of exotic birds. Sexual images pile up in comic profusion: Vacarro, booted, carries a whip; he fetches cool water from a well for

Baby Doll—water which we are told doesn't always come; he joins
Baby Doll on the garden swing; he rides her nursery rocking-horse; she
cuts a lemon to make him a refreshing drink and pricks herself with
the knife so that the blood trickles down her arm.

Caught in cold print, this symbolism comes over as obvious. But it
is visual not conceptual, and it is intended to be funny. It is the old old
tale of the virile lover who steals another man's wife, a mocking of
cuckolds and a celebration of manly prowess. Archie, neither as rich
nor as powerful as a magnifico, is a latter-day Pantaloon. The image is
completed in the final sequence (EXTERIOR. NIGHT) when Archie's
impotent pot-shots fail to disturb the lovers hiding in the pecan tree:
Silva cracks nuts in his mouth and shares them with Baby Doll who
had previously found this practice unhygienic.

★   ★   ★

The same ability to clothe intangible relationships in clearly visual
form is something that we find again and again in Tennessee Williams's
stage plays. It is at its most cinematic (in almost too obvious a sense)
in the second scene of Act II of *Sweet Bird of Youth*. The entire back
wall of the stage turns into a gigantic television screen from which Boss
Finley, the malevolent Southern demagogue, dominates the whole
scene, including the play's 'hero' Chance Wayne. Towards the end of
the Act the screen takes over completely from the stage action. Chance
Wayne does not utter another word until the curtain comes down.

This attempt to turn the playhouse into a picture theatre is all of a
piece with Williams's frequent experiments aimed at overcoming the
leaden immobility of the naturalistic set. Williams often tries to create
on the stage the fluidity and the sense of simultaneity which the editing
process can give to the cinema. A case in point is the setting of *Summer
and Smoke*. The Reverend Winemiller's rectory and Dr. Buchanan's
office, two fragmentary and allusive interior sets, are on stage throughout the play, overhung by the exterior scene with the stone angel whose
brooding presence as a somewhat contrived symbol of Eternity informs
the whole action. Williams suggests:

> Everything possible should be done to give an unbroken fluid quality
> to the sequence of scenes.
>   There should be no curtain except for the intermission. The other
> divisions of the play should be accomplished by changes of lighting.
>   (Author's Production Notes)

A characteristic feature of Tennessee Williams's stage settings is not merely the leaving out of inessentials of architecture—this is after all one of the commonplaces of modern scenic design—but a striving to overcome the division between interiors and exteriors. The inside of houses and their environment are often shown at one and the same time. The gain in fluidity thus obtained for the unfolding of the action resembles the filmic devices of the straight cut, the change of focus, the pan or the tracking shot. The inside-outside pattern may combine in one stage picture the characteristics of the medium shot and the very long shot. For *Sweet Bird of Youth* Williams makes the following scenic suggestion:

> The stage is backed by a cyclorama that should give a poetic unity of mood to the several specific settings. There are non-realistic projections on this 'cyc', the most important and constant one being a grove of royal palm trees . . . During the daytime scenes the cyclorama projection is a poetic abstraction of semi-tropical sea and sky in fair spring weather. At night it is the palm garden with its branches among the stars . . .   (Author's Note)

In front of this panoramic setting and in deliberate contrast to it there is, in Acts I and III, the hotel bedroom with its shut-in atmosphere, the luxurious prison where the Princess finds herself in bed with Chance Wayne, the no longer quite so young gigolo. The contrast between cyclorama and foreground in the two scenes of the second act—Boss Finley's house and the cocktail lounge of the Royal Palms Hotel—is a shade less violent.

The recurrent contrast in feeling between exterior and interior in these fragmentary or transparent sets indicates something in Williams's intentions over and above the theatrical convenience of rapid scene changes. (This point does not arise particularly in *Sweet Bird* anyway.) There is the playwright's desire to strip away the social façade from his characters and to lay bare the person hidden inside. In this he is perhaps doing no more than O'Neill had already done in *Desire Under the Elms*, where both the inside and the immediate environment of the Cabot farm are shown on stage. But O'Neill, too, achieved a kind of cinematic flow in his New England tragedy—a flow lost, paradoxically enough, in the heavy-footed screen version of the play.

The set of *The Night of the Iguana* offers a similar contrast between the Mexican rain forest that surrounds the Costa Verde Hotel and the

veranda of the hotel itself, which occasionally affords a sort of X-ray
view into the small cubicle bedrooms when they are lit from within at
night, softly romantic against the menacing jungle. We see into the
innermost being of the lost souls gathered together at the Costa Verde.

Again, simultaneity and the exterior-interior pattern are found in
a recent play, *The Milk Train Doesn't Stop Here Any More*. The set
embraces the library and the bedroom of the villa of the fabulously
wealthy Mrs. Goforth, the terrace in front of the villa as well as the
bedrooms of two further small villas on her estate. But compared to
previous plays, there is a retreat here from cinematic fluidity to a
distinctly more theatrical definition of the place of action. Williams
still distinguishes interior from exterior scenes by means of lighting
changes, but the various acting areas in interior scenes are laid open by
the removal of screens that otherwise mask them. The folding and unfolding of these screens is entrusted to a pair of stage assistants derived
from the kabuki theatre. (A turning to Oriental stage conventions had
already been foreshadowed in *The Night of the Iguana*: in Act III the
enigmatic Hannah Jelkes, dimly lit up in her cubicle, dons a kabuki
robe, holds a gold-lacquered Japanese fan and strikes something like a
kabuki dancer's pose—for no clearly perceptible reason.)

If the author's eye cuts through the walls of rooms and penetrates
into the hearts of his characters, the stress he lays on the abiding
presence of nature serves as a counterpoint to the human scene. Frequently he uses the sky to cast a poetic light over an action that, without some such mitigation, would verge on the sordid. The 'eternal'
elements in the picture put human agonies in their proper perspective
and offer the spectator some aesthetic relief. Thus we read in the
Author's Production Notes for *Summer and Smoke*:

> There must be a great expanse of sky so that the entire action of
> the play takes place against it . . .
> During the day scenes the sky should be a pure and intense blue
> (like the sky of Italy as it is so faithfully represented in the religious
> paintings of the Renaissance) and costumes should be selected to form
> a dramatic colour contrast to this intense blue which the figures
> stand against. (Colour harmonies and other visual effects are tre-
> mendously important.)
> In the night scenes, the more familiar constellations, such as Orion
> and the Great Bear and the Pleiades, are clearly projected on the
> night sky, and above them, splashed across the top of the cyclorama,

is the nebulous radiance of the Milky Way. Fleecy cloud forms may also be projected on this cyclorama and made to drift across it. Colour harmonies are tremendously important—for their own sake as well as expressionistically. Similarly Antonioni uses colour in *The Red Desert* partly to create pleasing abstract designs and partly to project a vision of the world as perceived by the fear-ridden, distraught Giuliana. But the author-director in the cinema controls the expressive value of his colours in a way that the mere playwright cannot hope to do.

In his Notes for the Designer to *Cat on a Hot Tin Roof*—a play which one would not place among his most cinematically influenced works—Williams admits the anaesthetizing qualities he so often wishes his colour schemes to have:

> ... I once saw a reproduction of a faded photograph of the veranda of Robert Louis Stevenson's home on that Samoan Island where he spent his last years, and there was a quality of tender light on weathered wood, such as porch furniture made of bamboo and wicker, exposed to tropical suns and tropical rains, which came to mind when I thought about the set for this play, bringing also to mind the grace and comfort of light, the reassurance it gives, on a late and fair afternoon in summer, the way that no matter what, even dread of death, is gently touched and soothed by it. For the set is the background for a play that deals with human extremities of emotion, and it needs that softness behind it.

The, by now sadly cliché'd, description of camerawork as 'painting with light' has its precise application here. A good deal of what the words in other plays would convey of the author's point of view is hinted at instead by means of light, colour and atmosphere. Here is another example of what the Germans call *Lichtregie* written into the directions of a play in order to give the following scene a particular emotional slant:

> The light has been gradually, steadily dimming ... There is, in effect, a division of scenes here, though it is accomplished without a blackout or curtain. As SHANNON and MAXINE enter Nonno's cubicle, HERR FAHRENKOPF appears on the now twilit verandah. He turns on an outsize light fixture that is suspended from overhead, a full pearly-moon of a light globe that gives an unearthly lustre to the scene. The great pearly globe is decorated by night insects, large but gossamer moths that have immolated themselves on its surface: the light through their wings gives them an opalescent colour, a touch of fantasy.   (*The Night of the Iguana*, Act II)

The atmospherics in Williams's plays do not always suggest 'eternity' or conjure up lyrical moods. Sometimes they are employed in the service of the pathetic fallacy. The thunderstorm in the rewritten (Kazan-inspired) Act III of *Cat on a Hot Tin Roof* echoes the clamorous battle within the Pollitt family; and its dying away at the end of the play visually and aurally underlines the upbeat finale. The thunderstorm that concludes Act II of *The Night of the Iguana* provides an image of Shannon's end-of-the-road situation and his plea for help:

> . . . a fine silver sheet of rain descends off the sloping roof, catching the light and dimming the figures behind it. Now everything is silver, delicately lustrous . . . The rainfall increases . . . SHANNON lowers his hands from his burning forehead and stretches them out through the rain's silver sheet as if he were reaching for something outside and beyond himself. Then nothing is visible but these reaching-out hands. A pure white flash of lightning reveals HANNAH and NONNO against the wall, behind SHANNON, and the electric globe suspended from the roof goes out, the power extinguished by the storm. A clear shaft of light stays on Shannon's reaching-out hands till the stage curtain has fallen, slowly.

Close-up, four-second fade-out: easily done on film, feasible but not quite so telling in the theatre. Williams evidently felt some twinges of doubt himself, as he writes in a footnote to the above directions:

> In staging, the plastic elements should be restrained so that they don't take precedence over the more important human values. It should not seem like an 'effect curtain'.

But such an 'effective' image is bound to be underlined by the very fact that the scene closes on it. The image is valid enough in itself. Shannon, the defrocked priest, has just uttered his desperate blasphemous challenge to God to strike him dead with his lightning: and nothing has happened. The real doubt in one's mind is whether the gesture can be realized altogether satisfactorily on the stage, with its fixed distance between actor and audience.

The film may direct its appeal primarily to the eye; but Williams's careful orchestration of sound—music as well as effects—is almost as deeply indebted to the cinema as are some of his visual devices. Admittedly, sound effects in the playhouse are as old as the hills. (Who would dream of omitting Shakespeare's sennets and alarums?) The American theatre has always been particularly sound-conscious: witness the tomtoms that pound away like a heartbeat through *The Emperor Jones*. But the film has gone much further in its complex orchestration of effects, effects laid against the right frame, exact down to one twenty-fourth of a second. Williams often uses sound as he does light, i.e. atmospherically. A recurrent effect which no doubt represents his sense of life as a perpetual struggle is the noises of the jungle. Piercing bird cries resound through the rain forest in *The Night of the Iguana*. A similar sound strikes one as rather *voulu* in that eminently Gothic play, *Suddenly Last Summer*. The barbarousness of the Venable household is echoed a shade too obviously by the jungle tumult of 'harsh cries and sibilant hissings and thrashing sounds in the garden as if it were inhabited by beasts, serpents and birds, all of savage nature'.

★　　★　　★

Various cinematic elements in Williams's playwriting can be seen plainly enough in *A Streetcar Named Desire*. The structure of this drama is not that of the well-made play—a closely knit action, the tying and unravelling of more or less clearly defined problems, the building up of suspense. There are of course some such conventional elements in *A Streetcar*. But it is more closely related to the epic play—epic not so much in the Hollywood sense of wide-screen grandeur nor quite in the Brechtian sense which implies detachment: but epic as narrative. '. . . each scene of *A Streetcar Named Desire*', says Alan Downer, 'is a miniature play, whose theme and characters will be reiterated by the miniature plays that succeed it, the cumulative effect of the whole depending upon Williams' skill in probing more and more deeply into the nature and motives of each of his characters'.[4] The narrative comes in eleven slabs of action; it shows the crushing of a human being, Blanche Dubois. It derives its tension from the mounting line of hysteria in each scene, with Blanche's being raped by Stanley as the climax; scene xi—when she is carried off to the mental hospital— is only the final confirmation of her destruction, which has by then been accomplished, the last nail in her coffin. Since the pattern of the drama is not the conventional act structure but something close to the film sequence, it is not surprising that the play translated exceptionally well to the screen.

In working on the first production of *A Streetcar*, Elia Kazan, who was later to direct the film version as well, gave each scene a label or

[4] *Op. cit.*, p. 30.

potted argument. This procedure—somewhat reminiscent of Brechtian practice—was designed to bring the action into focus. The 'miniature plays' of Kazan's breakdown all revolved around Blanche:

1. Blanche comes to the last stop at the end of the line.
2. Blanche tries to make a place for herself.
3. Blanche breaks them apart, but when they come together, Blanche is more alone than ever!
4. Blanche, more desperate because more excluded, tries the direct attack and makes the enemy who will finish her.
5. Blanche finds that she is being tracked down for the kill. She must work fast.
6. Blanche suddenly finds, suddenly makes for herself, the only possible, perfect man for her.
7. Blanche comes out of the happy bathroom to find that her own doom has caught up with her.
8. Blanche fights her last fight. Breaks down. Even Stella deserts her.
9. Blanche's last desperate effort to save herself by telling the whole truth. The *truth dooms her.*
10. Blanche escapes out of this world. She is brought back by Stanley and destroyed.
11. Blanche is disposed of.[5]

It is natural enough that such a sequence structure needs all the help that stage atmospherics—an imaginative setting, the play of light and shade, the overtones of sound montage—can provide. The feel of New Orleans, its very smell, is evoked in order to anchor the action in its environment and at the same time to draw from it the aesthetic values, the softening of too unbearable a reality, that we find repeatedly in Williams's stage directions. Here, too, the sky serves as a background nostalgic, luminous, pure—a dream perhaps of an unsoiled childhood now irretrievably lost. The scenic indications suggest a beauty strangely at odds with the strident events of the play.

The section is poor but, unlike corresponding sections in other American cities, it has a raffish charm. The houses are mostly white frame, weathered grey, with rickety outside stairs and galleries and quaintly ornamented gables to the entrances of both. It is first dark of an evening early in May. The sky that shows around the dim

[5] Elia Kazan, *Notebook for A Streetcar Named Desire*, in T. Cole & Helen Krich Chinoy, *Directors on Directing* (1963), pp. 365-6.

white building is a peculiarly tender blue, almost turquoise, which invests the scene with a kind of lyricism and gracefully attenuates the atmosphere of decay. You can almost feel the warm breath of the brown river beyond the river warehouses with their faint redolences of bananas and coffee . . .   (Scene i)

The stage design is on the exterior-interior pattern; this makes possible swift changes of focus, and it relates the destructive goings-on in the Kowalski ménage to the surrounding world of corruption. The author's glance pierces the walls of the house; it bores into the agony of the uprooted and helpless Blanche. With its 'heroine' cast wholly in the role of a victim, the play fails to reach tragic stature (no matter what claims may have been put forward for it in this respect). In fact, Williams is careful to distance her by showing up her foibles, her unconscious invitation of rape by Stanley, the sheer nagging awfulness of her presence in her sister's house which almost swings one's sympathy over at times to the zestful animality of the Kowalskis.

Just the same, it is necessary to insist that *A Streetcar Named Desire* revolves, or should revolve, around Blanche. Kazan's direction of the original production and of the film has cast a permanent veil over the way in which we see the play in our mind's eye; he has—very skilfully, to be sure—distorted the subtle shape and equipoise of the play. Although in his scenic breakdown he did in fact place Blanche at the core of the action, the balance of sympathy and interest somehow worked out differently in production. This was largely a matter of casting. It is now very hard not to think of Marlon Brando as *the* definitive Stanley. But Brando, as Harold Clurman has pointed out, is an actor 'of acute sensitivity. None of the brutishness of his part is native to him: it is a characteristic he has to "invent". The combination of an intense, introspective, and almost lyric personality under the mask of a bully endows the character with something almost touchingly painful.'[6]

The result of Kazan's casting—clearly an aspect of an interpretation which reached the peak of ambiguity in the rape scene—was to throw audience reactions into confusion. To quote Clurman again:

For almost more than two-thirds of the play . . . the audience identifies itself with Stanley Kowalski. His low jeering is seconded by the audience's laughter, which seems to mock the feeble and hysterical decorativeness of the girl's behavior. The play becomes the

[6] *Lies Like Truth* (1958), pp. 77–8.

triumph of Stanley Kowalski with the collusion of the audience, which is no longer on the side of the angels.

But how could what was a fault of the (in other respects highly effective) original production lead to a continuing misinterpretation of the play? Precisely to what degree we are supposed to be on Blanche's side, or whether indeed so simple a question of identification arises at all is not easy to determine in the face of Williams's attitudes. Is there not some ambivalence in the text itself that suggests an undercurrent of sympathy with the Kowalski way of life? The visual indications seem to denote at any rate some degree of aesthetic approval of it. Thus, Scene iii is described in the following terms:

> There is a picture of Van Gogh's of a billiard-parlour at night. The kitchen now suggests that sort of lurid nocturnal brilliance, the raw colours of childhood's spectrum. Over the yellow linoleum of the kitchen table hangs an electric bulb with a vivid green glass shade. The poker players . . . wear coloured shirts, solid blues, a purple, a red-and-white check, a light green . . . There are vivid slices of watermelon on the table . . .

This does not imply an out-and-out moral endorsement any more than Agnès Varda condones the adultery of her happy carpenter in the colour film Le Bonheur. But in both instances the sheer sensuous delight of the physical environment of the 'gaudy seed-bearer' cannot fail to affect the spectator's attitude: Stanley's rude vitality is pictured in glowing hues.

The light of heaven falls impartially with the same brightness on the just and the unjust, the weak and the strong, on joy and despair and degradation. Or does it fall a shade more luminously on the sordid side? When Stella whose 'eyes and lips have that almost narcotized tranquillity that is in the faces of Eastern idols' from a life of mindless non-stop sex, is discovered at the beginning of scene iv, she is 'serene in the early morning sunlight'. The smouldering tensions of scene viii —Mitch has failed to turn up at Blanche's miserably unsuccessful birthday supper—has this curious visual counterpoint:

> The view through the big windows is fading gradually into a still-golden dusk. A torch of sunlight blazes on the side of a big water-tank or oil-drum across the empty lot toward the business district which is now pierced by pin-points of lighted windows or windows reflecting the sunset.

And in scene xi, when Blanche is taken off to the asylum, we see that the 'building is framed by the sky of turquoise'. Lyrical softening? A shift of sympathy? Or savage irony? Williams makes a strong appeal through the eyes to emotions intense rather than clearly defined. Still, the pastel tones and half-lights that attach to Blanche seem intended to carry some positive overtones, whereas the primaries associated with Stanley, though vivid, are crude and garish.

The 'sound track' of *A Streetcar* is also conceived emotively rather than naturalistically. Perhaps more clearly than the imagery it creates empathy with Blanche. In so far as the effects help to establish atmosphere, it is largely *her* atmosphere. They reflect her impressions, her lacerated feelings. 'Effects' here include the scraps of dialogue which drift in from the street by way of acoustic impressionism without any special narrative function. At the opening of the play the Tamale Vendor, the Sailor, the Negro Woman and other floating voices swiftly create the sleazy locale in which Blanche is about to find herself trapped. In scene v when Blanche has told Stella what Mitch is beginning to mean to her, the Negro Woman outside cackles hysterically and in an indistinguishable mumble propositions a Young Man. Her laughter is an acoustic comment on Blanche's marital hopes and forms the sound link to the following scene—Blanche's nymphomaniac encounter with the same Young Man. Again, the Tamale Vendor's cry of 'Red hots!' and the Mexican Woman's funereal, '*Flores para los muertos*' are comments on Blanche's condition. They exist objectively but at the same time they reflect her state of mind.

The train noises that punctuate the action are even more subjective. They give a menacing quality to Stanley's quiet entrance into the house and cover his stealthy withdrawal, in scene iv; they are heard behind Blanche's telling Mitch the story of how she drove her young homosexual husband to suicide. The rush of the oncoming train, a symbol of massive destruction, is heard shortly before the rape.

Two kinds of music battle for possession of Blanche's mind—the Varsouviana heard when she last danced with her husband, and the blue piano from a near-by dive. The former music is wholly subjective: it occurs whenever Blanche's mind drifts back into the past. It comes in, most pathetically, just as the Doctor and the Matron are about to enter her room to take her away. More objective than the memory-laden polka, the blues music has a subjective aspect as well. Kazan is of course partly right in saying, 'The Blues is an expression of the loneliness and

M

rejection, the exclusion and isolation of the Negro and their (opposite) longing for love and connection . . . Thus the Blue piano catches the soul of Blanche, the miserable unusual human side of the girl which is beneath her frenetic duplicity, her trickery, lies, etc.'[7] But that is only part of the story. The jazz drifting in from outside also stands for the hostile forces closing in on Blanche. Set off by the train noise, the rape scene develops to the accompaniment of a mounting jazz rhythm which hits its climax as Stanley carries Blanche off to the bed. The trumpet and drums from the night-club around the corner are at once real in themselves and subjective, a noise in Blanche's mind, *and* symbolical of the forces that are crushing her. The different functions of the music support each other.

The overtonal use of effects is not, of course, unprecedented in the theatre. Chekhov used similar devices with great skill. We recall the fire-alarm in *The Three Sisters*, the distant sound as of a string breaking —bird of ill omen or mine disaster?—in the outdoor Act of *The Cherry Orchard*. But the as it were filmic precision of Williams's sound directions runs along similar lines to what John Grierson many years ago called the creative use of sound in the cinema.

As Blanche's mind gives way under the pressure of events, the sounds become increasingly inward, more like effects passed through echo boxes or strangely distorted. Before the rape, the 'night is filled with inhuman voices like cries in a jungle'—that typical Williams simile again!—and the visual accompaniment reads like instructions for special effects photography: 'Lurid reflections appear on the walls around BLANCHE. The shadows are of a grotesque and menacing form . . . [They] move sinuously as flames along the wall spaces . . .'

Complete acoustic subjectiveness is reached in the final scene when the sinister Matron confronts Blanche. 'The "Varsouviana" is filtered into weird distortion, accompanied by the cries and noises of the jungle.' The Matron speaks, and her chilly 'greeting is echoed and re-echoed by other mysterious voices behind the walls, as if reverberated through a canyon of rock.' It is only when the more humane Doctor comes in and courteously persuades Blanche to go with him quietly that the terrible noises subside.

If *A Streetcar Named Desire* can be shown to possess distinctly cinematic features in terms of plot structure as well as visual and sound treatment, that is not in any way to deny its theatricality. It simply

[7] *Directors on Directing*, p. 371.

means that Williams has borrowed and adapted a number of devices from a dramatic sister art and naturalized them on the stage.

★ ★ ★

Very different in form and feeling is *Camino Real*, which differs from *A Streetcar Named Desire* in another respect also: it was never much of a success on the stage, either in the United States or in Britain. *Camino Real* represents yet another aspect of Williams's attempts not merely to go beyond naturalism but to break away altogether from the stolid immobility of the stage. In his Foreword to the play, Williams makes a humorous comparison between it and Walt Disney's *Peter Pan* which was being shown in New Haven at the time of the pre-Broadway try-out of *Camino Real*. The analogy lies in the cinematic quality of linked and fluid images. He says:

> To me the appeal of this work is its unusual degree of freedom. When it began to get under way I felt a new sensation of release, as if I could 'ride out' like a tenor sax taking the breaks in a Dixieland combo or a piano in a bop session. You may call it self-indulgence, but I was not doing it merely for myself. I could not have felt a purely private thrill of release unless I had hope of sharing this experience with lots and lots of audiences to come.
>
> My desire was to give these audiences my own sense of something wild and unrestricted that ran like water in the mountains, or clouds changing shape in a gale, or the continually dissolving and transforming images of a dream.

For all its imaginative freedom, *Camino Real* is part of a long theatrical tradition—the dream play. In fact, a good deal of it recalls *A Dream Play* by Strindberg, which in its Prologue features the very clouds that Williams evokes as an image of freedom. Strindberg's play, according to the author, 'sought to reproduce the disconnected but apparently logical form of a dream'.[8] When *A Dream Play* was first produced in Stockholm in 1907, the resources of the theatre of the time were not equal to the demands made upon it. One cannot but agree with Elizabeth Sprigge when she says, 'A realistic presentation is not only very costly but very cumbersome . . . what a film the play would make!'[9] Similar cinematic elements can be found in later dream plays. Toller's *Masses and Man* (1921) alternates realistic with dream

[8] *Six Plays of Strindberg*, by Elizabeth Sprigge (1955), p. 193.
[9] *Idem*, p. 191.

scenes, both of them conceived in expressionist terms. *The Life of the Insects* by the Čapek brothers (1923) found its image of human life in the dream of a tramp asleep in the woods; but the allegorical form of this play places it in a category somewhat different from other more fluid, less rationalistic dramas.

A free, dreamlike association of images has, of course, been a characteristic film form at least since the 'twenties. A continuous line of avant-garde experimentation in the cinema stretches all the way from René Clair's *Entr'acte*, Buñuel's *Un chien andalou* and Cocteau's *Le sang d'un poète* to the American surrealist Maya Deren's films or Richter's *Dreams That Money Can Buy*. Resnais' *La dernière année à Marienbad* exploits the free play of mental associations, Bergman's *Wild Strawberries* plunges from old Professor Borg's waking reality into his dream life. It is in the nature of the medium that films can embody the flow of subconscious images much more boldly and truthfully than the stage.

Camino Real, then, is a dream play with all that this implies in cinematic fluidity. Like Strindberg's prototype it presents the author's own stream of consciousness. In a narrower sense the action of the play is dreamt by Don Quixote, the incarnation of impractical idealism and outdated notions of honour, who has fallen asleep in the plaza of this vaguely Latin American, or at any rate exotic, town. What passes through his mind in this place where the symbolic fountain has gone dry, is a nightmare in which characters from world literature such as the Lady of the Camelias and the Baron de Charlus mingle with historical figures like Byron and Casanova; with folklore creations like the all-American hero Kilroy; with symbolical creatures like the Street Cleaners who represent death; with expressionist typifications of general attitudes or situations such as The Survivor, The Dreamer or La Madrecita; or with freely invented persons like A. Ratt (a schoolboy joke this) and the broodingly ubiquitous Mr. Gutman (surely this is a pun too?) who appears to direct the action as if he were a universal puppeteer. Gutman calls out the blocks (cell blocks? road blocks?) into which the play is loosely divided, scene divisions of the via dolorosa of the innocents of life like Kilroy. On the wall of Gutman's Siete Mares Hotel hangs a phoenix painted on silk, a visual reminder of the death-and-resurrection theme which runs right through the play. It comes most openly to the surface in Blocks Fifteen and Sixteen when Kilroy, apparently claimed by the Streetcleaners and with his solid gold heart cut out of him on a dissection table, rises again and becomes Don Quixote's squire.

Most dream plays seem to tend towards pessimism, perhaps because of the inherent irrationality of the form. The freedom of absurdity is a dubious blessing. As Goya noted a long time ago—the sleep of reason breeds monsters. So the conciliatory ending of *Camino Real* inevitably remains unconvincing. When the fountain flows again with the waters of fertility and, as Don Quixote announces, the violets of tenderness have broken the rocks in the mountains, we feel unprepared for this rose-tinted conclusion. The flow of images may seemingly be free; but it cannot arbitrarily flow in any direction whatever.

Perhaps Tennessee Williams, like so many film script writers who have little or no control over the actual making of 'their' films, left too much of the shaping of the play in performance in the producer's (i.e. Kazan's) hands. 'The action,' writes Eric Bentley, 'has of itself next to no meaning. It has meaning only as created by actor and director. In *Camino Real*, Mr. Williams is not a dramatist but a scenario writer.'[10]

One's suspicion that the notion of cinematic freedom was not helpful here in clarifying the issues of the play but rather seduced the author into merely playful image-making, is reinforced when we read in the Foreword:

> Elia Kazan was attracted to this work mainly, I believe, for . . . its freedom and mobility of form. I know that we have kept saying the word 'flight' to each other as if the play were merely an abstraction of the impulse to fly, and most of the work out of town, his in staging, mine in cutting and revising, has been with this impulse in mind: the achievement of a continual flow.

But these three cinematic F's—flight, flow and freedom—cannot take the place of meaning in the theatre. Images, as Williams himself asserts in this Foreword, should not be a mere self-indulgence on the dramatist's part. But that, alas, is very largely what they are in *Camino Real*, for all its isolated moments of genuine communication.

★   ★   ★

Quite the most cinematic of Williams's plays is *The Glass Menagerie* —which is not surprising seeing it was first conceived in screen terms.

[10] *The Dramatic Event* (1956), p. 108.

A 'memory play', it employs the double vision, both realistic and romantic, that Miller was to cast over *A Memory of Two Mondays*. It has a narrator who introduces and comments upon the action, as does Alfieri in *A View from the Bridge*. Miller may have been influenced in the latter play by Williams and other exponents of the first-person-singular style of dramatic narration; at any rate, both Miller and Williams have adapted that oldest of cinematic tricks, the flashback, to the stage.[11] *The Glass Menagerie* is infinitely more subjective than either of Miller's plays: it contains sizable slabs of autobiography. Just as Thomas Lanier Williams had worked during the Depression as a clerk for the International Shoe Company in St. Louis, Tom, the narrator, works for the 'Continental Shoemakers' in the same city; he lives an intense imaginative life (we have already mentioned his movie-going habits) and he attempts to write in order to achieve some sort of inner freedom from a stifling environment, exactly as Williams had done at that period in his career. And just as Tom's sister Laura cannot cope with life and is frightened of all human contacts, retreating into the fantasy world of her glass toys which symbolize her fragility (and to a lesser extent, that of Tom and Amanda as well), Williams's sister Rose was suffering from schizophrenia in real life; in 1937 she was committed to a mental hospital. Finally, Amanda Wingfield—surely one of Williams's most three-dimensional creations—contains recognizable features of his own mother.

The memory action is seen from Tom's point of view—opening and finishing as it were in close-up on the narrator. The feeling that runs through the play justifies the flashback device. This cinematic breaking up of the flow of time casts a veil of nostalgia over the events of the past; and as Williams points out in his Production Notes to *The Glass Menagerie*, nostalgia is the play's first condition. The feeling matters more than the mere outer action. The typical interior-exterior setting serves the double purpose of peeling away the defences that Laura has built up against the world and of penetrating into the mind of the narrator, Tom. The vision of the play is dim with tears, with feelings of loss, sorrow, guilt and resentment. The fire-escape, a perfectly literal piece of domestic architecture, also stands for escape from family ties.

[11] On the problem of the narrator and similar devices in modern drama, see the excellent essay by O. Büdel: 'Contemporary Theatre and Aesthetic Distance', *PMLA* (1961), pp. 277–91.

The scene is memory and is therefore non-realistic. Memory takes a lot of poetic licence. It omits some details; others are exaggerated, according to the emotional value of the articles it touches, for memory is seated predominantly in the heart. The interior is therefore rather dim and poetic. (From the stage directions for scene i)

More than most plays, *The Glass Menagerie* would suffer from being presented without any technical aids. Its delicacy, its dependence for theatrical effectiveness on tone rather than plot do not make it a suitable vehicle for, let us say, sceneryless production. In building up the atmosphere for the play, Williams falls back to quite an exceptional degree on sensitive lighting. He has spelt out his requirements in the Production Notes:

Shafts of light are focused on selected areas or actors, sometimes in contradistinction to what is the apparent centre. For instance, in the quarrel scene between TOM and AMANDA, in which LAURA has no active part, the clearest pool of light is on her figure. This is also true of the supper scene, when her silent figure on the sofa should remain the visual centre. The light upon LAURA should be distinct from the others, having a peculiar pristine clarity such as light used in early religious portraits of female saints or madonnas. A certain correspondence to light in religious paintings, such as El Greco's, where the figures are radiant in atmosphere that is relatively dusky, could be effectively used throughout the play.

If this atmosphere is produced by what in camera terms would be low-key lighting and soft-focus photography, including the frequent use of a diffusion disc, Williams also gives us the stage equivalent to certain standard opticals. The memory action fades in, like the beginning of the normal film sequence, by the light coming on gradually behind the gauze fourth wall that at first separates the Wingfield interior from the auditorium; at the end of Tom's introductory speech, the wall is flown slowly. The reverse occurs as the play finishes: Laura blows out the candles and the gauze wall is dropped back into the scene again—fade-out. Not only the beginning and the conclusion of the play but all of its seven scenes (with the exception of scene v which brings down the interval curtain) follow the same pattern. Williams actually uses the film term 'fade out', and he says of the dying away of the light in the final scene, in a sense slightly different from its technical meaning in films: 'THE SCENE DISSOLVES'. The fading in and out of light as such is, of course, not peculiar to Williams's stagecraft; but he uses it in an almost cinematic way to represent thought processes, the rhythm of Tom's memory.

Few critics have paid any attention to Williams's intended use of projections in the play, largely I suppose because they are always omitted in production. His idea here is obviously rather different from Brecht's alienating use of a similar device: Williams is far from opposing emotional audience involvement as such. Brecht claimed these very un-Williamsian virtues for the projection of titles (at a fairly early stage in the development of his theories, in 1931):

> The orthodox playwright's objection to the titles is that the dramatist ought to say everything that has to be said in the action, that the text must express everything within its own confines . . . But this way of subordinating everything to a single idea . . . is something that the new school of play-writing must reject . . .
>
> Some exercise in complex seeing is needed . . . As he reads the projections on the screen the spectator adopts an attitude of smoking-and-watching.[12]

Certainly it is no part of Williams's intentions to create an audience of cigar-smoking children of the scientific age. But are there not at least some hints of a Brechtian function—a 'literarization' of the drama —in what he had hoped the titles would do for the play?

> In an episodic play, such as this, the basic structure or narrative line may be obscured from the audience; the effect may seem fragmentary rather than architectural. This may not be the fault of the play so much as a lack of attention in the audience. The legend or image upon the screen will strengthen the effect of what is merely illusion in the writing and allow the primary point to be made more simply and lightly than if the entire responsibility were on the spoken lines. Aside from this structural value, I think the screen will have a definite emotional appeal, less definable but just as important.
> (Production Notes to *The Glass Menagerie*.)

The atmospheric use of titles may be un-Brechtian but the title as a pointer to the meaning of a scene is not. Williams's motivation even in this latter respect was of course different from Brecht's—a fear that the text on its own might not quite make the intended impact. One can see the reason for this fear. *The Glass Menagerie*, structurally, is in

[12] From *The Literarization of the Theatre*, in *Brecht on Theatre*, tr. with notes by J. Willett (1964), p. 44.

essence a short story, or if you like a one-act play, expanded to full-length proportions. Its core, the actual storyline, is contained in Laura's confrontation with the Gentleman Caller, i.e. in scenes vi and vii. All the previous scenes are narrative, not dramatic. This loose welding together of scenes derives a good deal from filmic structure which—as in much of Antonioni's and Fellini's work, for instance—can sustain interest by the recording of atmosphere or the observation of the minute details of behaviour.

The analogy with Brecht's titles may not take us very far in evaluating Williams's screen device. It does, however, suggest a certain irony in the author's viewpoint which is only too easily ignored in production. Another comparison may make this even clearer. The screens—which, it is to be noted, are to carry images as well as legends—bear a striking resemblance to, and were quite probably inspired by, silent film titles. As a matter of fact, some of them read exactly like such titles: 'AFTER THE FIASCO—' . . . 'YOU THINK I'M IN LOVE WITH CONTINENTAL SHOEMAKERS?' . . . 'I DON'T SUPPOSE YOU REMEMBER ME AT ALL!' . . . 'A PRETTY TRAP' . . . or (a very authentic note this)—'TERROR!' Some titles are obviously, deliberately, preposterous. In scene vi a title reads, 'AH!', in scene vii there is a title, 'HA!' Like silent film titles, these legends supply thought processes or they comment on the action. Sometimes a transparently ironical point is made (and here we are quite close to the epic-theatre title), e.g. 'SUSPENSION OF A PUBLIC SERVICE', flashed on the screen just as the electric light goes off in the Wingfield flat. Images too are frequently given an ironical colouring, as when a young man with a bunch of flowers or a glamour-magazine cover are projected to symbolize Amanda Wingfield's pathetically unreal expectations and aspirations, or when Jim O'Connor's brasher but probably just as unrealistic ambitions are represented by a picture of an executive at a desk. Sometimes the images supply a naïve touch of poetry: blue roses are shown on the screen to underline the fact that 'Blue Roses' had been Jim's nickname for Laura at high school, a misunderstanding of 'pleurosis'.

On the whole we need not regret the practice of omitting the projections when *The Glass Menagerie* is produced. But they do point to a greater detachment on the author's part than is sometimes supposed, a detachment that keeps his nostalgia from becoming too cloying.

Another touch of silent film technique is very movingly introduced at the end of the play. Tom has at last decided to make the final break with his family. While the screen legend reads, 'AND SO GOOD-BYE . . .' a silent mime takes place on stage.

> The interior scene is played as though viewed through sound-proof glass. AMANDA appears to be making a comforting speech to LAURA who is huddled upon the sofa. Now that we cannot hear the mother's speech, her silliness is gone and she has dignity and tragic beauty. LAURA's dark hair hides her face until at the end of the speech she lifts it to smile at her mother. AMANDA's gestures are slow and graceful, almost dancelike, as she comforts the daughter.

This passage works like a piece of silent film, or more accurately, like a non-synchronous sequence in a sound film where instead of a naturalistic track we hear the narrator's voice. As in a film we are moved not by the persons themselves but by the images of persons— images here filtered through Tom's vision. As the two women attain the perspective of memory in his, and thereby in the audience's, mind we are reconciled to the structural deficiency in the play of which the author was himself so clearly aware.

★ ★ ★

Has the injection of filmic elements into Tennessee Williams's dramatic writings been beneficial or harmful? Any borrowings from related arts that can add to the vocabulary of the drama must surely be welcomed—as long as they do not run counter to the basic laws of the stage. The technical facilities of the modern theatre enable the playwright to do certain things not possible before, or at any rate not possible to the same level of perfection; and Tennessee Williams's acute visual and aural sensibility enables him to take full advantage of these facilities, with a consequent enrichment not merely of the form of his drama but of its content as well. But there is a danger in using the incidentals of drama—atmospherics, picture-making, the building up of sound effects—to disguise profound structural weaknesses. Even *The Glass Menagerie* and *A Streetcar Named Desire*, still to this day Williams's best plays and certainly his most successful ones, are not altogether immune to criticism on this score.

Actually, the cinematic qualities in Williams's drama have been getting progressively weaker over the years. We have seen that *The Glass Menagerie* owes its inception to a prior film script. *A Streetcar Named Desire* goes back to an early phase in Williams's career: the seeds of the full-length play can be found in two one-act plays, *The Lady of Larkspur Lotion* and *Portrait of a Madonna*. Similarly, *Ten Blocks on the Camino Real*, written in 1942, foreshadows the later nightmare of the Royal (or Real) Highway. It was in this formative period of his development as a playwright that Williams was most keenly influenced by cinematic ideas. Later plays, such as *Suddenly Last Summer* or *The Night of the Iguana*, have reverted to a much more theatrical mode. His recent play, *The Milk Train Doesn't Stop Here Any More*, is not marked any more by a sense of cinema than most plays being written nowadays. Are these plays any better for their greater theatricality (in the strict sense of the word)? Hardly.

If it is true that cinematic devices may at times have blemished the work of Tennessee Williams, it is also true that they were an integral part of his playwriting at its freshest and most creative.

Note

Biography. Edward Franklin Albee was born in Washington on 12 March, 1928. He was educated at various boarding schools, including the Valley Forge Military Academy, and Choate School from which he graduated. He worked subsequently in New York as a continuity writer for radio music programmes; for Bloomingdale's department store; for G. Schirmer, the music publishers; in an hotel; and, for the period 1955–8, as a messenger boy for the Western Union Telegraph Company.

He began to write for the theatre in 1958. These early plays received their first performances in West Berlin and off-Broadway, and at this time Albee made no secret of his dissatisfaction with the Broadway theatre. With the production of *Who's Afraid of Virginia Woolf?* in 1962, however, Albee achieved a great Broadway success, and has won numerous drama awards. He lives in Greenwich Village.

Works, with place and date of first performance. The Zoo Story (1959; West Berlin); *The Sandbox* (1960; New York); *The Death of Bessie Smith* (1960; West Berlin); these were published together in 1960. *The American Dream* (1961; New York); *Who's Afraid of Virginia Woolf?* (1962; New York); and *Tiny Alice* (1964; New York); all these were published in the year of their first performance. Albee's adaptation of *Ballad of the Sad Cafe* was first published in Boston (1963). Since the following chapter was written, two further plays have been published: *Malcolm* (based on a novel by James Purdy; 1966; New York) and *A Delicate Balance* (1966; New York).

The short early plays were published in England in *The Zoo Story and Other Plays* (1962), and *Who's Afraid* in 1964; quotations in this chapter are from these editions. *Zoo Story* is in the Penguin, *Absurd Drama*, ed. M. Esslin (1965).

Criticism. M. Esslin's *The Theatre of the Absurd* (1962) discusses the work of many dramatists referred to in this chapter; French 'absurd' plays are considered in L. C. Pronko's *Avant-Garde* (1962). R. N. Coe's small book, *Ionesco* (1961), is particularly illuminating on the ideas informing Ionesco's work; his plays are quoted from the collected translations by D. Watson and D. Prouse, published by John Calder (1958, etc.). R. Schechner has a short but radical controversy about *Who's Afraid* with the play's Broadway and West End director, A. Schneider, in *Tulane Drama Review*, 19 (1963). L. Baxandall has an essay on 'The Theatre of Edward Albee' in *Tulane Drama Review*, 28 (1965), and F. T. Driver in *The Reporter* (2 January, 1964).

IX

Albee and the Absurd: 'The American Dream' and 'The Zoo Story'

BRIAN WAY

★

As the American dramatist is often torn between a desire for the apparent security of realism and the temptation to experiment, so in Edward Albee's work, we see a tension between realism and the theatre of the absurd. *The Death of Bessie Smith* is a purely realistic play, and *Who's Afraid of Virginia Woolf?* is, for all its showiness, no more than a cross between sick drawing-room comedy and naturalistic tragedy. *The Zoo Story, The Sandbox* and *The American Dream* are, on the face of it, absurd plays, and yet, if one compares them with the work of Beckett, Ionesco or Pinter, they all retreat from the full implications of the absurd when a certain point is reached. Albee still believes in the validity of reason—that things can be proved, or that events can be shown to have definite meanings—and, unlike Beckett and the others, is scarcely touched by the sense of living in an absurd universe. Interesting and important as his plays are, his compromise seems ultimately a failure of nerve—a concession to those complementary impulses towards cruelty and self-pity which are never far below the surface of his work.

Albee has been attracted to the theatre of the absurd mainly, I think, because of the kind of social criticism he is engaged in. Both *The Zoo Story* and *The American Dream* are savage attacks on the American Way of Life. (I put the phrase in capitals to emphasize that this is not necessarily the way people in America actually live—simply that it is a pattern to which many Americans tend to conform, and, above all, that in the comics, on television, in advertising, and whenever an agency projects the personality of a politician, this is the way in which Americans are assumed and expected to live). Earlier satirists,

189

like Sinclair Lewis and H. L. Mencken, had made their attack through a heightened, but basically realistic, picture of representative men and social habits—Babbitt and the business-world, Elmer Gantry and religion—but this method is no longer appropriate. The American Way of Life has become a political slogan and a commercial vested interest since the war, and is maintained and manipulated through a conscious process of image-building carried out mainly by the mass-media of communication. A would-be social critic of today has to concern himself with these images rather than with representative men, and for the deflation of images realism is not necessarily the most effective artistic convention.

The American Way of Life, in the sense in which I am using the phrase, is a structure of images; and the images, through commercial and political exploitation, have lost much of their meaning. When the Eisenhower family at prayer becomes a televised political stunt, or the family meal an opportunity for advertising frozen foods, the image of the family is shockingly devalued. The deception practised is more complex than a simple lie: it involves a denial of our normal assumptions about evidence—about the relation between the observed world and its inner reality. This is why the techniques of the theatre of the absurd, which is itself preoccupied with the devaluation of language and of images, and with the deceptive nature of appearances, are so ideally suited to the kind of social criticism Albee intends. It is for this reason, too, that he has felt able to use the techniques of the theatre of the absurd, while stopping short of an acceptance of the metaphysic of the absurd upon which the techniques are based. It is possible, clearly, to see the absurd character of certain social situations without believing that the whole of life is absurd. In Albee's case, however, this has meant a restriction of scope, and his plays do not have the poetic quality or imaginative range of *Waiting for Godot*, for instance, or *The Caretaker*, or *Rhinoceros*.

★   ★   ★

The absurd, then, in so far as it interests the student of literature, presents itself for discussion on two levels: first, there is an underlying vision of the universe, a vision memorably expressed by Kafka and the existentialists as well as by the dramatists of the absurd; and secondly, a number of forms of writing and strategies of presentation generated by the underlying vision.

A writer's vision is absurd when the arbitrary, the disconnected, the irrelevant, non-reason, are seen to be the main principle or non-principle of the universe. Pascal, whom existentialists sometimes claim as a precursor, has expressed the vision most succinctly when he writes:

Je m'effraie et m'étonne de me voir ici plutôt que là, car il n'y a point de raison pourquoi ici plutôt que là, pourquoi à présent plutôt que lors.[1]

Jean-Paul Sartre has the most complete and celebrated account of the experience in *La Nausée*, where Roquentin sits on a park bench and stares at the root of a chestnut tree. When, later, he tries to characterize the experience, the word Absurdity comes to him:

Un geste, un événement dans le petit monde calorié des hommes n'est jamais absurde que relativement: par rapport aux circonstances qui l'accompagnent. Les discours d'un fou, par exemple, sont absurdes par rapport à la situation où il se trouve mais non par rapport à son délire. Mais moi, tout à l'heure, j'ai fait l'expérience de l'absolu: l'absolu ou l'absurde. Cette racine, il n'y avait rien par rapport à quoi elle ne fût absurde . . . Absurde: par rapport aux cailloux, aux touffes d'herbe jaune, à la boue sèche, à l'arbre, au ciel, aux bancs verts. Absurde, irréductible; rien—pas même un délire profond et secret de la nature—ne pouvait l'expliquer. Évidemment je ne savais pas tout, je n'avais pas vu le germe se développer ni l'arbre croître. Mais devant cette grosse patte rugueuse, ni l'ignorance ni le savoir n'avait d'importance: le monde des explications et des raisons n'est pas celui de l'existence. J'avais beau répéter: 'C'est une racine'—ça ne prenait plus. Je voyais bien qu'on ne pouvait pas passer de sa fonction de racine, de pompe aspirante, à *ça*, à cette peau dure et compacte de phoque, à cet aspect huileux, calleux, entêté. La fonction n'expliquait rien: elle permettait de comprendre en gros ce que c'était qu'une racine, mais pas du tout *celle-ci*.[2]

[1] 'I am frightened and amazed to see myself here rather than there, since there is no reason at all why "here" rather than "there", why "now" rather than "then".' Quoted by P. Foulquié, *L'Existentialisme* (Paris, 1952), p. 39.

[2] 'A gesture, an event, in the cosy little world of men is never absurd except relatively: in relation to the circumstances which accompany it. The words of a madman, for example, are only absurd in relation to the situation he is in, but not in relation to his delirium. But I, just now, experienced the absolute: the absolute or the absurd. There was nothing in relation to which this root was not absurd . . . Absurd: in relation to the pebbles, the tufts of yellow grass, the dry mud, the tree, the sky, the green benches. Absurd, irreducible: nothing—not

Both Pascal and Sartre describe vividly the arbitrary, dislocated quality of experience—the sense of living in a world where nothing has any fundamental connection with anything else. Sartre goes a stage further when he exposes the irrelevance and the futility of reason—the reason in which the naturalist writer has supreme faith—and the completely illusory nature of rational explorations. When one says to oneself 'It's a root' and continues in a generalizing abstracting way to explain to oneself what it is that a root does in relation to the tree and the earth, one is deceiving oneself if one imagines that the process brings one any nearer to understanding *that*—that object which is unique, stubborn (entêté), and, as Roquentin says a little later, 'beneath any possible explanation' ('au-dessous de toute explication'). There is no transition from the world of explanations to the world of the absurd; from the notion that a root is a suction pump to the thing itself—the bark tough and close as a seal's skin, the greasy stubborn horny thing before Roquentin's eyes.

A writer for whom experiences are as dislocated and unrelated as this must clearly deny the logic of cause and effect, the logic on which naturalistic drama is based. Sartre expresses this denial in a particularly interesting way in the sequence of reflections from which I have already quoted:

> Des arbres, des piliers bleu de nuit, le râle heureux d'une fontaine, des odeurs vivantes, des petits brouillards de chaleur qui flottait dans l'air froid, un homme roux qui digérait sur un banc: toutes ces somnolences, toutes ces digestions prises ensemble offraient un aspect vaguement comique. Comique . . . non: ça n'allait pas jusque-là, rien de ce qui existe ne peut être comique; c'était comme une analogie flottante, presque insaisissable avec certaines situations de vaudeville.[3]

---

even a profound secret delirium of nature—could explain it. Obviously I did not know everything, I had not seen the seed develop, nor the tree grow. But in front of this great gnarled foot, neither ignorance nor knowledge had any importance: the world of explanations and reasons is not that of existence . . . It was useless for me to repeat: "It is a root"—that didn't fit any longer. I saw very well that one could not move from its function as a root, as a suction pump, *to that*, to that tough close seal's skin, to that greasy, horny, stubborn appearance. Its function explained nothing: it allowed one to understand in a general way what a root was, but not at all what *this* was' (*La Nausée* (Paris, 1942), pp. 168–9).

[3] 'Trees, midnight blue pillars, the happy chatter of a fountain, vivid scents, light warm vapours floating in the cold air, a red-haired man digesting his lunch

'Comique . . . non . . . une analogie flottante . . . avec certaines situations de vaudeville'—incidents, that is, which have the logic of music-
hall slapstick, but which are not necessarily funny. In music-hall acts
and in the slapstick situations of the early cinema we see constantly this
denial of the logic of cause and effect on which Sartre's analogy is
based: in *City Lights* a statue is being unveiled; we expect a dignified
climax to a public ceremony, but instead we find Chaplin cradled in
the statue's arms making frantic efforts to climb down. Similarly in
Ionesco's *Rhinoceros*, in which the citizens of a French provincial town
are being rapidly transformed into rhinoceroses, the telephone rings,
and Bérenger picks it up, with certain reasonable expectations as to
whom his correspondent will be:

BÉRENGER. Perhaps the authorities have decided to take action at
    last; maybe they're ringing to ask our help in whatever measures
    they've decided to adopt.
DAISY. I'd be surprised if it was them.
[*The telephone rings again.*]
BÉRENGER. It is the authorities, I tell you, I recognize the ring—a
    long-drawn-out ring, I can't ignore an appeal from them. It can't
    be anyone else. [*He picks up the receiver.*] Hallo? [*Trumpetings are
    heard coming from the receiver.*] You hear that? Trumpeting! Listen!
[*Daisy puts the telephone to her ear, is shocked by the sound, quickly
replaces the receiver.*]
DAISY [*frightened*]. What's going on?
BÉRENGER. They're playing jokes now.
DAISY. Jokes in bad taste!

                                                        (p. 99)

Bérenger, an inveterate believer in the logic of cause and effect, a man
who is certain he lives in a meaningful universe, picks up the telephone
and instead of the reassuring voice of the authorities hears the trumpet-
ing of rhinoceroses. It is indeed, as Daisy says, a joke in bad taste—
'Comique . . . non . . . une analogie flottante . . . avec certaines
situations de vaudeville.' There could be no more vivid dramatic
instance of what it means to live in an absurd universe.

---

on a bench: all this drowsing and digestion taken as a whole had a vaguely
comic aspect. Comic . . . no, it didn't go quite as far as that, nothing which
exists can be comic; it was like a fleeting analogy, almost impossible to grasp,
with certain music-hall situations' (*La Nausée* (Paris, 1942), p. 167).

The absurdist habit of mind, then, is overwhelmingly intellectualist, metaphysical even. It constantly asks the question 'What is the meaning of life?', and finds as an answer, 'There is no meaning', or, 'We do not know', a discovery which may be horrifying or comic, or both. The theatre of the absurd has responded to this metaphysic by evolving new dramatic forms,[4] and the second stage of my analysis of the absurd will be an examination of these.

For the playwright who accepts without reservations that he is living in an absurd universe, the loss of faith in reason which is at the heart of this vision and the conviction that the rational exploration of experi-ence is a form of self-deception, imply a rejection of those theatrical conventions which reflect a belief in reason. Characters with fixed identities; events which have a definite meaning; plots which assume the validity of cause and effect; dénouements which offer themselves as complete resolutions of the questions raised by the play; and language which claims to mean what it says—none of these can be said to be appropriate means for expressing the dislocated nature of experience in an absurd world. In terms of formal experiment, then, the theatre of the absurd represents a search for images of non-reason.

★   ★   ★

Albee has used these images of non-reason in his attack on the American Way of Life without, as I have said, accepting the underlying vision which generated them. His work belongs to the second level of the theatre of the absurd: it shows a brilliantly inventive sense of what can be done with the techniques, but stops short of the metaphysic which makes the techniques completely meaningful. Nevertheless, *The American Dream* and *The Zoo Story* are the most exciting produc-tions of the American theatre in the last fifteen years, and I propose to analyse them in detail in such a way as to bring out particularly what they have in common with other absurd plays and where they diverge from them.

In *The American Dream* (1961), Albee is closer to Ionesco than to any other dramatist. Like Ionesco, he sees the absurd localized most sharply in conventions of social behaviour. For both dramatists, the normal currency of social intercourse—of hospitality, or courtesy, or desultory

[4] Perhaps it would be more accurate to say that it is an attempt to bring together a number of old theatrical devices in a new way; see 'The Tradition of the Absurd' in Esslin, pp. 233–89.

chat—has lost its meaning, and this 'devaluation of language', to use Martin Esslin's invaluable phrase, is an index for them of the vacuity of the social life represented. The inane civilities exchanged by the Smiths and the Martins in *The Bald Prima Donna* enact the complete absence of human contact which is the reality beneath the appearance of communication. We see similar effects in *The American Dream* in the opening exchanges:

DADDY. Uh . . . Mrs. Barker, is it? Won't you sit down?
MRS. BARKER. I don't mind if I do.
MOMMY. Would you like a cigarette, and a drink, and would you like to cross your legs?
MRS. BARKER. You forget yourself, Mommy; I'm a professional woman. But I will cross my legs.
DADDY. Yes, make yourself comfortable.
MRS. BARKER. I don't mind if I do. (p. 28)

Ionesco and Albee use this method of exposing the essential meaninglessness of most middle-class language and gesture as a basis for much wider effects than the mere deflation of certain speech-habits. In Ionesco, particularly, it becomes a major principle of dramatic construction. He subjects conventional patterns of behaviour, the clichés of which much everyday speech is entirely composed, and the most complacent and unthinking of our normal assumptions and attitudes, to a disturbing shift of perspective: he places them in grotesque situations where they are ludicrously inappropriate, and their meaninglessness is stripped bare. *Amédée* (1954) is probably his most elaborate exercise in this technique. Amédée and Madeleine Buccinioni, a middle-aged bourgeois couple, have shut themselves up in their Paris apartment for fifteen years in order to conceal the corpse of a man Amédée may have murdered. The corpse has grown a white beard and long fingernails and toenails over the years, but during Act I, its rate of growth is suddenly accelerated, presenting Amédée and Madeleine with an acute problem:

MADELEINE. The neighbours must have heard.
AMÉDÉE [*stopping*]. They *may* not have done. [*Short silence.*] There's not a sound from them! . . . Besides, at this time of day . . .
MADELEINE. They must have heard something. They're not all deaf . . .
AMÉDÉE. Not *all* of them, they couldn't be. But as I say, at this time of day . . .

MADELEINE. What could we tell them?

AMÉDÉE. We could say it was the postman!

MADELEINE [*turning her back to the audience and looking towards the rear window*]. It was the postman who did it! It was the p-o-stman! [*To* AMÉDÉE]. Will they believe us? The postman must have gone, by now.

AMÉDÉE. All the better. [*Loudly shouting to the rear of the stage.*] It was the p-o-stman!

MADELEINE.⎱ It was the p-o-stman! The p-o-stman!
AMÉDÉE. ⎰

[*They stop shouting, and the echo is heard.*]

ECHO. The p-o-stman! The p-o-stman! P-o-stman! O-o-stman!

AMÉDÉE [*he and* MADELEINE *both turning to face the audience*]. You see, even the echo is repeating it.

MADELEINE. Perhaps it isn't the echo!

AMÉDÉE. It strengthens our case, anyhow. It's an alibi! . . . Let's sit down.

MADELEINE [*sitting down*]. Life's really getting impossible. Where are we to find new window-panes?

[*Suddenly, from the adjoining room, a violent bang is heard against the wall;* AMÉDÉE, *who was about to sit down, stands up again, his gaze rivetted on the left of the stage;* MADELEINE *does the same.*]

MADELEINE [*uttering a cry*]. Ah!

AMÉDÉE [*distractedly*]. Keep calm, keep calm!

[*The left-hand door gradually gives way, as though under steady pressure.*]

MADELEINE [*not far from fainting, but still standing, cries out again*]. Ah, Heaven help us!

[*Then* AMÉDÉE *and* MADELEINE, *dumb with terror, watch two enormous feet slide slowly in through the open door and advance about eighteen inches on to the stage.*]

MADELEINE. Look!

[*This is naturally an anguished cry, yet there should be a certain restraint about it; it should, of course, convey fear, but above all, irritation. This is an embarrassing situation, but it should not seem at all unusual, and the actors should play this scene quite naturally. It is a 'nasty blow' of course, an extremely 'nasty blow', but no worse than that.*]   (pp. 176–8)

The dialogue is composed entirely of clichés, and is dominated by mundane bourgeois attitudes—chiefly the anxiety to preserve appearances before neighbours, and the desperate determination to act as if everything were normal. (Ionesco's final stage direction, of course, underlines this.) As so often in absurd drama, the language and the action contradict each other. The grotesque horror of the situation is played off against the ludicrous pretence at maintaining a sense of the ordinary suggested by the language. When middle-class clichés and stock attitudes are shown to be so evidently meaningless in this situation, one is directed to the conclusion that they are in fact meaningless in all situations, and that only the blindness of habit conceals this fact from us.

Albee develops the situation in *The American Dream* along similar lines. He sees the American Way of Life as one in which normal human feelings and relationships have been deprived of meaning. The gestures of love, sexual attraction, parental affection, family feeling and hospitality remain, but the actual feelings which would give the gestures meaning have gone. To show this in sharp dramatic terms, Albee constructs a situation of gestures which are normally supposed to have meaning but, as transposed by him, are seen to have none. As soon as the family tableau of Mommy and Daddy, the overtly homey middle-aged couple, and Grandma, their apparent tribute to the duty of caring for the aged, is presented, we see what Albee is doing:

MOMMY. We were very poor! But then I married you, Daddy, and now we're very rich.

DADDY. Grandma isn't rich.

MOMMY. No, but you've been so good to Grandma she feels rich. She doesn't know you'd like to put her in a nursing home.

DADDY. I wouldn't!

MOMMY. Well, heaven knows *I* would! I can't stand it, watching her do the cooking and the housework, polishing the silver, moving the furniture. . . .

DADDY. She likes to do that. She says it's the least she can do to earn her keep.

MOMMY. Well, she's right. You can't live off people . . . I have a right to live off you because I married you, and because I used to let you get on top of me and bump your uglies; and I have a right to all your money when you die. And when you do, Grandma and I can live by ourselves . . . if she's still here. Unless you have her put away in a nursing home.

DADDY. I have no intention of putting her in a nursing home.

MOMMY. Well, I wish somebody would do something with her!

DADDY. At any rate you're very well provided for.

MOMMY. You're my sweet Daddy; that's very nice.

DADDY. I love my Mommy.   (pp. 21–2)

The characters are isolated from each other in little worlds of selfishness, impotence and lovelessness, and all warmth of human contact is
lost. It would be inaccurate to say that the gestures of love and connection ('You're my sweet Daddy'—'I love my Mommy') are deflated;
their meaninglessness is exposed by tagging them on as afterthoughts
to phases of the action where they are—as here—ludicrously in-
applicable.

This method of scene-construction determines not only the local
effects of *The American Dream*, but the major patterns of the play.
Albee is disturbed and agonized by the extent of the dislocation of
people's relationships and the imprisoning isolation of which these
scenes are images. The play's central image of this failure of human
feeling and contact is sterility—the inability to beget or bear a child—
and as its title suggests, Albee tries to give the image the widest possible
social reference. He implies that the sterility which the audience sees in
his characters is typical of the society as a whole, and is created and
perpetuated by the society. For him, the American Way of Life
systematically eliminates, in the name of parental care, and social and
moral concern, every trace of natural human feeling and every potenti-
ality for warm human contact from those who have to live by it, and
especially from the young.

When Mommy, Daddy and Grandma, and the quality of their lives,
have been firmly established, Mrs. Barker, a representative of the
Bye-Bye Adoption Service, calls on them. She forgets why she has
called (a common motif in absurd plays, underlining the arbitrariness
and irrelevance of all action in an absurd world, though little more
than a gimmick here). Grandma, to help her, gives her a 'hint'—the
story of 'a man very much like Daddy, and a woman very much like
Mommy', and 'a dear lady' very much like Mrs. Barker. It is a story
of individual sterility:

> The woman who was very much like Mommy, said that she and
> the man who was very much like Daddy had never been blessed
> with anything very much like a bumble of joy . . .
> . . . she said that they wanted a bumble of their own, but that the
> man, who was very much like Daddy, couldn't have a bumble; and
> the man, who was very much like Daddy, said that yes, they had
> wanted a bumble of their own, but that the woman, who was very

much like Mommy, couldn't have one and that now they wanted
to buy something very much like a bumble.   (p. 40)

It is also a story of that collective sterility which eliminates natural
impulses in others. Mommy and Daddy buy 'a bumble of joy', and its
upbringing is a series of mutilations at their hands:

GRANDMA. . . . *then*, it began to develop an interest in its you-know-
what.

MRS. BARKER. In its you-know-what! Well! I hope they cut its
hands off at the wrists!

GRANDMA. Well, yes, they did that eventually. But first, they cut off
its you-know-what.

MRS. BARKER. A much better idea!

GRANDMA. That's what they thought. But after they cut off its you-
know-what, it *still* put its hands under the covers, *looking* for its
you-know-what. So, finally, they had to cut off its hands at the
wrists.   (pp. 40–1)

The child's eyes are gouged out, it is castrated, its hands are cut off,
its tongue is cut out, and finally it dies. In this brilliant sequence of
dramatic writing, Albee has given us a fable of his society, where all
the capabilities for connection—eyes to see, sexual organs with which
to love, hands to touch, and tongue to speak—are destroyed, and the
victim of the socializing processes of the American Way of Life,
humanly speaking, dies. And it is all done in the name of affection and
care. Once again, the gestures of human contact survive grotesquely
in the coyness with which the sexual act and the begetting and rearing
of children are described ('being blessed with a bumble of joy', 'its
you-know-what'), and the gestures are seen to be hideously and
mockingly at odds with the reality.

Towards the end of the play, the victim himself appears—the 'twin'
of 'the bumble of joy'. He is a young man with all the external marks
of youth and vitality, handsome, muscular and self-confident. Grandma recognizes in him immediately the American Dream. But just as
the gestures of parental love have been only a sham, his outwardly
vigorous youthful appearance is only a shell. His life is a terrible
emptiness, a series of deprivations identical with the mutilations
practised on his 'twin' brother:

I don't know what became of my brother . . . to the rest of myself
. . . except that, from time to time, in the years that have passed, I

have suffered losses . . . that I can't explain. A fall from grace . . . a departure of innocence . . . loss . . . loss. . . . Once . . . it was as if all at once my heart . . . became numb . . . almost as though I . . . almost as though . . . just like that . . . it had been wrenched from my body . . . and from that time I have been unable to love . . .

And there is more . . . there are more losses, but it all comes down to this: I no longer have the capacity to feel anything. I have no emotions. I have been drained, torn asunder . . . disembowelled. I have, now, only my person . . . my body, my face. I use what I have . . . I let people love me . . . I accept the syntax around me, for while I cannot relate . . . I know I must be related *to* . . . (pp. 50–1)

This moving speech is one of those moments of total illumination in absurd drama (Aston's account of his experiences in the psychiatric ward in *The Caretaker* is the finest example) where a character, for a moment, sees the entire hopelessness and confusion of his existence before lapsing once more into the 'syntax around' him. The Young Man has to accept that syntax—the meaningless gestures of human affection and contact—when he is adopted, or re-adopted, by Mommy and Daddy. While they celebrate with Sauterne, Grandma observes sardonically from the wings: 'Well, I guess that just about wraps it up. I mean, for better or worse, this is a comedy . . .' The bad Sauterne is drunk, and sterility, impotence, lovelessness and disconnection are masked with the gestures of celebration, conviviality and family-love, suggesting as they do all that is lacking—the physical warmth of sex and parenthood, and the meaningfulness of people being together. Only the gestures remain, these gestures which have been simultaneously canonized and deprived of meaning by the publicists of the American Way of Life: the politicians, the admen, the columnists and the TV commentators.

It is significant that the only character in *The American Dream* with any vitality or attractiveness is Grandma—and she is 'rural', from an older way of life. The way in which she is juxtaposed against the Young Man who is the American Dream seems to symbolize a society in which the natural order of life has been reversed, in which the younger one is the less chance one has of being alive.

These patterns and images occur elsewhere in Albee's work. His sense of human isolation and despair is the central preoccupation of *The Death of Bessie Smith* (a bad play, it seems to me), and in *The Sandbox*, which parallels the situation of *The American Dream* most interestingly, though on too cramped a stage. The image of sterility is very prominent in *Who's Afraid of Virginia Woolf?*, but is used there much less effectively than in *The American Dream*. Apart from its spectacular ability to amuse and shock, *Virginia Woolf* has a certain emptiness—no incident or image in it has reference to anything wider than the neuroses of its characters.

His first play, *The Zoo Story* (1959), however, contains some very fine dramatic writing. Again it is an exploration of the farce and the agony of human isolation. When the play opens, Peter, a prosperous youngish man in the publishing business, is reading on a bench in Central Park, New York. Jerry, who describes himself as a 'permanent transient', insists on talking to Peter. Peter tries to brush him off, to get on with his reading, but Jerry forces Peter to confront him fully as a human being, working first on his curiosity, and then provoking him by insults and blows. When Peter is sufficiently enraged, they fight. Jerry, in an improbable and sentimental catastrophe, puts a knife in Peter's hand and impales himself on it. He succeeds in forcing Peter out from behind the shelter of his possessions (symbolized by the park bench over which they ostensibly fight) and his middle-class complacency, into a real confrontation with the isolation and despair of the human condition. If Jerry is a 'permanent transient', Peter is, after the killing, at least 'dispossessed':

> You won't be coming back here any more, Peter; you've been dispossessed. You've lost your bench, but you've defended your honor. (p. 142)

And Jerry, in turn, even if it has cost him his life, has at last made 'contact' with another being.

It is because human isolation is so great, and because the 'contact' which would end it is so formidably difficult to obtain, that Jerry went to the zoo:

> Now I'll let you in on what happened at the zoo; but first, I should tell you why I went to the zoo. I went to the zoo to find out more about the way people exist with animals, and the way animals exist with each other, and with people too. It probably wasn't a fair test, what with everyone separated by bars from everyone else, the animals for the most part from each other, and always the people from the animals. But if it's a zoo, that's the way it is. (p. 135)

The entire human condition, for Jerry, is a zoo story of people (and animals) forever separated by bars.

In its finest scene, the long speech in which Jerry describes his attempt to form a relationship with his landlady's dog, *The Zoo Story* offers a superb example of what I call pseudo-crisis—the second pattern of absurd writing that is central to Albee's work. In classic drama, crisis is one of the most important means by which the action is significantly advanced. In *Othello*, for instance, when Iago tells Othello that he has seen Desdemona's handkerchief in Cassio's hands, a whole complex of tensions is brought to a head, and after this crisis, the catastrophe is measurably nearer, and Othello is demonstrably a stage further on his course of violence and madness. In the absurd play, on the other hand, what I call a pseudo-crisis occurs when a similar complex of tensions is brought to a head without resolving anything, without contributing to any development or progression, serving in fact to demonstrate that nothing as meaningful as progression or development can occur, emphasizing that complexity and tension are permanent and unresolvable elements of a world of confusion. Lucky's speech in *Waiting for Godot* is perhaps the most elaborate and extreme occurrence. Harold Pinter's work, too, is full of pseudo-crisis, the funniest instance, perhaps, being Davies's account of his visit to the monastery at Luton in search of boots (*The Caretaker*).

Jerry's long speech in *The Zoo Story* has all the marks of pseudo-crisis. It is used here to explore Albee's preoccupation with man's failure to make contact with others, and the drying up of those feelings that should provide connection. Jerry lives in a rooming-house where the landlady's dog attacks him every time he comes in. He is fascinated by the dog's hatred; he responds to it with obsessive force: it is a challenge—the dog is intensely concerned about him and if he can meet the challenge he may be able to create out of it the contact he is looking for. He decides that first he will try to kill the dog with kindness, and if that fails he will simply kill it. He feeds it hamburgers; its animosity doesn't diminish, and so, at the climax of this pseudo-crisis— a farcical and yet poignant parody of the love-hate situation in romantic fiction—he gives the dog a poisoned hamburger. Nothing really happens, nothing is resolved. The dog doesn't die, nor does it come to love Jerry; for a moment Jerry and the dog look at each other, but then the dog withdraws from contact with him; even the pressure of its hatred has gone—'We neither love nor hurt because we do not try to reach each other,' Jerry says, trying to express the agony of his need:

I loved the dog now, and I wanted him to love me. I had tried to love and I had tried to kill, and both had been unsuccessful by themselves. . . . I hoped that the dog would understand.
. . . it's just that if you can't deal with people, you have to make a start somewhere. WITH ANIMALS! (*much faster now, and like a conspirator*) . . . Don't you see? A person has to have some way of dealing with SOMETHING. If not with people . . . SOMETHING. With a bed, with a cockroach, with a mirror . . . no, that's too hard, that's one of the last steps. With a cockroach, with a . . . with a . . . with a carpet, with a roll of toilet paper . . . no, not that either . . . that's a mirror, too; always check bleeding. You see how hard it is to find things? With a street corner, and too many lights, all colours reflecting on the oily-wet streets . . . with a wisp of smoke, a wisp . . . of smoke . . . with . . . with . . . with love, with vomiting, with crying, with fury because the pretty little ladies aren't pretty little ladies, with making money with your body which is an act of love and I could prove it, with howling because you're alive; with God. How about that? WITH GOD WHO IS A COLOURED QUEEN WHO WEARS A KIMONO AND PLUCKS HIS EYEBROWS, WHO IS A WOMAN WHO CRIES WITH DETERMINATION BEHIND HER CLOSED DOOR . . . with God, who, I'm told, turned his back on the whole thing some time ago . . . with . . . some day, with people . . . (JERRY *sighs the next word heavily*) People. With an idea; a concept. And where better, where ever better in this humiliating excuse for a jail, where better to communicate one single, simple-minded idea than in an entrance-hall? Where? It would be a START! Where better to make a beginning . . . to understand and just possibly be understood . . . than with . . . than with A DOG. Just that; a dog . . . A dog.

(pp. 130–2)

The dramatic structure of this part of Jerry's speech reflects very closely the rhythms of pseudo-crisis—the excitement, the tensions, rising to the shouted climax ('WITH GOD WHO IS . . .'), and then slipping away into the lax despairing tempo of its inconclusive end ('with . . . some day, with people'). The hopelessness of this is quickly recognized, and Jerry reverts to his attempt with the dog, but this, too, has failed and proved nothing. In this final downward curve of the pseudo-crisis everything is conditional and hypothetical ('It would be A START! Where better to make a beginning . . . to understand, and just possibly be understood . . .').

In this early play, there is an attempt, too, to relate Jerry's agony to the wider social pattern—to see it as a product of the American Way of Life:

> I am a *permanent transient*, and my home is in the sickening rooming-houses on the West Side of New York City, which is the greatest city in the world. Amen.   (p. 133)

In spite of the bitter force of this, however, it is clear that the impulse of social criticism has only been very partially translated into dramatic terms. Jerry's outburst here tells the audience how to react; it is almost a piece of editorializing, and doesn't have the persuasiveness of art, the sense that ideas have become vision and are being enacted.

At such moments in *The Zoo Story*, and most of all, of course, at the moment of Jerry's melodramatic and sentimental death, we are left with a sense of dissatisfaction whose root causes are to be found in that compromise with the experimental theatre that seems to me so characteristic of American dramatists. The action and the dialogue are dislocated, arbitrary and absurd (pre-eminently in Jerry's story of the dog) up to the moment of Jerry's death, and then all the traditional assumptions of naturalism flood back into the play. It is postulated, quite as firmly as in any Ibsen social drama, that a catastrophe is also a resolution of the situation of the play, and that events, however obscure, ultimately have a definite and unambiguous meaning. Jerry spends his dying breath telling us what the play means as explicitly as does Lona Hessel at the end of *Pillars of Society*. This sudden reversion to a faith in the validity of rational explanations makes previous events in the play seem arbitrary in a wholly unjustifiable way: they can no longer be seen as appropriate symbols of life in an absurd universe. The slightest hint that events in an absurd play are amenable to everyday explanation is completely destructive of their dramatic effectiveness. If it were possible to say of Vladimir and Estragon, or of Davies, that they are crazy bums who should be locked up, *Waiting for Godot* and *The Caretaker* would be ruined. In spite of some striking effects, it is possible to entertain this suspicion about Jerry, and it is largely because of this misguided attempt to exploit the advantages both of the theatre of the absurd and of realism, that *The Zoo Story* misses the greatness which at times seems so nearly within its grasp.

The American Dream does not show so straightforward an evasion of the absurd as *The Zoo Story*, but it lacks even more completely the metaphysical dimension. One can perhaps best begin accounting for its limitations by noting a distinction which Martin Esslin makes most perceptively: first there is—

> . . . the experience that Ionesco expresses in plays like *The Bald Prima Donna* or *The Chairs*, Adamov in *La Parodie*, or N. F. Simpson in *A Resounding Tinkle*. It represents the satirical, parodistic aspect of the Theatre of the Absurd, its social criticism, its pillorying of an inauthentic, petty society. This may be the most easily accessible, and therefore most widely recognized, message of the Theatre of the Absurd, but it is far from being its most essential or most significant feature.
> Behind the satirical exposure of the absurdity of inauthentic ways of life, the Theatre of the Absurd is facing up to a deeper layer of absurdity—the absurdity of the human condition itself in a world where the decline of religious belief has deprived man of certainties.
>
> (pp. 291–2)

The American Dream is effective only within the limits of the first category. It is too exclusively and merely a satire of American middle-class aspirations and self-deceptions. It is, above all, a play about Other People, not about ourselves: when we laugh at Mommy and Daddy, we are laughing at emotional and sexual failures which we do not recognize as our own and in which we refuse to be implicated, whereas when we laugh at Davies, or at Vladimir and Estragon, we are laughing at our own illusions and recognizing our own acts of hubris, self-deception and failure. Since *The American Dream* doesn't implicate us, it never becomes tragic. Harold Pinter has said of his own play:

> As far as I am concerned *The Caretaker* is funny up to a point. Beyond that point it ceases to be funny, and it was because of that point that I wrote it.[5]

Albee never reached this point except perhaps for the brief moment I have noted where the Young Man's sense of loss is met with Grandma's compassion. But we do not otherwise have to regard the characters—certainly not Mommy and Daddy—as tragic or even terrifying: they enact for us a certain attitude to America in 1960; they do not go beyond it to tell us anything about the human condition.

In one important sense, *The American Dream* does not belong even to the 'satirical, parodistic' category of absurd plays. It is, like *The Zoo Story*, a play which reaches a definite conclusion and which implicitly

[5] Letter to *Sunday Times* (14 August, 1960); quoted Esslin, p. 218.

claims that its events have an unambiguous meaning. Grandma's 'hint' to Mrs. Barker is a fable of almost diagrammatic directness and simplicity; by contrast, the Fireman's fables in *The Bald Prima Donna* are absurd parodies, satirizing the assumption that a tale has a 'moral', and further, undermining our confidence in the kind of popular wisdom represented by the morals of Aesop's fables.

Above all, at the end of *The American Dream*, Grandma can tell the audience:

Well, I guess that just about wraps it up. I mean, for better or worse, this is a comedy, and I don't think we'd better go any further. No, definitely not. So let's leave things as they are right now . . . while everybody's happy . . . while everybody's got what he wants . . . or everybody's got what he thinks he wants. Good night, dears.

Her remark, 'Well, I guess that just about wraps it up', is ironical only in the most external sense—in the sense that Mommy and Daddy and the Young Man and Mrs. Barker, who have all just drunk 'To satisfaction', are in for some unpleasant surprises. As far as Grandma and the audience are concerned the situation really is wrapped up, and the play has proved its point as self-consciously as any theorem. Again, *The Bald Prima Donna* is a significant contrast, ending not with a proof but returning in a circle to the point at which it began.

It is only when one compares *The American Dream* with the greatest absurd plays that the real damage done by this compromise between reason and the absurd can be fully reckoned. In the first place, many of the local effects seem to be, in retrospect, merely tricks. The way in which it handles argument will illustrate what I mean. The metaphysic of the absurd, as I have said, involves a loss of faith in reason and in the validity of rational explorations of experience, and one of the most characteristic forms of writing of the absurd theatre, developed to represent this on the stage, is the systematic pursuit of the irrelevant. Absurd plays are full of arguments which lead nowhere, or which parody the processes of logic, or which are conducted from ludicrous premisses. At the beginning of *The American Dream* Mommy's account of her argument in the department store as to whether her hat was beige or wheat-coloured is a clear instance of this. But it does not symbolize anything deeper: far from being an index of a world in which everything is too uncertain to be settled by argument, it takes its place in a play which, from its determination to prove a point, is naïvely confident in the power of argument. It therefore seems, in retrospect, no more than a trick to get the play started. By comparison, the argument in *Rhinoceros*, as to whether the animals which charged down the street had one horn or two, is funnier and also infinitely more disturbing: it represents the last feeble efforts of ordinary men to cling to their reassuring certitudes as their world founders into chaos, and, as they themselves, through turning into rhinoceroses, are about to lose their very identities. Albee's work lacks this imaginative dimension, to say nothing of the compassion, horror and despair, implicit in the periodic speculations of Vladimir and Estragon on the nature of Godot.

But it is in dénouements, as I have pointed out, that Albee diverges most clearly from the absurd, and it is here that the divergence does him most harm. His plays are tightly 'wrapped up', where the best absurd plays leave us with an extended sense of the uncertainties of our condition. The quiet heartrending close of *Waiting for Godot*—

VLADIMIR. Well, shall we go?
ESTRAGON. Yes, let's go.
They do not move.

—or the end of *The Caretaker*, where Davies and Aston look ahead into their bleak future, a future in which Davies will never 'get settled down and fixed up', and in which Aston will never build his shed, have all the dramatic and poetic power Albee lacks. Perhaps the most relevant comparison is with the lyrical closing moments of *Amédée*, where Amédée, as he floats up into the sky, makes a speech to the crowd:

Ladies and Gentlemen . . . Please don't think . . . I should like to stay . . . stay with my feet on the ground . . . It's against my will . . . I don't want to get carried away . . . I'm all for progress, I like to be of use to my fellow men . . . I believe in social realism . . .

As well as being delightfully comic, Amédée's flight into space even while he utters all the positivist nostrums by which man tries to keep his feet on the ground, is an exquisite poetic image, where Albee's narrow cocksureness is poetically dead.

When all these limitations of scope have been noted, however, it is only fair that one should return to an assertion of the importance of Albee's good qualities in the American theatre. If it is true that he inhabits a finite world, he does so with brilliance, inventiveness, intelligence and moral courage.

Note

Editions. The principal dramatic works of the playwrights considered in this chapter are:

Paddy Chayefsky: *'Marty'* (in R. E. Sheratsky and J. L. Reilly, *The Lively Arts* (1964); *The Middle of the Night* (1957); *The Tenth Man* (1960); *Gideon* (1960); and *The Passion of Joseph D.* (1964)—the last four published by Random House, New York.

Frank Gilroy: *Who'll Save the Plowboy?* (1962) and *The Subject was Roses* (1965), both from Random House which has also published *about those roses or How not to Produce a play and succeed* (1965) which contains production notes for the play.

William Hanley: *Mrs. Dally Has a Lover and other plays* (Dial Press, 1963); and *Slow Dance on the Killing Ground* (Random House, 1964).

Murray Schisgal: *'The Typists' and 'The Tiger'* (Coward-McCann, New York, 1963; London ed., Cape, 1964); and *Luv* (Coward-McCann, 1965).

For Albee, see the prefatory note to Chapter IX.

Of further interest for those seeking recent plays are the paperback anthologies, R. Corrigan's *New American Plays* (1965) and E. Parone's *The New American Theatre* (1965).

Criticism. See prefatory Note for Chapters I and III.

X

Today's Dramatists

RICHARD A. DUPREY

★

BY surveying a few writers one can see something of the general situation of today's dramatist. We can further see the range of his undertakings as he provides us with an interestingly varied approach to life and to the theatre which mirrors it. Those who seem to afford us the best comprehensive picture of today's situation are Edward Albee, Paddy Chayefsky, Murray Shisgal, William Hanley and Frank Gilroy. In this group too we also see, either in the man or his apparent influence, some hint as to the direction of future development in our theatre.

Beyond this group of five, there are surely other playwrights who have shown promise or who have achieved a degree of accomplishment that could warrant their inclusion in such a discussion. For example, Le Roi Jones, the young Negro playwright, has elicited a great measure of comment, favourable and otherwise, with his two short plays, *The Toilet* and *Dutchman*. They're bitter plays, etched in acid, which dare to use words hitherto excluded from our stage vocabulary. If for no other reason, it might seem desirable to mention Jones in this chapter for his part in returning the hard-core shocking word to the stage.

Le Roi Jones is quite talented as a writer. It's ridiculous to write him off as a mere user of scatalogical terms for shock effect. His choice of topic precludes such an oversimplification. In an age of racial tumult, when charity and justice have become such an issue, Jones and James Baldwin, who fashioned *Blues For Mister Charlie* for the stage, are fascinating for whatever insight they bring to one of our nation's most critical problems. Such is not, however, so much a consideration of their craft as it is a question of sociological attitude. As playwrights, despite the fascinating techniques they may borrow, we can find their technical attitudes, their areas of style, their additions to the accepted vocabulary of our stage, better demonstrated in the previously mentioned quintet.

Looking then in an entirely different direction, how can one fail to mention, at least by name, Neil Simon and Jean Kerr? Though neither has done anything of note beyond the superficial stand-up kind of humour represented in *Come Blow Your Horn* and *Barefoot in the Park* for Simon, and *Mary, Mary* and *Poor Richard* for Mrs. Kerr, their Broadway successes qualify them for notice as we peruse the slim roster of playwrights. One can, with careful picking, find a measure of reasonably worthwhile social comment in their work: Simon has written tellingly about today's secular American Jewry and Jean Kerr manifests a number of wise insights on marriage and intellectualism.

Continuing on in a hurried recitation of playwrights who might have been included, there's the brilliant deviser of play titles, Arthur Kopit, who strains wildly to match his brilliantly promising titles with even so much as adequate plays. One can't seriously or gracefully suggest that anyone who penned such titles as *On The Runway of Life You Never Know What's Coming Off Next*, *The Day The Whores Came Out to Play Tennis* and *Oh Dad, Poor Dad, Mama's Hung You in the Closet and I'm Feeling So Sad*, lacks a considerable facility with words. Perhaps too, the audacity of his wild, *Poor Dad* would warrant his inclusion in a more exhaustive study. Though it's impossible to call Kopit an important writer, his works are being performed.

We might also have included Lorraine Hansberry whose untimely death cut short what might have proved a most fascinating career as a playwright. Her *Raisin in the Sun* was an excellent play, shot full of human insights that transcended any racial concerns. Then there's William Gibson whose powers as a writer of prose fiction seem to adapt even more brilliantly for the stage. His *Two For the Seesaw* and his later, well-known triumph, *The Miracle Worker*, were written for the commercial theatre and emerged as considerable commercial successes. Gibson also stated in his work *The Seesaw Log* many of the things that demand saying about the craft of the playwright in today's theatre. And there's Sidney Michaels whose *Dylan* proved to be one of the most dramatically stirring offerings of recent seasons though it fell quickly as a victim to America's 'hit or bust' mentality. Michaels, with *Ben Franklin in Paris*, a dull musical, seems to have switched allegiance to make his mark.

All of these playwrights are most interesting, but for the sake of orderliness and because they constitute adequate mirrors to the whole of what's going on, we'll touch but the five. In their number we see the major drift of our theatre reasonably well defined. We get some hint of the dominant influences and the most urgent problems of theatre in the United States today. Perhaps these five constitute a kind of microcosm for us, through which we may perceive the whole subject of the dramatist in our life.

Working hard at it throughout the first half of the twentieth century, we here in the United States have succeeded in making the theatre, traditionally a place for enchantment and mystical evocation, literal minded and somewhat constipated with fact. Insisting that every play be rooted in credible reality and yammering constantly about the need for motivation, we have abandoned the mystery of the theatre. We have forsaken the inexplicable for the logical. We have created a theatre based on philosophy—a rational system—and kicked out the immeasurable fascination of mystery once thought to be the artist's birthright.

Perhaps one might expect such to have happened. A theatre normally mirrors a society's plight and doesn't function as an antidote to it. Our age is hipped on science and even though the scientist himself still grants that mystery remains, most of us look upon all things as measurable and demonstrable.

Following out of all of this, it seems it was inevitable that there should have been a reaction. It was inevitable that *some* dramatists should object to the literalism of our theatrical conventions and create new ones—a set of conventions reclaiming the mysterious and that which goes beyond logic. To a degree, this has happened as it happened on the Continent. (I don't mean to infer at this point that all our present generation of writers are absurdists intent on putting the torch to objective truth, relation of character to situation and Lessing's long treasured ideal of 'internal probability': the five I have chosen here to represent the whole macrocosm of our theatre represent a genuine diversity of approach to technique and life.) There is, however, a drift among our serious playwrights towards a conviction that goes far past the point of ordinary realism which too has had its day. There is what appears to be a general dissatisfaction with the generally easy conclusion, the established attitude. This 'drift' is not a pronounced one. We Americans are, for the most part, too conservative to go all the way with a theatre of mystery, of incantation and magic. But we can become enamoured of the strange and the bizarre. Perhaps such has become a need in our scientific society.

★   ★   ★

Perhaps most influential in this process one might call 'the reinstatement of mystery' is Edward Albee. Since his *Zoo Story* appeared several years ago as a double bill off Broadway with Samuel Beckett's *Krapp's Last Tape*, Albee has provided a hurricane of controversy. Alternately hailed as a veritable genius and derided as a dramaturgical charlatan, Albee has continued to write serious plays and has been produced extensively *on* Broadway, *off* Broadway and way off Broadway in the so called tributary theatre. Though his *Ballad of a Sad Cafe* and *Tiny Alice* failed at the box office and received vicious handling from some of the critics, there is still a considerable weight of opinion that asserts Albee to be America's most exciting dramatist, well on his way to becoming our major playwright.

Though Albee is most often considered a genuine card-carrying member of the Absurdist Movement, it is most difficult to assign any fixed position—to identify any particular point of view to him in regard to dramatic technique. In technique he has shown himself thus far eclectic. Only in his consistently pessimistic point of view does there appear to be any genuine consistency shown in his work.

His first play, *The Zoo Story*, falls into the Absurdist category. It belongs there because, in the words of Martin Esslin (most adept at identifying and tagging Absurdists), he '. . . attacks the very foundations of American optimism' (p. 225). Secondly, it belongs there because it explores the limitations and the debased state of verbal communication. Peter, Albee's complacent citizen, and Jerry, his tortured young outcast, cannot reach one another. They are unable to engage in meaningful dialogue. And if we are to assign major characteristics—distinguishing marks—to the Theatre of the Absurd, a concern with the devaluation of language is clearly one of these.

Albee however, despite the sympathy he clearly shows towards what might be called 'the Absurdist position', doesn't stay with this approach to the problem of recreating life on stage. *The Death of Bessie Smith*, though it too deals with disillusionment, is a stern piece of realism. It can't be comfortably categorized with *The Zoo Story*, *The American Dream* or *The Sandbox*, all of which seem to fit in neatly with the works of the European Absurdists. It's a free-wheeling, terribly cruel drama this man writes. It has an unconscionably sadistic point of view. It tosses Lessing away to half adopt Artaud, and it thumbs its nose at the motivations that the realistic theatre has come to demand.

However, just as Albee seems to have adopted a particular artistic orientation, he seemed to reverse himself. Not only does he consent to full-scale Broadway production after having loudly indicted Broadway as a totally bankrupt institution, but he adopts the conventions of the naturalistic stage in *Who's Afraid of Virginia Woolf?*

In a certain sense we might call Edward Albee 'a spitter'. Like August Strindberg, Albee's most brilliant writing is demonstrated when he places two characters, boiling with hate, in a face-to-face confrontation. He has a talent for invective—a genuine gift for reproducing insult. His characters claw at one another fascinatingly. Though his talent for such hatefulness pales in comparison with that of Strindberg, he sears effectively with it. Though it fails to measure up even to the same sort of thing demonstrated in O'Neill's *Long Day's Journey Into Night*, there's no question but he writes an incandescent fight.

In *Who's Afraid of Virginia Woolf?*, it's as though he had agreed to the proposition that invective is the mainstream of his dramaturgical talent, for he sustains the bitterness throughout and writes a marathon quarrel. There are no real changes of pace, no substantial scenes of gentleness or good humour to contrast with the pyrotechnic displays of bad temper and out-and-out malice. There is nothing but a number of very brief periods—little breathers—in which the combatants may catch their breaths to go on to even more nasty and furious things.

Actually, *Virginia Woolf* is a sustained family quarrel. It's a lengthy and harrowing family altercation written with considerable incandescence and with real linguistic virtuosity. It's not so much a play as it is a triumph of another order. Lee Baxendall outlines what Albee's intention seems to be in a fascinating article in the *Tulane Drama Review* (1965). He suggests that there is, in this particular play, a rejection of the creative principle, a railing at the fatherhood of God through the archetypal family breakdown.

Virginia Woolf proved to be both a box office success and a theatrical sensation. One might say that Albee, with his blazing dialogue and his frankness of speech, had won a battle. But in winning this fight, the dramatist can sometimes place himself in a vulnerable position. He risks further reverses. Regardless of the degree of his virtuosity, he can find himself in possession of an attractive formula—one that's worked out well—and may learn to depend on it.

Albee seems to have given way to just such an insidious temptation in *Ballad of the Sad Cafe*, adapted from Carson McCuller's work. In *Ballad* he has extended the spitting match and portrayed it in physical terms between weirdly assorted human types. From the hulking, unhappy woman to the dwarf, these are strange people—cruelly malformed characters. They are vivid, but do they reach us? Do they touch us?

The grotesqueness, the feverishness, of *Ballad*'s combatants take us too far from the indictment—however audacious—of normally well-thought-of people that sold *Who's Afraid of Virginia Woolf?* to a sensation-seeking, scandal-bibbing public. The bitter attack on the college community, on the devoutly bourgeois American college professor, is one thing: the professor is enough of a household god so that the dramatist may peck away at him. Man has always been delighted to hear the apparently wise, pious, rich, talented, educated, successful or august individual debunked. But with the human dregs characterized in *Ballad of the Sad Cafe*, there's nowhere to go. As one disgusted theatregoer put it within earshot of me, 'Who in hell cares about nuts like that? I want to see people.' Eugene O'Neill discovered a long time ago how hard it is to walk *that* tightrope. The playwright seeks vividness and excitement in his characters but must not banish credibility.

In *Tiny Alice*, the vitriolic hate scene is still with Albee though he seems to have buried it now under the debris of his intellectual pretensions. As before, the scene of violent vocal argument constitutes his greatest strength. On the other hand, it seems to prove the source of his greatest weakness. During the very first scene of this turbidly symbolic play, Miss Alice's lawyer, a Mephistophelean character, and the Cardinal, a cruel portrait of a Renaissance prelate, engage in what has become for Albee, the obligatory scene. In this confrontation, we are again struck by Albee's gift for finding the right vicious word, the barb, the clever death-blow to pride, the civilized yet barbaric indictment on one's fellow creature. But as the play continues, the contrivance, the preposterously unsatisfactory characterizations and the junior high school blasphemy fail to measure up to the early scene's promise and we are left feeling that Albee's muse is the most short-winded of the sisters.

Philosophically, Albee's plays both celebrate and curse sterility.

Surely there's no fecundity to be found anywhere in his work. There's no hope of anything better to come out of the dismal situation. One almost imagines he is hearing the hateful wail of a bitter, barren woman who curses all the pregnant for the filled womb she lacks. This ipecacuanha of the soul brings nothing important up. It just retches painfully and to no purpose.

Yet Edward Albee the playwright has his strengths and he fills a definite place in our theatre. Though he's strongly literary in his approach to 'the art of the immediate' as Ghéon called it, over fond of puns and elliptical constructions, he is clearly a theatricalist. He has absorbed a great deal from the older and in a certain sense purer forms of theatre, the vaudeville stage, the burlesque spectacle and the fight— bulls, human beings, whatever. Unlike T. S. Eliot (*Tiny Alice* does conjure up elements from *The Cocktail Party*, though Albee's angels are fallen ones), Albee uses the stage dynamically for the most part and is not tempted by poetry. He is not content to elicit images merely for the mind, but uses the artifices of stage convention to involve the emotions.

To an extent we may accuse Albee, like far too many other dramatists of our time, of using the stage for therapy and for seeking self-justification. It was, for example, disturbing when Arthur Miller, a fine journeyman playwright, drifted away from the Ibsenesque objectivity he had made his *forte* to write the self-justificatory piece, *After the Fall*. It was as though the man had forsaken his earlier approach to the creative act and had instead cribbed his analyst's couch-side notes, cast them into a kind of free-form Expressionism, and then staged the whole porridge as is, without any real attention to the abstractive process that is part of true art. I feel that Albee is guilty of the same sort of thing.

Obviously, many a writer has used his craft as a means for exorcizing his own personal devils. It's similarly clear that this constitutes at least a portion of any artist's motivation. The artist seeks to extend his personal vision into some form that invites the agreement of others—that confirms his own life-hypothesis. But it has always appeared that the audience, or the critic who seeks to be its just spokesman, has a right—a duty even—to praise or indict a work on the basis of whether or not he can make the exorcism apply to the commonality of men, not only to himself. When the artist chooses his means of communication and when he goes forth to seek his audience, he should tacitly agree that as he serves himself, he must also seek to serve that audience he chooses.

Has Albee properly and honestly faced up to any such ideal? He writes for a tribe—a limited tribe—and, though his plays have achieved a degree of acceptance outside New York and the côterie audience often to be found there, *Virginia Woolf* has made a substantial number of ticket-sales on the basis of audacity and on the promise of hearing four letter words in public and in mixed company.

Edward Albee seems feverishly dissatisfied with the world and with the society in which we now live. Some take this as an assertion which makes Albee of fantastic value to our stage. There's no denying the fact that a society needs critics in order to regain or to preserve its health. There's no question at all that the earnest and honest writer who is dissatisfied with the world has an obligation to himself and to his fellows to shout in the hope of changing it. There are times when one gets the impression that only the iconoclasts of Absurdism or such part-time Absurdists as Albee are manifesting this kind of dissatisfaction.

★   ★   ★

But it's not necessarily so. As a matter of fact, one may challenge the validity of such questioning when it is built on so pessimistic a point of view that the question is asked in the same breath with a statement that there are no answers to be had. Thus Paddy Chayefsky, a man who, despite his youth, is sometimes considered outside the present genera-tion of dramatists, offers another dimension of dissatisfaction with things the way they are. Happily, it appears to be a more enlightening dissatisfaction—a more hopeful kind of criticism. It seems less criticism Chayefsky offers than a measure of self-knowledge—the accepted basis for self-improvement. Like Berthold Brecht, into whose stylistic area Chayefsky seems to have moved, his theatre seems intent on illumina-tion and consequent judgment.

Chayefsky began in the realistic theatre. Coming from what was once, however briefly, a legitimate training ground for playwrights, television, he created works like the much-praised *Marty* which sought with a stringent selectivity to photograph the dulling elements in a prosaic and tedious world. Strangely though, as Chayefsky made this kind of comment about our world and our society, we didn't feel like indicting him. First of all, with his eye for humane detail, he made it *less* tedious, *less* wearisome. Then too, he made his criticisms with such sympathy for his fellow man and with so many flashes of warm humour that we felt someone was on our side. An experience was being shared with us. We were not witnessing aesthetic masturbation.

Paddy Chayefsky is still a young man. In recent efforts he has grown progressively away from the realistic school that first sustained his talents and has shifted his direction on to a pathway that seems to parallel the direction taken by our theatre as a whole. Though his last two efforts on Broadway, *Gideon* and *The Passion of Joseph D.* failed to ring the gong of financial success, he still appears the leading strongman of our currently productive dramatists. We may say this because in Chayefsky's work there's a genuine humanistic commitment, an effective eclecticism as regards technique, an ability to see humour as an effective and credible counterpoint to the most serious of problems, an understanding of what's bothering the contemporary Jew (who still makes up the most influential and loyal segment of the American theatre audience) and a physical and intellectual vigour that promises additional years of creativity.

Further, Chayefsky is a brave man. He is intellectually outspoken and he is confident of his own considerable powers as a dramatist. He is not afraid of the large-scale project, as evidenced by *Gideon* and *The Passion of Joseph D.*, and yet he retains enough from his period of television apprenticeship so that he owns a considerable eye for detail—meaningful detail. Providing only the continuing availability of a producer with vision, patience and money, Chayefsky will continue to do important things for our stage.

Occasionally one is able to see a Marlowe-like quality in the best of Chayefsky's work. As in the great Elizabethan, we detect a certain chill grandeur in Chayefsky. Though his Jewishness enables him to come up with a simple, homely quality one doesn't detect in Marlowe, the comparison seems an otherwise good one. The satiety of Marlowe's Faust provides, for example, an interesting comparison with Joseph D.'s impatience with and dissatisfaction with God. Lacking Mephistopheles, the twentieth-century Faust sacks cities and plays at God through politics and murder.

The new Chayefsky dates back to *The Tenth Man*, a contemporary tale about a Dybbuk, a transitory spirit that moves restlessly from place to place, from one being to another. In this play, superficially realistic and rich in Yiddish humour, Chayefsky is off on a spiritual search that parallels some of the theological speculations of the late Martin Buber. Chayefsky has spoken and hinted about the dilemma of the modern Jew who seeks to serve the flinty and jealous Yaweh of the Old Testament and who yet seeks accommodation to the role of humanist.

o*

How can one serve so jealous a Deity and still see great value and significance in man's estate? Chayefsky faces this problem squarely— uncompromisingly—in *Gideon*. He shows us The Angel of God wrestling with Gideon for an ideal. The play concludes with God and man at odds with one another. Of this alienation of creature and Creator one of the players is given the line, 'Perhaps someday God and man may . . . with this conceit, we end the play.'

Gideon is a fine play and though it becomes somewhat heavy-handed here and there and though it requires actors of heroic stature (again a reminder of Marlowe) it has an innate tension, a Gordian knot of inner struggle, that makes it exciting. There's real conflict to be found in the work.

Most recently, in a disastrously unsuccessful production, Chayefsky presented *The Passion of Joseph D*. This work, peculiarly mixing styles, sought to outline and explore the spiritual and emotional problems of Joseph Stalin who found it necessary to forsake God as a young seminarian because God didn't seem good enough and because God's code of morality as the young man saw it, couldn't serve the needs of his peasant nature. As a substitute deity, Joseph D. adopts Lenin and under the shadow of this new divinity, the young man rises to a fantastic pinnacle of power, wresting what he wants out of life with the passion of a wild beast. But the new god also fails and now Stalin, *man of iron*, whom all gods have failed, has to find a replacement for his second master. History records, along with Chayefsky, that the lost beast Stalin finds something in his own breast which he sets up in place of the objects of his former worship. Only death will ultimately stop his fancy, his ambition, his passion.

If Chayefsky seeks to purge his own Dybbuks in these plays, he at least turns up issues, problems, fears, that afflict the commonality of men. He treats them too, these problems, with an objectivity that keeps the playwright from obtruding. Perhaps one may legitimately say of Chayefsky that he's accepted to a far greater degree than Albee has, the idea that the theatre is properly a collaborative art. In a sense, he is able to see the audience as a partner to the collaboration. Despite the considerable weight of his intellectual and spiritual concerns, Chay- efsky is capable of writing fine theatre.

★   ★   ★

Unlike Chayefsky, who has swung to experimentation with Expressionism and many of the devices of Brecht's kind of Epic Theatre, and Albee, who plays dazzling word-games and flirts with European Absurdism, there are other American playwrights who have stayed closer to the realistic conventions. They use an almost strained kind of literalism as the vehicle for their vision.

Murray Schisgal is an interesting example of this type of theatre workman. Schisgal has raised an intriguing new voice in our theatre. He has demonstrated to us that a playwright can write eloquently and yet have 'an ear'. His plays are crammed with the clichés of the time—clichés of action as well as those of word—and yet they seem dazzlingly original. Under the surface of what, at one quick look, appears to be everyday language, there is anguish and irony. Schisgal has a way of taking the compassionately curious, deep inside his characters.

Schisgal writes primarily about love and loneliness. His work is deeply rooted in anguish though one suspects that like Tennessee Williams he is one of those seekers after love who has never really tasted or understood the draught they so feverishly seek. His thirst prompts him to hunt, but he doesn't quite know the nature of what it is he's hunting.

Schisgal's major work, *Luv*, is a marvellously funny play. A great deal of its humour seems imposed from without by the much admired directorial touch of Mike Nichols. But a great deal comes from within. Schisgal sees the absurdity of many of man's greatest trials and the preposterous manner in which we make our own beds of thorns. There's nothing cruel about Schisgal's humour. There's a brand of compassion that runs through it and we feel that where there's a longing for something better, even when it's not found, there's no real sterility. Though Harry and Ellen and Milt talk about—even attempt—suicide, one knows that they'll continue to live in the world, limping along and trying to suck whatever happiness they can from the rind of their young dreams.

Murray Schisgal is also known for two shorter works, *The Typists* and *The Tiger*. They too render the familiar newly eloquent through a manner of realism that seems to go far beyond realism and its limitations. *The Typists* is a particularly interesting play. It reminds one somewhat of Thornton Wilder's *The Long Christmas Dinner*. The convention is that of taking one significant aspect of man's life and using it to miniaturize virtually the whole life-span: Wilder has taken a festive dinner—the *agape*; Schisgal, in keeping with our no-nonsense era, has taken work.

The typists, a man and a woman, seem to live their whole lives, happy, sad, agonizing, funny, before us. And as quitting-time draws near, we are shown something of the bravery and pathos of our earthly existence. Banality becomes precious and oddly noble. *The Typists* is a rare and compassionate play and in its *caesuras* while the pair pause for breath, somehow spent, searching awkwardly for the next thing to say, we are touched.

The Tiger offers a measure of pathos as well, but does strike us as being too pat a trick. A young man, a would-be Raskalnikov, intent on showing his mastery of life, abducts a suburban housewife. His intent is clearly to terrorize the young woman and to rape her. Thus he will manifest himself as a kind of Nietzschean superman. As the would-be tiger pours out his longings to this young woman, confiding in her his dream of being a great free beast in the jungle of existential freedom, we see the victimizer gradually becoming the victim as the woman puts *her* claws out; and we see the young man's rape reverse its direction and we see him trapped in a kind of illegitimate domesticity just as frightful as the one he had always dodged to avoid. Once again Schisgal finds a measure of pathos in the human condition and though he leaves his characters somewhat worse for the experience, there's a warmth in the man's work that leaves one thinking there's a kind of nobility to be found in our petty machinations.

★   ★   ★

William Hanley is not so kind. Hanley, known principally for his *Slow Dance on the Killing Ground* and *Mrs. Dally Has a Lover*, is, somewhat like Edward Albee, troubled by the difficulties involved in communication. As a playwright, he communicates clearly enough with a kind of embellished, almost flowery realism. But he holds out little hope that man can really, effectively, communicate with his fellow. As a matter of fact he raises—perhaps not fully meaning it—the perfectly valid question of whether or not we have anything that's worth communicating.

Slow Dance on the Killing Ground brings together a bizarre combination of characters. We are given a candy-store owner, supposed victim of Hitler's camps, and a young Negro with a fantastic IQ and an even more fantastic imposture. The third party of the piece is a young woman—a college girl—lost on her way to an abortionist. These three oddly assorted characters, each with a kind of secret, are drawn together in the tentative oasis of the candy store. Outside there is the killing ground, the world where, as Hanley seems to see it, there is danger and chaos and terror and fear. Inside, all of these things are present too, but there is a measure of sanity. The people see each other too clearly to constitute any *real* threat to one another except that they *do* rip each other's masks away and this may—in the playwright's eye—constitute an even more deadly kind of demolition than the violent extinction waiting out on the streets of the 'killing ground'.

Slow Dance is what its title suggests. It is a dance, chilling and deliberate. It's also slow while Hanley details maddeningly the little things that go to make up a life of what has been called 'of quiet desperation'. Yet there's an ominous build to the piece that shows something of the genuine tragic flavour. Though the characters seem deficient in dimension and resonance, the texture of tragedy is very much present. Outside all is howling and madness. Within the small, very limited circle of light, reason and charity have a chance, even if only for a few passing moments.

Mrs. Dally is quite different. In this play, Hanley shows no interest in the larger issues of life—anything that might come close to the tragic. Here instead, the focus is on the small personal adjustment we seek to make in relations with others in this lonely world. The play appears closely related to much of what Tennessee Williams has written about the lack of genuine love in our society. Hanley has not, however, come anywhere close to Williams in the eloquence of his language, in the credibility *or* vividness of his characters.

* * *

Finally, in our set of five, there's Frank D. Gilroy. Gilroy won the 1965 Pulitzer Prize for Drama with his *The Subject Was Roses*. Peculiarly enough, *The Subject Was Roses* is a realistic, three-character, one-set, domestic drama that deals also—harking back to our discussion of Albee—with family failure. I say *peculiarly* because of our theatre's general movement away from—beyond—realism. *The Subject Was Roses* is specifically realistic.

Gilroy is, however, remarkably eloquent and as one listens to his dialogue, one is reminded that the realistic drama need not be derivative or in any way second class. Even if realism has become nearly bankrupt in years of reiteration, there is still room for the exceptional realistic playwright who is both accurate to life and who is sufficient master of the play form to make the statement he wants to make. Gilroy manifests precisely this kind of talent. With judicious embellishment of the ordinary, Gilroy makes a far more significant statement about the breakdown of communication between people, the manner in which we lash out at those we most love, the urgency of the human heart, than any other playwright of our day here in the United States. His manner is deceptively simple. He has caught the texture and rhythm of life and has transferred it with skill and feeling to the stage.

Gilroy treats of the demolition of a family that has been held together by habit and custom—without real love or understanding. A young man comes home from military service. He finds himself unable to adjust to his parents and they discover, in the process of seeking their son once more, that their love has atrophied as well. It's a curious, tense play that seems to manifest love by its absence. There are clearly times when one can better see love by the nature of the vacuum left when it dies. Perhaps this is, in a manner of speaking, like Tennessee Williams and Eugene O'Neill's efforts to show the shape of God by the size of His footprints.

Tim and John and Nellie are utterly believable and yet he has not overburdened them with the kind of bizarre qualities that keep us from suffering with them. So often the playwright, lacking confidence in the characters he has chosen, will embellish them with peculiar traits to make them more 'theatrical'; there are times when he does this to the point that the audience will no longer recognize them as brothers. But Gilroy has held himself away from this dramaturgical trap. His characters are vivid enough, but they are human. They are likeable and yet he's built into them a moral resonance. There's some credible span between their best qualities and their worst.

Since *The Subject Was Roses* opened on 25 May, 1964 at the Royale Theatre, things have not gone especially well for it in the commercial sense. Like another Pulitzer Prize winner of several seasons back, Tad Mosel's *All The Way Home* (adapted from James Agee's book, *A Death in the Family*), Gilroy's play has struggled to stay alive. Only the announcement of the Pulitzer Prize seemed to sustain the play and business has never improved to the point of being especially satisfactory.

★   ★   ★

If one were to seek a synthesis in regard to the playwrights discussed here and all the other American dramatists they represent, one would have to point out that the American playwright seems far more reluctant than his European brother to shuck off the realistic convention. Even Chayefsky and Albee, working with Expressionistic elements, maintain a considerable wealth of realistic detail. Schisgal and Hanley, like a great many lesser lights, have so used repetition and the banal that they seem to have crossed to a point far beyond realism into what might call, for lack of a better term, Overstated Realism.

As for content, virtually all of the American playwrights today seem obsessed with the problems of human communication. It may be that this has worked at cross purposes with their dreams of eloquence, for most seem far more absorbed with the *process* of communication than with the development of any philosophical burden of thought to be communicated. We have few examinations into the nature of truth like those to be found in Genet and Beckett, except possibly for *Tiny Alice*. Our writers are talking constantly about the communication of *feelings*—almost never about *visions*. Somehow, all this seems markedly narcissistic.

There's little question in anyone's mind today that there are vast gulfs between human beings—gulfs that can be bridged by the creative artist. As a communicator of vision, the artist has been busy fulfilling such a function for centuries. Similarly, many of these gulfs constitute emotional alienation. For example, the race situation is almost exclusively an emotional situation. America's crisis of colour has little to do with ideology. It's based almost exclusively on emotional criteria. And thus we can't indict James Baldwin or Le Roi Jones for the bitterness written in their own work. We can't indict them for reporting a situation that really exists. Nor can we legitimately cast stones at Albee's *Zoo Story* for exploring the difficulty of communicating. It's a genuine problem for all. There is a point, however, at which the theme seems to break out of bounds—run wild. When we emphasize the problem of communication to the point where we are no longer eager to communicate, we lose the craft of good artifice. Imitation is still the key to theatrical craft. We needn't bore the audience in order to properly depict a bore.

In mitigation we should remember that today's dramatists are, for the most part, denied the *sine qua non* for the fashioning of a first-rate theatrical talent: they lack companies with which to work, stages upon which to flounder. The concept of resident playwright has made little headway in universities. Occasional foundation grants have been made and the playwrights have dutifully watched rehearsal and participated in discussion; but their works remain infrequently done and even after their initial productions, when they finally are produced, there is little opportunity for further exposure.

If history can be said to teach us anything, it demonstrates that the successful playwright is always the product of a working theatre. He is always a writer who has been afforded an opportunity to explore the kinetic theatre in production. Such opportunity is almost never available today; the solutions so far tried are inadequate.

One can only wonder whether we will discover our new playwrights soon—playwrights who will evidence something healthy in our society by proving that there are some who care enough and know enough and feel enough to look objectively and yet constructively on the world in which we live. We need men who will continue to put the theatre forth as a service for mankind—a celebration of the mysteries of his existence. This is, of course, a big order and it will take theatres and zealous producers to run them.

Or perhaps our theatre will continue to atrophy and we will continue as theatrical mechanics and the parents of attractive chorus girls.

Index

[*This index excludes information, systematically arranged for reference purposes, given in the notes before each chapter.*]

225